THE BAFFLED PARENT'S GUIDE TO

COACHING YOUTH
HOCKEY

Look for these other Baffled Parent's Guides by Ragged Mountain Press

THE BAFFLED PARENT'S
GUIDE TO
COACHING YOUTH
HOCKEY

Bruce Driver
Stanley Cup Champion

with Clare Wharton

Ragged Mountain Press/McGraw-Hill

Camden, Maine • New York • Chicago • San Francisco
Lisbon • London • Madrid • Mexico City • Milan
New Delhi • San Juan • Seoul • Singapore • Sydney • Toronto

*To the two hockey parents who brought me into this world and also taught me
everything they know about the sport—thanks, Mom and Dad! Gary, thank you for
being the role model who drove my passion to play. Clare, thank you for your vision
and including me in your plan to write this book. I'd especially like to thank Tracy,
my wife of twenty years, who put up with me during my fifteen-year NHL career and
still supports my desire to coach today. Lastly, to our two children, Whitney and
Dillon, thank you for letting me be a coach—and not Dad—when we are on the ice!*
BRUCE DRIVER

*To my husband, Larry, and my children, Carrie and Todd,
for their unwavering support, love, and encouragement.*
CLARE WHARTON

The McGraw·Hill Companies

1 2 3 4 5 6 7 8 9 10 DOC DOC 0 9 8 7 6 5

© 2005 by Ragged Mountain Press

Library of Congress Cataloging-in-Publication Data
Driver, Bruce.
  The baffled parent's guide to coaching youth hockey / Bruce Driver with Clare Wharton.
     p.   cm. — (The baffled parent's guides)
Includes index.
  ISBN 0-07-143011-3
  1. Hockey for children—Coaching. I. Wharton, Clare. II. Title. III. Series.
  GV848.6.C45D75 2005
  796.962´077—dc22   2004014118

Questions regarding the content of this book should be addressed to
Ragged Mountain Press
P.O. Box 220
Camden, ME 04843
www.raggedmountainpress.com

Questions regarding the ordering of this book should be addressed to
The McGraw-Hill Companies
Customer Service Department
P.O. Box 547
Blacklick, OH 43004
Retail customers: 1-800-262-4729
Bookstores: 1-800-722-4726

Photographs by Larry A. Wharton.
Illustrations by Deirdre Newman.
Rink diagrams by L. Peter Zeidenstein.

Contents

Part One

Coaching 101: Everything You Need to Know about Coaching Youth Hockey

Part Two

Drills: Foundations for the Growth of Players and Coaches

Preface: In Canada, Every Kid Plays Hockey

I grew up in Toronto, Canada, where basically everybody plays hockey. All the neighborhood kids gravitated to my parents' double driveway because of its size. We spent every day stickhandling with tennis balls, shooting on anyone willing to play goalie, and skating, always skating. I remember the park down the street from my house, where each winter the town would erect a skating rink. My father and neighbor filled the rink with a fire hose and tended to it with shovels, and off we went. From the time I was three, almost every free minute was spent skating. When I started school, I couldn't wait to race home, complete my homework (or sometimes not), and head for the rink at that park. I always looked forward to weekends because I could skate all day, or at least until my parents called me in for lunch and supper.

All my friends played for one reason: they loved the game. Of course, we all had dreams as well. When we scored, we envisioned that the next puck we got in the net was the winning goal of the seventh game of the Stanley Cup finals. But our motivation for playing was simply to have fun. My father coached hockey and taught me things that I carried into my days in the National Hockey League. My parents provided incredible support for both me and my older brother who also played hockey. Their support never included pressure; I know I wouldn't have lasted as long as I did had I felt pushed to play. Because I loved the game, I joined my first team when I was four and continued to play in Toronto until I was eighteen. The minor hockey system in Toronto is the largest and probably the best known in the world. I was fortunate to be a part of the Toronto Marlies AA teams when we won an amazing four city championships in a row. I then played for the Wexford Raiders, a Bantam A team, for two years, but I really wasn't certain how long I was going to continue playing. I was drafted by the Oshawa Generals, a Major Junior A team, but left near the end of training camp for a Tier 2 Junior A team back in Toronto.

My good fortune continued when I was accepted at the University of Wisconsin, playing my first two years for one of the best coaches in the country, "Badger Bob" Johnson. Bob took a coaching job with the Calgary Flames before I began my junior year, but our new coach, Jeff Sauer, continued Bob's winning tradition. My team won two national championships and one second place in the three years I played for Wisconsin. I considered it a joy to play the sport I loved and receive an excellent education at the same time.

In hockey, as in life, you never know where the next opportunity will present itself. After completing my junior year at college, I was asked to try out for Team Canada for the Sarajevo Olympics of 1984. Our first training camp took place in June of 1983, the beginning of a whirlwind tour of games that stretched all across the globe to such places as Sweden, the USSR, Germany, and Austria. In fact, even though the tryout team was based in Calgary, only five games of the fifty-five we played that year were home games. Although I still regard those months as the longest hockey tryouts I've ever faced, playing hockey around the world was nothing short of amazing. Actually, I did not find out until the middle of January that I had made the Olympic team. My excitement only doubled when I got to the Olympic Village, meeting other young athletes from every sport and attending Olympic events. Team Canada made it to the bronze medal game, and as disappointing as it was to lose that game, we proved we were a young group of Canadian kids who played better than everyone expected.

Once again, I found myself faced with a decision. I could return home and wait until the fall to begin my senior year at college, or I could accept an invitation from the New Jersey Devils to try out for the team. I accepted the invitation, playing only four games with the team before we were eliminated from the playoff race. Again, disappointment brought opportunity. I was then sent to play for their farm team, the Maine Mariners, who were fighting for a playoff spot when I arrived. We not only managed to make the playoffs, but we went on to win the championship and the coveted Calder Cup. The Calder Cup win capped the longest year of my playing career, spanning from June 1983 to May 1984. The following year, I was called to the Devils' training camp and won a spot on the team, the beginning of a fifteen-year career in the National Hockey League.

Throughout my NHL career, I always tried to learn from the lessons of success and disappointment. 1988 was the first year the Devils made it into the play-offs by winning the last regular season game in overtime. But the Cinderella play-off run ended when we lost game seven to the Boston Bruins in the semifinals. When we failed to make the play-offs the following year, I realized that success never comes easily and can never be taken for granted. In the next few years, we were bounced from the first round of the play-offs, but our determination grew. Losing an emotional seven-game series in 1994 to the New York Rangers, our cross-river rivals, actually helped us the following year. We won the Stanley Cup in 1995 because of our renewed focus and determination that was born from the previous year's defeat.

When I retired from professional hockey after concluding my career with the New York Rangers in 1998, I realized that along with a natural ability to play hockey, luck had helped station me at the right place at the right time. I now play recreational hockey with new friends but have switched positions from defenseman to goalie. I coach youth hockey as well and thoroughly enjoy it. By coaching children, I get to teach them the skills, but equally as important, I pass along what I learned growing up in Toronto: always play for fun.

From Player to Coach

I began coaching youth hockey because both my son and daughter wanted to get on the ice. Playing hockey was their idea, not mine. Because I was fortunate enough to have been taught by so many talented coaches during my career, I could incorporate their valuable lessons into my own style of instruction. Right now, I'm involved in coaching at Pee Wee, high school girls' varsity, and Junior A levels. I emphasize skill development rather than team strategies with the younger players. Kids should be taught how to play the game properly so they can progress to the next level. The emphasis should be on fun and learning, not winning games. I've found it's best to wait until the Bantam, Midget, and high school levels to introduce a lot of advanced team concepts and hockey strategies.

One of the things that sets hockey apart from other sports is how much money parents must spend on equipment and ice time. But there are many skills that can be developed away from the rink, which coaches tend to overlook. Encourage kids to stickhandle tennis or street hockey balls around inverted pails or shoot pucks against boards. Be creative and have fun.

Collaboration

Clare Wharton is a former high school English teacher turned freelance journalist who has worked as a reporter and feature writer for various New Jersey newspapers and parenting publications. After earning a master's degree as a Reading Specialist, she worked as an English tutor in an adolescent crisis unit. She became interested in hockey when her son began playing at the age of seven. After ten years as a full-fledged "hockey mom," Clare developed a growing enthusiasm for hockey by watching and attending New Jersey Devils' games.

Remaining in contact with her friends from the world of youth hockey, Clare learned that the extremely talented defenseman she had watched throughout his NHL career had become a much-admired youth hockey coach. When the opportunity arose for her to write about the sport she had grown to love, Bruce Driver was her first choice.

Introduction: Welcome Aboard, Coach

So, you're a Baffled Parent. The last thing you clearly remember was your son or daughter asking to play youth hockey. It sounded like a great idea. Perhaps you played hockey yourself or simply enjoy watching the game. Or maybe you don't even know the difference between offsides and icing. It didn't much matter until you suddenly found yourself selected to coach your child's team. Now what?

This book is for you.

Everything written here will guide you to become a successful coach. This book is geared for teaching six- to fourteen-year-old players the game of hockey. Not only will you learn hockey basics, but you'll learn how to teach them as well. You'll understand and be able to convey the true meaning of sportsmanship and teamwork. And best of all, you'll learn to relax, have fun, and enjoy the many rewards of coaching.

Every child learns in a different way and brings a different level of athletic ability to the rink. I'll show you how to challenge your players so each child can progress to the next level of play. I'll explain how to encourage even the shyest child and use the energy of the most enthusiastic. You'll discover ways to approach mixed as well as single-gender teams. Whatever team or level you're responsible for, you'll be able to instruct, encourage, and mold a team into one that will play well and have fun in the process.

How to Use This Book

Coaching Youth Hockey: The Baffled Parent's Guide explains the skills required to play youth hockey, offering detailed drills, techniques, and suggestions for instruction. Though it's best to begin by reading the book in its entirety, you can refer to each chapter for advice on specific challenges. Part One provides all the nitty-gritty information you'll need to coach your team. Chapter 1, Creating an Atmosphere of Good Habits, will walk you through establishing yourself as coach. If you're not quite clear on the rules of the game, read Chapter 2, Before Hitting the Ice: Hockey Clear and Simple. If the thought of organizing an entire season is overwhelming, see Chapter 3, Setting Up the Season. If you're uncertain about the skills necessary to play hockey, refer to Chapter 4, Essential Skills and How to Teach Them. Worried about what to say to your new team and where to begin? Chapter 5, Goaltending, explains the special skills your goalie will need, and Chapter 6, Offense and Defense, focuses on offensive and defensive fundamentals. Chapters 7 and 8, The Practice and Sample Practices, will tell you how to organize and conduct your practices, providing a detailed time frame for the many drills that are included for teaching the principles. In Chapter 9, The Game, you'll learn how to have a stress-free first game and help your players have fun on the ice. Chapter 10, Dealing with Parents and Gender Issues, addresses problems that might arise with parents and challenges that different genders can create.

In Part Two, you'll find every drill necessary for the growth and happiness of your players and *your* peace of mind. Remember that no matter at what level you're coaching, the fundamental drills (Chapter 11) should be an integral part of every practice. Offensive and defensive drills (Chapters 12 and 13) are included; you determine how many of each type your team should work on at each practice. You'll notice that unlike many other sports, hockey requires that players transition quickly from offense to defense depending on what's happening on the ice. Therefore, Chapter 14, Game Situation Drills, provides the drills necessary for players to become versatile and proficient in every situation.

● *beginner*

●● *intermediate*

●●● *advanced*

Drills are assigned difficulty levels of "beginner," "intermediate," and "advanced." Beginner drills are generally for six- to eight-year-olds; intermediate drills are for nine- to ten-year-olds who should have mastered most of the essential skills; advanced drills are for eleven- to fourteen-year-olds who already excel at skating, stickhandling, shooting, and checking. Keep in mind that kids learn the game and develop their motor skills at different ages. Use the drills that best address the needs of your team and your individual players, regardless of age group.

Some chapters conclude with a Question and Answer section to guide you through dealing with any perplexing situation that might arise during the season. If you're still having trouble mastering hockey terminology, use the information sidebars and glossary as your hockey dictionary. The section on referee signals will explain each call. If you're looking for additional insight about youth hockey organizations or online sites, check the Resources. And the detailed index will help you locate advice on specific problems. Use all the information provided to adapt to your own needs, questions, and unique style.

A Word on Coaching Style

All the drills and techniques included in this book are ones that have worked best for me since I began coaching youth hockey. In other words, they best fit *my* style, but you may want to develop your own. Coaching styles can vary greatly, but one thing they should all emphasize is respect. First and foremost, teach your players to respect you, themselves, the other team, and the officials. Their win-loss record is much less important than the way they conduct themselves on and off the ice. In addition, your primary objective should be to bring each child to his or her best level of play through hard work and encouragement. When players look back at the time they spent playing hockey, they probably won't remember how many games their team won or lost during a particular season, but they will remember if they had fun doing so.

Kids love the competitive, fast-paced aspects of the game, so I incorporate mini-competitions during practices. I'll sometimes have the losing competitors do extra skating sprints or push-ups, but these are designed to heighten the level of competition rather than be seen as a punishment. Again, if you don't like the idea of intra-team competitions or if you feel it hurts rather than helps your players, feel free to eliminate them completely.

As coach, you're also your players' role model, so use your responsibility wisely. Kids are very eager to learn and just as eager to please. Make your expectations clear at the beginning of each season, practice, and game. Be patient because not all kids grasp new concepts and drills at the same time. Be quick to praise them for a good effort, be understanding when they fail, and be willing to give as much time as necessary to help each individual contribute. Working as a team provides as many lessons about life as it does about hockey. Children will learn the enormous satisfaction they can derive from helping one another, working together toward a common goal, and involving 100 percent of their effort and abilities. Your reward as coach will be in guiding them to these realizations.

There are five key points for being a good coach:

Come prepared for the expected . . . and the unexpected. Make certain you have a well-made plan for every game and practice. Select drills based upon the skills your team needs to learn, but include fundamentals at every session. Your practice plan should include the time allotment for each drill or activity. A backup plan is a must. You may have been promised a full-ice practice, only to learn you're sharing the ice with another team. You may find that someone else is using the extra cones and nets you were planning to use for a relay. Hope for the best, but plan for the monkey wrenches.

Remember to bring everything you'll need, such as your coaching board, whistle, water bottles, pucks, cones, first-aid kit, and handouts. Good organization on your part will help keep each child involved, interested, and clear about your expectations.

Be adaptable. Sometimes things that look good on paper just don't cut the ice. If you see your team is struggling with a particular drill, you may either have to modify it or substitute a completely new drill. You can easily judge when your kids are becoming bored; don't hesitate to insert a scrimmage or mini-competition to restore their enthusiasm.

Kind words go a long way. No one likes to be criticized or humiliated. Remember that kids are eager to learn and to please. As their coach, you're expected to instruct, correct, and challenge. However, you must be sensitive in your approach. Be generous in your praise when a child has mastered a particular skill; choose your words carefully when a player makes an error.

Enthusiasm is contagious. Show your players how pleased you are to be their coach. Your high energy level will ignite their passion to become better players and teammates. Remember that practices are just as important as games. You must convey that there's no place you'd rather be and no other group of kids with whom you'd like to share your knowledge.

Get to know each player. A good coach knows that a team is made up of individuals, each with his or her own unique personality. Through careful observation, you'll learn how best to raise the skill and personal confidence level of each child. One player may enjoy demonstrating a new drill for teammates. Another may be horrified at the thought. Your responsibility is to motivate players to feel good about one another's strengths as well as their own. Children can learn a great deal from each other as well as from you. As you guide them to interact positively, they will truly become a "team."

PART ONE

Coaching 101: Everything You Need to Know about Coaching Youth Hockey

CHAPTER 1

Creating an Atmosphere of Good Habits

In order to have an enjoyable season, it's necessary to lay out the ground rules right from the beginning. Tell your players exactly what you expect of them. They should always give you their full attention, arrive on time, and work hard in practice. Respect is a big part of learning to be a team player in hockey as in life. Remind them that respect must be given to their teammates, referees, and opponents as well as their coach.

You should be the primary role model for your team. Everything you require of your players you should require of yourself, but you should also go "the extra mile." For example, get to the rink ahead of your players, be prepared with a written plan for the game or practice, and make certain that you have everything you need to make the plan work. If your drills require cones or pylons, make certain they're already at the rink or bring them with you. If you'd like to use extra goal nets at a particular session, check with the rink ahead of time to be certain they're available.

Because ice time is a costly and precious commodity, you'll need to make the most of each practice. Being well prepared means you can use every minute fully and wisely. Your players will take their own responsibilities seriously because they take their cues from you.

Children need consistency to understand that certain behaviors will always be expected while others will never be tolerated. For example, you'll always expect all your players to have all their equipment each time they show up for a game or practice. Explain that just as carpenters would never come to work without their tools, hockey players must always have all their equipment, and it all should be in good condition. (Read more on equipment in Chapter 3, Setting Up the Season.) In the same vein, you can't tolerate disrespectful behavior from anyone. If you announce that players will lose ice time in a game if they are hostile to an opponent, you must be certain this applies to star players as well as those with less skill.

Recognize that each child is unique. Although you need to treat your players equally in regard to behavioral issues, decide what works best to chal-

"Oreo" Coaching

While attending a coaching certification program, I learned an interesting metaphor for effective coaching. Picture an Oreo cookie. The first outer layer should be a positive message regarding what your player has done right. Use the center layer to suggest ways to improve, and then have the concluding layer contain an encouragement. For example, "Johnny, that was a good try. But if you position the puck in the middle of your stick blade, you'll be able to complete the pass better. Good effort! You'll make the pass correctly next time."

lenge their physical and emotional differences. Some players are eager to demonstrate a new drill or be the first to sprint around the ice five times. Others are shy and dislike having the spotlight shining on them. Find ways to bring out the best in everyone. If you remember that every child likes to receive praise for a job well done, you'll see even the quietest player strive to improve. Likewise, make it a point to provide individual challenges. Have players of the same or a higher ability level compete against each other. Just make certain that players with fewer skills are never embarrassed or lose their love of the game because a challenge is too far above their present skill level.

An established routine helps everything (and everyone) run smoothly. Your whistle is one of your most powerful tools. You'll use it to stop or change a drill or to bring your players together for further instruction. Whatever its use at the time, your players should know that your whistle is the signal for their undivided attention. Use the locker room for teaching. When all your players are dressed, go over any new drills they'll be learning once they hit the ice. Employ your coaching board to diagram and illustrate the drill and then be ready to answer questions. Give careful consideration to the age group you're dealing with and work within their attention span.

Establish Your Identity as Coach

What should your players call you? That's really your decision, but I've found everyone on the teams I work with (including myself) is comfortable calling me Coach, Coach Bruce, or Coach Driver. If you prefer a stricter environment, you might require your players to address you as "Mr.," or "Mrs.," or "Ms.," but explain that you require that out of respect, not out of a desire to establish yourself as drill sergeant.

Questions and Answers

Q. What do I do with a child whose parents want him to play, but he himself appears disinterested?

A. Try to get the child involved. Ask him to set up the goal nets before practice begins or fill the water bottles. During practice, skate next to him for a short time and encourage his participation. It's possible that the problem isn't that the child is disinterested, but rather that he's feeling inadequate about his skill level. Of course, there will occasionally be children who simply wish they were elsewhere. Explain to the team that every player needs to contribute his or her personal best at all times. It hurts everyone if you constantly stop practice to capture this child's attention or discipline inappropriate behavior. This is the time to address his parents in a calm, straightforward manner. If league officials are available, they can provide added insight when you meet with the parents.

Q. What do I do with a child who is consistently late?

A. When coaching youth hockey, remember that none of your players are old enough to drive a car, so sometimes they really have no control over when they arrive. In your first meeting with parents and in the welcome letter you provide (see the sample letter on page 25), emphasize the importance of being punctual. When players are late, impose some small form of forfeit so your players understand the need to respect your rules. If the lateness continues, call the parents to determine the reason and take part in finding a solution.

There are many early morning practices in hockey because that's when the ice is most readily available. I've discovered that a great method for getting kids to practice on time, especially in the early morning hours, is to begin practice with a scrimmage. I split the players into two equally talented teams, throw two pucks on the ice, and let the kids play. Kids love to scrimmage so much that it motivates them (and in turn, their parents) to be punctual.

Q. What do I do when a child is inattentive or consistently fools around during practice?

A. First of all, when you're speaking with your team, minimize the distractions. If you're sharing the ice with another team, position yourself and your assistant coach against the corner boards and have the players face you. That way, their focus will be on you, not what may be happening at the other end of the ice. If specific players are not paying attention, use their names when describing a drill; for example, "Pat, this drill involves skating around the face-off circles." You can also ask an inattentive player a question that pertains to the situation or have her demonstrate the next drill. If none of this appears to have any effect, don't hesitate to speak to the player after practice and, if necessary, her parents. This is also a great time to remember the valuable support that your assistant coach can provide. While you're speaking or demonstrating a drill, your assistant can quietly remind players to "listen to the coach" or "pay attention to what we're doing."

Q. How do I deal with players who make fun of players who are less skilled?

A. Instead of making the situation a punishment, create a learning, rewarding experience for the more-skilled players by explaining that the strength of a team depends on everyone's efforts. Encourage those with greater skills to work with the less-skilled players. Remind players that everyone is there to learn, and that some just learn faster than others. Point out how the most admired athletes are ones who take on the role of leader and put the team first by helping everyone improve through encouragement, not criticism. You'll find that your skilled players will begin to feel good about doing something as important as helping their teammates improve.

Before Hitting the Ice: Hockey Clear and Simple

If you ask a child why he loves to play hockey, he'll probably tell you about the excitement found in skating and scoring goals. Visit any skating arena during a public session and watch the joy in a child's eyes the first time she lets go of her parents' hands and skates alone. Or stand alongside a frozen lake and watch a game of pond hockey, where kids hustle to shoot pucks into a makeshift goal net, raising their sticks in triumph when they get something past the goalie. There are few rules in these games, but each child certainly uses the basic skills of skating, passing, and shooting. I like to teach these skills with beginning hockey players and introduce the rules of the game gradually. Some rules are added at specified levels, so there is really no need to overwhelm younger players with all of them at once.

Four years ago, a good friend asked if I would help him coach his Pee Wee house-league team for an upcoming tournament. The challenge was having only two practices to prepare. Each player was at a different skill level, but that was really less important than what they all had in common: they wanted to be there and they wanted to learn. During the practices, I taught them a defensive and an offensive zone system. I explained that if they understood these concepts and enacted them, they would do well. We played three games at the tournament, winning one, losing one, and tying one. It was amazing watching those kids play and thinking of all they had absorbed in two days because they were so eager to learn.

When you begin coaching, you'll discover most players have enthusiasm for learning and a strong desire to play. Build on both these qualities, and as your players progress, their skills will progress with them. This chapter will help you understand the essentials of hockey from rules to offensive and defensive basics.

The Ice Rink

A hockey rink is a rounded rectangle approximately 85 feet across and 200 feet long. It's surrounded by either painted white wood or a fiberglass wall called the *boards*. The *centerline* (marked A) divides the ice into two parts. The two *blue lines* (marked B) are positioned on either side of the centerline approximately 27 feet from it. Thirteen feet from the end boards are red lines called the *goal lines* (marked C); the *goal nets* sit on these lines. In front of each goal net is the *goal crease* area where the ice is painted blue and enclosed with a red line. Players cannot make intentional contact with the goalie when the goalie is in this crease.

The end of the rink where your goaltender defends the net—from the end boards to the nearest blue line (B)—is called a team's *defensive zone*. The center ice section between the blue lines is called the *neutral zone*, and the area farthest from the defending goal is the *attacking* or *offensive zone*. Nine circles (one is blue, eight are red) designate where face-offs occur. Circle 1 designates the area for face-offs that begin the game and each period and that restart the action after a goal is scored. Circles 2 to 9 are for face-offs after a stoppage in play or after a penalty. The *slot* is the area in the middle of the ice between the face-off hash marks and the top of the offensive zone face-off circles. The *high slot* is the area in the middle of the ice at the top of the offensive zone face-off circles.

A hockey rink is approximately 200 feet long and 85 feet wide. The red centerline divides the rink in half. Nine circles designate where face-offs occur.

Bare Basics
Players and Positions

Each team is allowed a roster of seventeen skaters and two goalies. Team rosters usually consist of nine forwards, six defensemen, and two goalies for each game, though only six team members are allowed on the ice at any one time during a game. The left and right wingers and the center make up the forward line. The center is usually the player who takes face-offs; that is, she tries to control the puck so her team can gain possession. The main task of the forwards is scoring goals.

The job of the two defensemen is to prevent the opponent from scoring goals. Defensemen must be proficient at skating backward when their opponent is attacking into their defensive zone, but they must also be ready to change positions and pass to an awaiting forward when their team is on the offensive. The job of the goalie, often called the last line of defense, is to prevent goals from being scored.

Of course, no player can become proficient at hockey by performing only one task or position. Forwards often must help out in the defensive zone, defensemen are allowed to score goals, and although it is very rare, even goalies have delighted the crowd when they score into an empty net. Playing hockey is as much about "hockey sense" as it is playing position. A good player knows when to switch from offense to defense and vice versa.

Scoring

Each team attempts to score goals, which are awarded when a puck *completely* crosses the goal line. Offensive players are generally responsible for scoring goals; defensive players prevent the other team from scoring. Of course, a good player is one who can shift from offense to defense (and vice versa) when needed.

The team with the most goals scored is the winner. In most leagues, teams get two points for a win, one for a tie, and none for a loss. With the exception of Juniors (see the Age Classifications sidebar), if a game is tied at the end of three periods, a five-minute rest period is called, and then the game resumes for ten minutes of *sudden death* play. In other words, the team that scores first during that extra ten-minute period wins. If no goal is scored during the first ten minutes, additional ten-minute time periods are played until one team scores. Teams switch sides and defend the net at the opposite end of the rink after time has expired in each period of the game.

Playing Time

In some house leagues at the Mite and Squirt level, all players on the ice switch after two minutes of play, usually at the sound of a horn or buzzer. In travel leagues, in other house leagues, and above Squirt level, a single player or an entire line changes *while* play continues, called *changing on the fly*.

Younger skaters generally play three periods of ten minutes each. The time of each period increases as the players get older. For example, in Junior games, the three periods are usually twenty minutes long, with a short break (one or two minutes) between periods.

Officials

Referees officiate the game. There is usually one head referee who signals when a goal is scored and calls penalties. The two linesmen are in charge of

Age Classifications

Most house-league teams accept all the players who come out for the team. A travel team holds tryouts and accepts a limited number of players. In either case, teams are established according to a child's age as cited in the following charts:

USA HOCKEY—Youth Teams

Date of Birth	Age Category	Age Division
1986	18 years	Midget 18 or Under
1987	17 years	Midget 18 or Under
1988	16 years	Midget 16 or Under
1989	15 years	Midget 16 or Under
1990	14 years	Bantam 14 or Under
1991	13 years	Bantam 14 or Under
1992	12 years	Pee Wee 12 or Under
1993	11 years	Pee Wee 12 or Under
1994	10 years	Squirt 10 or Under
1995	9 years	Squirt 10 or Under
1996 and younger	8 and Under	Mite 8 or Under

USA HOCKEY—Girls' Teams

Date of Birth	Age Category	Age Division
1985	19 years	19 or Under
1986	18 years	19 or Under
1987	17 years	19 or Under
1988	16 years	16 or Under
1989	15 years	16 or Under
1990	14 years	14 or Under
1991	13 years	14 or Under
1992	12 years	12 or Under
1993	11 years	12 or Under
1994	10 years	10 or Under
1995	9 years	10 or Under
1996 and younger	8 and Under	8 or Under

HOCKEY CANADA—Minor Hockey Age Classifications

Age Division	Age Category
Pre-Novice	6 and Under
Novice	7 and 8
Atom	9 and 10
Pee Wee	11 and 12
Bantam	13 and 14
Midget	15 to 17
Juvenile	18 to 19
Over-Age Juvenile	20

face-offs and making the calls for icing and offside. However, at the beginning levels of hockey, two referees usually divide the officiating duties.

Basic Rules
Offside

A player is called offside when she crosses into the attacking or offensive zone of the opposing team in advance of the puck and makes contact with the puck. The offside rule prevents one player from shooting the puck to an awaiting player in the offensive zone.

Icing

Icing occurs when a player shoots the puck from his team's side of the center red line across the opposing team's goal line. Icing is permitted only when a team is serving a penalty and is "shorthanded," meaning they have at least one fewer player on the ice than the other team. Some leagues have in-house rules that use the defensive blue lines as the rule for icing.

Left: A player is called offside when she crosses into the attacking or offensive zone of the opposing team in advance of the puck and makes contact with the puck. The offside rule prevents one player from shooting the puck to an awaiting player in the offensive zone.

Right: Icing occurs when a player shoots the puck from his team's side of the center-line untouched across the opposing team's goal line. It is permitted only when a team is serving a penalty and is shorthanded. Some leagues have rules that use the defensive blue line as the icing line.

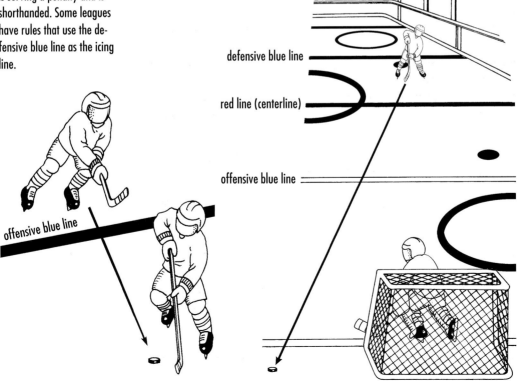

offensive blue line

defensive blue line

red line (centerline)

offensive blue line

Two-Line Pass

The only USA Hockey–sanctioned leagues that forbid a two-line pass (passing the puck across two lines to a teammate) are adult checking leagues. Hockey Canada does have a rule forbidding two-line passes, but has recently ruled that individual leagues may make their own decision on this infraction. Check with the International Ice Hockey Federation for country-by-country stipulations.

Penalties

A player is given two minutes in the penalty box for most minor penalties. When a penalty is called on the goalie, another player goes to the penalty box in her place. Some of the most commonly called minor penalties are:

Charging: Taking more than two strides or steps before checking an opponent. This can result in a five-minute penalty instead of two, at the discretion of the referee.

Cross-checking: Holding the shaft of the stick between the hands and using it to check an opponent. This penalty is usually two minutes unless the check is violent or a head shot, which increases the penalty time to five minutes.

Elbowing: Using the elbow to check an opponent. Although this is usually a two-minute penalty, an elbow to the head or an intent to injure guarantees a five-minute stay in the penalty box.

Holding: Grabbing the stick, jersey, or any part of an opponent's body.

Hooking: Using the stick to hook an opponent's stick or body.

Interference: Obstructing the progress of an opponent who does not have the puck.

Slashing: Using the stick to hit an opponent. Again, this can be a five-minute penalty instead of two.

Tripping: Using the stick or part of the body to trip an opponent.

Players receive a five-minute penalty for most major penalties, which include the following:

Boarding: Checking an opponent into the boards in a dangerous manner.

Checking: Not allowed below the Pee Wee level, so a penalty will be called.

Checking from behind: Pushing, checking, or cross-checking an opponent from behind. This is most dangerous when a player is slammed into the boards.

Fighting: Any form of fighting is not tolerated in youth hockey and will usually warrant suspension.

High-sticking: Holding the stick above normal shoulder height and using it to check an opponent. This is a penalty even if done unintentionally. Often a double minor or a major penalty is now called on a high-sticking penalty, with the offender serving four or five minutes in the penalty box.

Spearing or **butt ending:** Using either end of the stick to jab at an opponent.

The stiffest penalties called in hockey are imposed for various infractions during a game:

Misconduct: This usually involves the removal of a player from the game (other than a goalkeeper) for a ten-minute period. A misconduct penalty may be called when a player uses obscene or profane language, intentionally knocks or shoots the puck away from an official during a stoppage, deliberately throws equipment onto the playing area or, after receiving a penalty, refuses to go where a referee has ordered. However, another player is permitted to immediately replace the player who has been removed.

Game misconduct: A player or team official is suspended for the duration of the game. In this case, another player is permitted to immediately replace the offending player. This penalty usually carries a suspension for the next game that the team plays as well.

Match penalty: A match penalty is called when a player attempts to or deliberately injures an opponent. A player or team official is suspended for the duration of the game and immediately removed from the game. The penalized team immediately places a nonpenalized player (other than the goalkeeper) in the penalty box for five minutes. In some leagues, a player who receives a match penalty will be suspended from playing in any games or practices until league officials deal with the case.

Penalty shot: A player is awarded a penalty shot when she is fouled from behind while on a breakaway and prevented from getting a clear scoring opportunity. The player and defending goalkeeper are the only two players permitted on the ice. The puck is placed at center ice, and the shooter begins skating at her blue line. The goalie is allowed to move out of her crease once the player makes contact with the puck. The player must make forward progress to score a goal and is not permitted a rebound shot.

As the Game Progresses

Some people might find it difficult to follow a hockey game because there seem to be so many things happening simultaneously. If you keep the basic rules and penalties in mind, it becomes easy to understand what's happening.

A hockey game begins after a warm-up session where each team skates and takes practice shots on its own goalie. Both teams use half-ice only, staying exclusively on their half of the ice. At the sound of a horn or buzzer, the players on the starting lines take their positions on the ice. Play begins when the referee stands between the two teams' centers and drops the puck. Each center tries to win the *face-off* by gaining immediate control of the puck and passing it to one of the wingers or defensemen.

As play continues, you may see a linesman with one arm straight up signaling an offside and wonder why the play is continuing. This *delayed offside* means the linesman has seen a player on the team with puck possession skate into the offfensive zone before the puck, but he or a teammate has not yet touched the puck. If the player skates back into the neutral zone without touching the puck, no offside will be called. Even if the puck is never played by this player, a puck entering the net will not count as a goal if an attacking player is offside.

Hockey is a sport that has a *penalty box*, a designated area for rule breakers. When a penalty is called on a particular player, he or she must sit in the penalty box for the entire time of the penalty while play continues. His team plays short-handed, meaning it can only have five players on the ice instead of six. It is entirely possible to have more than one player in the penalty box at one time. Naturally, the more players a team has sitting in the penalty box, the greater its disadvantage in defending its goal, although the minimum number of skaters the offending team can play with on the ice is three. The team not being penalized goes on a *power play*. If the team scores, the offending player's penalty is terminated, and he comes out of the penalty box. However, if the player is serving a major penalty (carrying a five-minute penalty), he stays in the penalty box for the entire five minutes, giving the attacking team an opportunity to score more than one power play goal.

The only player who will never spend time in the penalty box is the goalie. Any penalty called on the goalie will be served by another member of her team. However, goalies can be ejected from a game for a match penalty or game misconduct.

You might also see something called a *penalty shot*, a free shot awarded in nearly every movie about hockey, but much less often in a real game. If an attacking player has a clear scoring chance but is fouled from behind, the referee may award a penalty shot. The fouled player gets the opportunity to come in alone from center ice on the goalie. A penalty shot can also be awarded if a player, other than the goalie, covers the puck with his hands or body in his own team's goal crease. The penalty shot is an exciting one-on-one test of wills and strategy for both the scoring hopeful and the goalie.

You've probably heard the term *pulling the goalie*. This generally happens during two specific situations. If a referee signals a penalty on one team but delays calling it because the other team has possession of the puck, a coach will often motion for the goalie to come to the bench. This allows the team to have an extra offensive player on the ice until the offending team touches the puck, at which time the referee will call the penalty. Likewise, goalies are often pulled near the conclusion of the game by a team that is trailing by a goal. The team then has a one-skater advantage as it attempts to score the tying goal but must make certain it defends its now-vacant net.

CHAPTER 3

Setting Up the Season

Much of your peace of mind as a coach will depend upon your organizational skills both on the ice and off. Have your practice and game schedule established well before the drop of the first puck. Don't be afraid to delegate responsibility to assistant coaches and your team manager. This will allow you more time to work with the kids, which is why you're there in the first place.

First Things First

The youth hockey winter season generally runs from October to April. Call the ice rink where you'll be practicing to find out the times and days for your team's practices. USA Hockey suggests that through Midget age (see page 15 for age classifications) there should be at least two practices for every game. In addition, the recommended maximum number of games per season is fifteen games for Mites, twenty for Squirts, thirty for Pee Wees, thirty-five for Bantams, and forty-five for Midgets. You'll also need to set up a schedule for both home and away games, which need to be coordinated with other teams in your league or division. This responsibility is usually handled by your team manager or league officials.

Of course, we all know about Murphy's Law. There will be days when you learn that if something can possibly go wrong, it will. There will be times when you arrive for your scheduled practice time, but another team has been mistakenly assigned to your time slot. Or you may travel to an away game only to find there are no officials for the game. Just remember that for every problem there is a solution, if you're willing to compromise and use creative thinking. Remember, too, that your players will be watching to see how you respond to problems. If you lose your temper or berate others when things don't go as planned, you set a poor example for your team and run the risk of losing their respect in the process.

The hockey organization for which you'll be coaching will determine

Tryouts

Every kid loves to play the game. However, most become very nervous when it comes to tryout time. Quite often, kids feel uncomfortable about all the comparisons that go on between peers. They should be reminded that children develop their motor skills at different rates so the most skilled player today may not be the most skilled player tomorrow!

Tryouts out at the recreational level should *never* exist. It's important that everyone who wishes to play receives that opportunity regardless of ability. Coaches should be responsible for the development of all the players, not just the more-skilled ones. Tryouts should be left for the more competitive leagues such as travel programs, club teams, and high school.

If you're coaching at a level that requires tryouts, it's important that you are organized and also that the players:

- have a complete understanding of what is expected at tryouts
- are provided with the same opportunity to make the team regardless of where they played the previous year
- are assessed according to your requirements (skill level and team play) instead of subjective reasons (they were on the team last season or friendships)
- are treated with respect

Make sure all players understand that you're assessing their ability to play hockey and not them personally. All players should be notified individually as to whether they made the team or not. It's important to clearly explain to players who don't make the cut their areas of strengths and weaknesses, and also give them a direction for improvement. Equally as important is to explain the expectations for each player who has made the team.

registration costs, times and dates of in-person registration, and the number of players on a given team. After registrations are complete, you'll receive a list with the names and phone numbers of your players. Call each parent, introduce yourself, and invite parents and players to the first meeting. You'll probably want to save the details about your coaching philosophy and expectations until the meeting, but make certain you tell parents about registration fees and additional costs. Explain each piece of equipment their child must have from the very start of the first practice so there's plenty of time for shopping. Hockey is a game that requires a great deal of protective equipment; no child can be permitted to play or even practice without it. Parents new to the game may not be aware that hockey is an expensive sport. However, some youth hockey organizations (occasionally in conjunction with corporate sponsors) now provide new or used equipment and scholarships so the game can be enjoyed by all.

Selecting an Assistant Coach

When selecting an assistant coach (or possibly several assistants), you'll want to choose someone who shares your enthusiasm for teaching young people.

Skills and Positions

Some youth players want to play a specific position while others are willing to try any position. I encourage all players to experiment in trying to learn more than one position. I find that players who have tried more than one position usually end up finding their niche. Also, players who learn many different positions gain a better understanding for the entire game and are less likely to criticize teammates when mistakes are made. There are many advantages to being a versatile player. Coaches are always looking to plug a hole in the lineup when there is an injury or absent teammate. Just as their bodies develop differently, youth hockey players develop their skills at very different rates. No one can project the future skill level of a youth hockey player.

Usually, coaches who confine players to one specific position at a very young age have their own agenda (winning), instead of the interests and development of their players. Don't get me wrong; I like to win as well, not for my own benefit, but for the self-esteem of my players. However, I stress that it's more important to learn the proper skills and use those skills to learn how to play the game. I tell my players all the time that as long as they play hard (give an effort) and smart (do the things that we as coaches are teaching them), then they will hear nothing but positives. Winning is not as important as having fun, learning the proper way to play the game, and improving.

1. If my team plays well but loses, I always tell them that I'm proud of the way they played.

2. If they play poorly (lack of effort and mental mistakes), they generally hear about it, though I always include a positive spin at the end.

3. If they play poorly but win, I always address the fact that winning doesn't mean that they played a good game. I speak to them about their lack of effort or concentration.

As coach, you should set a goal for yourself. A successful season for you should mean that you've helped make an improvement in each and every one of your players.

A person who enjoys the game of hockey but who is uncomfortable working with children would not be a wise choice. It's important that your assistant shares your coaching philosophies and is long on tolerance and patience. Often high school and college students are eager to become coaching assistants and may play hockey themselves. If so, your student assistant can demonstrate drills or teach one group of players while you're teaching another. Make certain that you have an open line of communication with your assistants so that if a problem develops, you can discuss and implement solutions you have mutually agreed upon. Your players will learn from the respect and give-and-go between you and your assistants.

The Many Hats of a Team Manager

It's a big job to be a team manager, so make certain when you ask for a volunteer that he or she is fully aware of the responsibilities. Your manager might take charge of the following jobs:

1. Establishing a phone or e-mail plan for whenever there's a change in the practice or game schedule. The manager may want to make all the calls

Recommended Starting Times for Games (USA Hockey)

Games should begin no later than:
    7:00 p.m. for Mites and Squirts
    8:00 p.m. for Pee Wees
    9:00 p.m. for Bantams
    10:00 p.m. for Midgets

or may ask three or four parent volunteers to call or e-mail a specified number of parents.

2. Formulating and distributing away-game directions at least a week in advance. The manager might determine if any parents have a problem providing transportation to or from games or practices, and then help in establishing carpools.

3. Setting up a time to determine player sizes and numbers for team jerseys. Orders are usually placed through local sporting goods stores, which often provide team discounts. The manager should follow up to ensure that sizes and player numbers and names are correct.

4. Arranging for team dinners, award ceremonies, and fund-raisers. The proceeds from fund-raisers can be used to defray the cost of ice time or the expense of accommodations when travel games necessitate overnight stays. Dinners and ceremonies usually include the parents as well as the players. They're a terrific way to highlight the growth of the team and cement the bonds of interaction and friendship.

Meeting the Parents

You'll want to schedule your first parent meeting before the season actually begins, either directly before the first practice or a week or so in advance. Have copies of the practice and game schedules along with a letter to parents (see sample on page 25). Explain the details of practices and games and, most importantly, your philosophy as a coach, including your behavioral expectations for players and parents alike. It has become an unfortunate reality that some parents have lost sight of the fact that children play sports to have fun. I believe that nowadays kids are put under too much pressure to compete, which makes the fun quickly disappear. Some parents will lose their tempers with their children, opposing teams, referees, and even the coach because the win-loss record has become too important. Help parents understand your coaching philosophy, which in my case is to give all players every opportunity to improve their game. I try to help my players advance their skill level and their mind for the game so they can progress to the next level. Never forget that hockey is a game. When the fun is taken out of playing, children quickly lose their desire to play.

When you're speaking with the parents, remind them that even

Calling All Volunteers!

If you have parents who want to be part of the team but don't want to help out on the ice, by all means use their enthusiasm to take over the administrative details. There are routine but important administrative aspects to running a team that could be taken over by a manager or several committed parents:

Phone/E-Mail Tree

Instead of having every kid call you whenever there's a change in the schedule, have one parent arrange a phone or e-mail tree. You can call or e-mail one designated person, who then initiates a reliable chain of communication for the rest of them.

Practice Transportation

A designated parent can be in charge of carpooling by checking that each player has a ride to practice and home again. Though many families won't need this help, the safety net it provides for those who do is reassuring. This parent should make certain that all players are picked up from practice before he or she leaves.

Fund-Raisers

Getting all of the necessary equipment can be somewhat expensive. Having team dinners, organizing fund drives, and arranging other fund-raising events are projects that an administrative parent can organize, with some of the duties delegated to other team parents as well.

Snack Duties

A small, nutritious snack after practices (off the ice only!) or a trip to the local pizza parlor after a game can be a helpful boost or well-deserved reward for your young players. A parent can be in charge of this service or can create a rotating schedule of parents who would be interested in helping. This is a fun and highly satisfying way that parents can be involved with the team.

though their child's participation is voluntary, you need parental cooperation to make the season run smoothly. For example, although everyone leads a hectic life, it's important that parents take their responsibility to the team seriously. This includes being on time and phoning the team manager if a child will be absent because of illness or an emergency situation. Though children must rely on their parents for transportation, they can't use their parents as an excuse. Generally, a small forfeit for latecomers such as extra laps or collecting the pucks and pylons after practice will send the required message that lateness is unacceptable. Of course, if tardy behavior becomes an established routine, speak with the parents personally and remind them that commitments to the team should be taken seriously.

Hockey Equipment

A vital issue when speaking to parents is the equipment their child will need to play hockey. Because hockey is a physical, fast-paced game, equipment needs to fit properly and be in good condition. I recommend buying equipment at a store specializing in hockey wear because the salespeople are highly knowledgeable about equipment and proper sizing. This list will help you understand what items are needed and how each should fit.

Sample Preseason Letter to Parents

Welcome to All Parents and Players:

It's time for another hockey season! My goals are to make the game of hockey fun, give all players a good understanding of how the game should be played, and work on improving their skills as hockey players. It is my philosophy that my assistants and I are on the ice to help as many children improve as possible. We will be teaching your child to learn how to properly play the game of hockey, and preparing them for the next level. I don't place a lot of emphasis on winning and losing, although everyone loves to win. I'm more concerned about whether or not the team is competing hard, how they're playing the game, and whether they're learning.

Parents need to be a good influence on their children. Please cheer on your son or daughter and their teammates, but please do not yell at the officials, the coaches, or the opponents. Understand that your behavior will certainly rub off on your children, and they will act as you do. Kids play hockey to have fun, so let's make it fun for everyone.

Hockey equipment can be expensive, but having the proper protection is certainly the most important aspect of your child's safety. Please seek out a store that specializes in hockey equipment to make sure that your child is properly fitted with all the protection he or she needs. My assistants and I will be happy to check and discuss any hockey equipment questions you may have at our first parent meeting.

I have only a few rules for all players (and parents):
Come ready to give your full attention at all practices and games!
Work as hard in practices as you will in games!
Respect your coaches, teammates, referees, and the opponent!
Be on time! And Have Fun!

Games: Please try to be in the locker room 30 minutes before all games. We would like all players dressed, sitting in the locker room, and ready to go 10 minutes before the scheduled game time so we can go over lineups and last-minute instructions for each game. For practices, we would also like to have all players ready 10 minutes early so we can explain practice drills in the locker room and save time on the ice.

We understand that your child's participation is voluntary, but we need your cooperation to make the season run smoothly. If you're going to miss a practice or game, I need to know in advance. Missing practices and games without a phone call may result in less playing time in future games.

Cancellation: Unless you hear otherwise, we'll always have practice or games. In the case of cancellation, players will be notified by means of the enclosed phone/e-mail contact list.

Must bring: Please make sure your child has a water bottle and all his or her hockey equipment. All equipment should be labeled with your child's name.

As coaches, we are volunteers and we enjoy what we do. We are not perfect. If you have a question or problem, please bring it to my attention.

Have your child come ready to play hard, learn, and have fun!

Thanks,
The Coach
1234 Oak Street
555-6789
coach@hockey.com

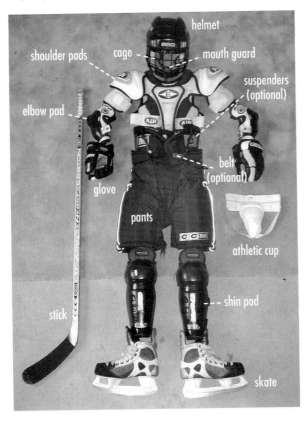

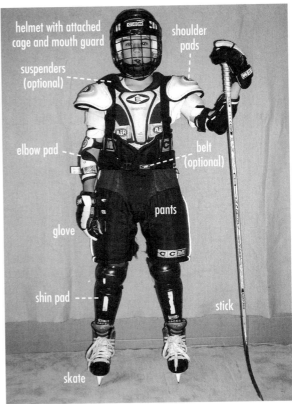

Left: A player's equipment.

Right: This youth hockey player is dressed in properly fitting equipment.

Athletic cup. Male athletic supporters are also referred to as *jocks*. Inside the supporter is a protective cup, which should be purchased in the appropriate size. Female pelvic protection is called a *jill*. Both the jill and jock are sized according to the measurement of the player's waist and should feel snug, but not tight.

Garter belt. These, too, are sold according to waist size and are used to hold up hockey socks.

Shin pads. They protect the shinbone and kneecap and should be made of hard plastic with a shin suspension and extra padding in the knee. The area between the kneecap and shin section should be flexible. Make certain the bottom of the pad does not reach beyond the top of the skate. Hockey socks are worn over the entire shin pad area.

Pants: Hockey pants are fitted according to waist measurements, usually 4 to 6 inches larger than the player's usual waist size. The upper, padded section of the pants should cover the hips, lower ribs, and kidneys. The leg section should extend to an inch or two above the knees, overlapping the top of the shin pads. There should be no space between the pants and shin pads.

Elbow pads: These must cover the elbow joint completely and be made from material that can adequately absorb shock.

Shoulder pads: Hard caps are molded to protect the shoulder tips with

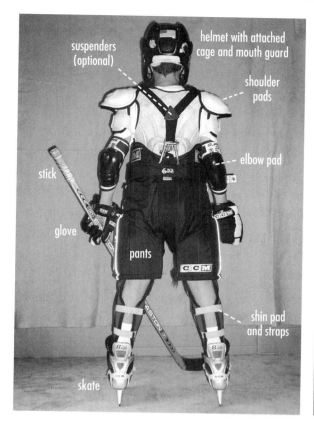

shock-absorbing material covering the upper arms, chest, and back. For female players, there is a combination shoulder and chest protector that provides extra protection in the breast area.

Gloves: Gloves should be well padded over the fingers, thumb, and back of the hand while at the same time should allow for some finger and thumb movement. Note that there should be no unprotected space between the shoulder pads, the elbow pads, and the hockey gloves.

Jerseys and hockey socks: Most organizations purchase jerseys and hockey socks by using an allotment from the registration fees. The team manager is often responsible for sizing and ordering. Both travel and club teams provide each child with two different colored jerseys; white jerseys are usually worn by the home team. Player names and numbers are imprinted on the back of the jersey for easy identification by officials and coaches. In most house-league programs, each team is required to have only one colored jersey, which must be different from all the others in their league.

Helmet: Helmets are worn to prevent brain and skull injuries and must be HECC (Hockey Equipment Certification Council) certified. Hockey Canada recommends that every minor player wear a helmet certified by the Canadian Standards Association (CSA). When properly fitted, the helmet will cover the forehead, temple, and base of the skull. It should not slip or be

Left: Hockey pants, shoulder and elbow pads, shin pads, and gloves must be fastened securely and be snug, but comfortable

Right: Players should check their equipment before each game or practice for signs of wear or damage.

Take Care of Your Equipment

Make certain helmet screws are tightened.

Rinse mouth guard after each use; keep in plastic case.

Check straps on shoulder and elbow pads for wear.

Check shin pads for cracks and torn padding.

Check gloves for holes.

Skate Care

After Each Use:

Wipe blades until completely dry.

Unlace skates and extend tongue to allow interior to dry.

Check for dull or nicked blades.

Make certain the rivets that attach the blade holders are secure.

so tight that it causes headaches. The chinstrap should be comfortably tight to ensure the helmet does not come off during play.

Face mask: These are available in clear plastic or wire cage styles and must be fastened securely to the helmet. They also must be HECC approved.

Mouth guard: This plastic device fits over the top teeth. A dentist can make a custom-fitted mouth guard, but bear in mind this will be rather expensive and will need to be replaced each year. Less expensive models are available that are softened when dropped into boiling water and then "fitted" by pressing over the top teeth. Colored mouth guards that are attached to the mask are required in the Pee Wee through Junior divisions of USA Hockey, but are not mandatory in Canada.

Sticks: To select a stick of proper length, place the bottom edge of the stick flat on the ice between the player's skates. The stick shaft should come between the player's chin and tip of his nose. Hockey stick shafts are made from a variety of materials such as hardwood or a combination of graphite, carbon, and Kevlar. Sticks also vary in length, diameter, weight, shaft blade, and blade flex, depending on customer preference. Blade curvature varies from nearly straight to a maximum legal limit of ½ inch. For youth hockey players, lighter sticks with more flex are best. Hockey tape should be used to tape the blade and upper handle of the stick to give the player better control when stickhandling, passing, and shooting.

Skates: Skates should be purchased *slightly* smaller (usually one size) than the player's shoe size. Some parents might be tempted to buy a larger than required size so their child can use the skates for a longer period of time. This not only hampers the child's skating development, but it can also cause injury to the back of the ankle from repeated friction between the skate and

Stick length is a matter of preference, but most hockey players prefer a stick that extends between the chin and tip of the nose when they hold it while wearing skates.

foot. Toes, heels, and the Achilles tendon area need good support and protection. Skates that fit properly should feel snug when the player is wearing one pair of socks, with only enough room for a pencil to fit between the heel and the back of the boot. Parents usually lace their child's skates when they are young, but as they get older, children are eager to become self-sufficient and lace their own. Although there are even lace-tightening tools available at hockey stores, some skaters still can't get their laces tight enough. Therefore, if you see one of your players skating with her ankles turned out, those laces need to be tighter! There should be enough room for toes to move. Keep in mind that properly fitted skates are the most important piece of equipment when it comes to improving a player's skating skills. If your child is falling frequently while turning or stopping, this usually indicates her skates need sharpening. Skate guards are recommended but not required. They prevent skate blades from becoming dull when a player is walking in skates on a non-ice surface.

Neck guards: Neck guards are required for Canadian youth hockey players but are optional in the United States. They protect the windpipe and the blood vessels in the neck and should be purchased according to neck size. Velcro closures allow the player to adjust the neck guard for a secure fit.

Hockey bag: A good hockey bag should be made of durable material and be large enough to carry all required equipment. Try to purchase a bag that has side pockets for mouth guards, hockey tape, a water bottle, and other miscellaneous items. Small towels are great for wiping skate blades. Extra helmet screws and a screwdriver are always a good idea.

Goalie Equipment

It should come as no surprise that goalie equipment is more specialized and more expensive than a typical player's. Goalkeepers require leg pads, kneepads, belly pads, a catching glove (also called a trapper), and a rectangular-shaped, protective glove called a blocker. In addition, specialized pants, shoulder and arm pads, a stick, and goalkeepers' athletic cup are required for both female and male goalkeepers. A goalkeeper's mask is not required, but a plastic throat protector attached to an approved hockey helmet with an attached facemask or goalkeeper's mask is mandatory.

Goalkeeper skates are also not required but are strongly recommended because they're

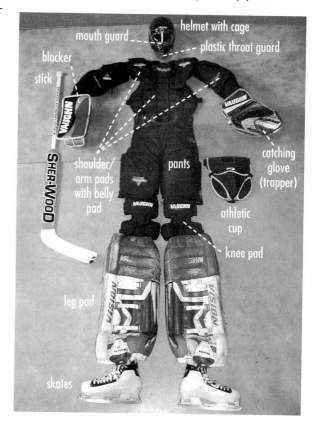

A goalie's equipment.

mouth guard
helmet with cage
plastic throat guard
blocker
stick
shoulder/arm pads with belly pad
pants
catching glove (trapper)
athletic cup
knee pad
leg pad
skates

made to protect the feet when stopping the puck from entering the net. For the best protection, it's important that the skates be properly fitted by a trained, knowledgeable salesperson.

Team Equipment for the Coach

Bring the following items with you to practice: a practice plan for both a full-ice and half-ice session in case you're sharing your practice time with another team, a coaching board with dry-erase markers, a first-aid kit, your list of parents' emergency contact phone numbers, a whistle, and your own equipment. You may want to use a separate bag to bring thirty pucks and cones for use in various drills.

Questions and Answers

Q. How do I go about setting up a practice and game schedule? Does the rink where I'm coaching have an established slot of times for practices? Do I personally call all the teams in my league to schedule games?

A. It really depends on what type of league your team is in. If you're coaching a house league or an in-house league, the league officials will set the schedule. There may be six teams playing in your league, so you'll probably play one game a week against one of those six teams. Practice times are set by the league, and each team usually holds one practice a week. If you're coaching a town team, your games will probably be scheduled by league officials, but the coach, the team manager, or whoever organizes the town's hockey program is responsible for scheduling practices. There is no set rule on this so it's best to check with your town's recreation department.

Travel teams are also organized according to leagues, though they are usually part of larger hockey organizations that are made up of a combination of in-house leagues and travel teams. The team manager usually books nonleague games, but the organization has one representative who books all the travel games for all the teams, working in conjunction with a league scheduler. In addition, many youth hockey associations have their own tournament directors whose sole responsibility is handling tournaments for each of its travel teams. Remember that if you're coaching a travel hockey team, there are more weekly practices and many more games. If different people are responsible for booking games, practice times, and tournaments, good communication between all the parties and the parents is a necessity.

Q. What are the most important things to include in my letter to parents?

A. It's important to stress your coaching philosophy, most especially that you believe kids should have fun. Include your expectations for both the kids and parents and a brief overview of what you're going to teach their kids and what you'd like their children to learn. In my letter, I stress that although winning is great, it's not my yardstick for a team's success. I am more concerned about how the kids play, if they're learning the game properly, and the positive lessons they can gain from working together as a team. It's vital that you are clear about your ground rules from the very beginning.

Q. When I hold my first meeting with parents, how do I present my philosophy and expectations without coming across as a dictator?

A. The overwhelming majority of parents will appreciate your willingness to coach their children. Once they see your enthusiasm for helping their children develop hockey skills and good work habits, parents will realize that you have their kid's best interests at heart and theirs, too. Have an open-door policy with parents so they can feel free to ask you questions or express their concerns. Be understanding when a parent tells you her child has to miss a practice or will be going away on a family vacation; however, explain that you do need to be notified in advance of the absence. Although youth sports require commitment, you never want the parents or kids to feel guilty about spending time together as a family, even when it means missing some playing time.

Unlike any other sport, the ice time necessary to play hockey is an expense for which parents pay. It makes sense to go over drills and game reminders in the locker room so ice time can be saved for skating. Remind parents that this is your motivation for requiring their children to be at the rink a half hour before a game or practice. Anything that can be explained in the locker room will result in more ice time for the players. In addition, if you have to repeat your instructions for latecomers, it hurts the whole team. It's been my experience that if the parents are the ones who are continually responsible for their child's tardiness, you only need to explain once how this hinders the team. If it's the child who is dragging his heels, speak with him directly. Sometimes kids tune out their parents' advice but will listen carefully to the same advice coming from another source.

I also stress the importance of kids respecting each other, the opposing team, and the officials. Tell the parents that you require the same behavior from them as you do from their children. If the rules apply to everyone and serve a purpose, you'll find most parents will comply with your instructions.

Q. I'm having trouble selecting an assistant coach who possesses both hockey and teaching skills. How can I find the right assistant?

A. Look for someone who enjoys teaching children. It's almost a prerequisite that he or she has played hockey before and has an understanding of the game, though someone could certainly be a fine coach without playing experience. My mother never skated, but she could coach any hockey team because she grew up in Canada and spent many of her nights bouncing from rink to rink watching her two sons play and her husband coach. She has a great grasp of and passion for the game.

Nowadays, there are many more people becoming involved with coaching youth hockey. Both USA Hockey and Hockey Canada have coaching certification programs that provide four certification levels for both perspective and current coaches. These programs provide not only an understanding of hockey but also solutions to dealing with situations both on and off the ice.

If you choose as your assistant a parent who has a child on the team, make certain he or she has the welfare of the entire team at heart. Explain that both of you are there to coach the entire team, not just your daughter or his son. Good coaching requires that every player be treated fairly, which becomes an additional challenge when personal interests are involved.

Q. No parent has stepped forward to be team manager. How do I get a willing volunteer?

A. Address this issue at your first parent meeting, preferably sooner. Many times you'll already know at least one of the parents on the team and will feel comfortable approaching this parent. Sometimes a parent will volunteer without your even asking. If you don't get a volunteer who wants to handle all the responsibilities, ask for one person to handle the phone calls if there are scheduling changes, another to be in charge of team dinners and functions, and someone else to be solely responsible for handling hotel arrangements and finances for tournaments. At your first meeting with parents, explain that if no one volunteers to be manager, you'll randomly assign a different parent each week to handle the phone calls, e-mails, scoring tables, and penalty box.

The use of computers has become a godsend for keeping parents updated about any additions or deletions in the season's schedule. Scheduling changes occur with great frequency, so parents need to be notified as soon as possible. Just make certain you let the parents know in advance if they'll be notified by e-mail, phone, or both.

CHAPTER 4

Essential Skills and How to Teach Them

The Fundamentals

There are few things more exciting than watching a skilled hockey player during a game. A good player can skate at breathtaking speeds, make passes with amazing accuracy, and score goals through a seemingly invincible line of defensemen and goalkeeper. But the essential skills of hockey—skating, passing, shooting, stickhandling, and checking—are acquired through years of practice, a great deal of repetition, and hours of hard work. No matter what level of competition players reach, they never stop working on the basics. Your job as coach is to help your players understand and practice these skills.

Skating

Skating is by far the most important skill that a hockey player needs to master. Tom McVie, my first NHL coach, lived by the motto "If you can't skate, you can't play." Skating is the first skill that needs to be mastered and must be worked on at each and every practice. (Note that children should *not* sign up to play hockey unless they have already had some skating lessons.) The better children become at skating, the more confidence they'll have as players.

Six Basic Skating Principles

There are six principles that make a player a good skater:

Low body position with knees bent. It is imperative to focus on players' body position as they learn to skate. Skaters should maintain the athletic, hockey position, meaning the knees are bent and the body is slightly flexed at the waist.

Head and chest up. Teach players to skate with their heads and chests in an upright position to maintain balance. Players who look at their toes while skating will have too much weight forward and will quickly lose their balance. "Heads-up" skaters will perform the other essential skills such as stickhandling, passing, and shooting at a higher level.

A hockey player's basic stance begins with the knees bent, the feet shoulder width apart, and the upper body slightly flexed at the waist. The player's head should be upright, with the eyes focused forward and the chest in an upright position to help maintain balance. The stick should be on the ice directly in front of the body.

Stick position. Players should skate with their stick on the ice in front of their body and not to the side. They should sometimes practice skating with just their top hand on the stick, although they should usually skate with both hands on the stick because they must always be ready to make a pass or give a target to receive one. In situations where high-speed skating is needed, as in forechecking, backchecking, breakaways, and some stick checking, players should have only one hand on their stick.

Edge control. Each skate blade has an inside and an outside edge. Proficient skating requires being comfortable on both edges. Edge control becomes especially important while turning and stopping.

Full extension. A short stride provides little power or speed. A powerful stride is achieved when a player fully extends the stride leg through to a flick of the ankle.

Recovery. The same fully extended stride leg must return under the midline of the body to provide support. If a player doesn't recover to the starting position, the next stride won't be as efficient.

Teaching the Principles: Six Skating Skills

There are six skating skills that your players need to learn: forward stride, starting and stopping, turning, backward skating, pivoting, and transition moves.

Forward Stride

The forward stride is made up of three steps: stride, glide, and recovery. The easiest way to teach the forward stride is to have your players watch a demonstration of the stride from two different vantage points: directly behind the skater and from the skater's side. As your players practice the forward stride, remind them to stay low using a good athletic hockey position with their knees bent at a 90-degree angle and keeping their head, chest, and back erect. They should extend the stride leg as they're pushing fully through on the inside edge of the skate, cutting a C shape into the ice. To conclude, players should then recover the stride leg back to the starting position while the opposite glide leg stays in place. Direct your players to move the arm

Left: From the basic hockey stance, the player turns the foot of one skate slightly outward and pushes off the inside edge to begin the stride, cutting the shape of the letter C into the ice.

Right: The stride leg pushes outward to full extension while the player uses the opposite leg to glide. It's important to maintain body position and balance.

Left: The recovery starts as the player begins cutting the second half of the C by pulling the stride leg back toward the starting position.

Right: The recovery finishes with the stride leg pulled back to the starting position and the player getting ready for the next stride. Again, the player maintains body position and balance.

Drills

- Forward Skating C Cuts
  F1
- V-Starts and Control
  Stops F3
- Two-Skate Power Stops
  F7
- Stickhandling While
  Skating F32

The V-start begins with an explosive forward movement from a stationary position. The player stays low with knees bent and the back, head, and chest erect.

Principles of the Quick Start

1. Toes are turned out with heels close together at a 45-degree angle
2. Knees are bent, with the head, chest, and back upright and erect
3. On inside edges of both skates, the player thrusts forward with power off one skate to a full extension
4. Upper body is in line with extended leg
5. Stride leg recovers low and quickly to the starting position
6. The player begins the next stride with the opposite leg

that's opposite their striding leg parallel to the stride, not across their body. Remind your players to have their stick remain on the ice in front of their body to receive a pass from a teammate.

Starting and Stopping

Starting is relatively easy to learn; stopping is not. Starting power comes from the thighs and knees; visualize exploding forward, not upward, from a stationary V-start position (see illustration). Remind your players to stay low with knees bent, back straight, head and chest up.

Your players should be thinking about making those first two or three strides powerful with full extension and with rapid, low leg recovery. These strides should carve marks in the ice at approximately a 45-degree angle, in line with the skating direction. The first few strides do appear to be short, but that's because there's little gliding. After your players have taken those first few steps, they should continue to stride fully to produce smooth skating. Your players will develop quick starts if they remember to use powerful thrusts forward, full extension, and rapid leg recovery.

Two types of hockey stops should be taught: the control stop and the two-skate power stop. The *control stop* is used when a player needs to make a complete, stationary stop. The *two-skate power stop* is used when a player needs to make a quick transition in skating direction.

Performing a control stop is often a difficult skill for beginners to master. Players should rotate shoulders and hips 90 degrees and have their knees deeply coiled like shock absorbers to absorb momentum and provide balance. Your players' feet must be shoulder width apart with slightly more of their weight toward the front foot. As they stop, players also need to stagger their skates (heel to toe) to maintain balance. Edge control becomes important in the next step. As they slow with knees still bent, their weight shifts more evenly over both feet, and the trailing skate straightens up to finish primarily on the inside edge.

If any players are struggling with stopping, you may want to teach them to snowplow, the method used by beginning skiers. Although this should not replace learning to stop properly, your players can gain confidence by turning their toes in and then sliding the forward foot around to finish the stop. Understand that this does not help them learn to stop on both the inside and outside edges at the same time; therefore, they should continue to work toward stopping properly. Also, explain that they'll need to

In a basic stop, the player slows her body with knees bent, body weight shifting over both feet, and the trailing skate straightening to a finish.

Principles of the Control Stop

1. The player rotates shoulders and hips 90 degrees with knees deeply bent to act like shock absorbers
2. Body weight is slightly more toward the front foot
3. Feet are shoulder width apart but staggered (heel to toe)
4. More weight is put on the inside edge of the front skate and less on the outside edge of the trailing skate
5. Body weight moves over both feet, and the trailing skate finishes more on the inside edge

Drills

- V-Starts and Control Stops F3
- Two-Skate Power Stops F7

Beginning skaters can use the snowplow technique to stop, and then they can progress to learning the control stop. Much like skiing, the player maintains bent knees, with the stick blade on the ice and the toes of the skates turned inward. A complete stop is achieved by pushing on the inside edges of both skates.

The progression to feeling the edges through to the control stop position happens as the player slides one foot forward to finish perpendicular to the original skating direction. While staying on the inside edge and sliding the front foot forward, the player transfers more weight toward the bent back leg to maintain balance.

stop as they face in different directions many times during an actual game, so they must practice stopping correctly facing both left and right.

The two-skate power stop is a more difficult skill to master than the control stop. Players should again rotate their shoulders and hips 90 degrees, with their knees deeply coiled like shock absorbers to absorb momentum

Principles of the Two-Skate Power Stop

1. The player rotates shoulders and hips 90 degrees with knees deeply bent to act like shock absorbers

2. The body leans backward slightly with feet shoulder width apart and staggered heel to toe

3. Body weight is distributed over the midline of the body

4. The player pushes on the inside edge of the front skate and also pushes with more strength on the outside edge of the trailing skate

5. While slowing to a stop, the player transfers weight totally onto the trailing leg as the front foot lifts and steps over the trailing skate to change skating direction

Hockey players often have to change directions quickly from a forward skating position. The player's hips, shoulders, and stick rotate 90 degrees, with the knees deeply bent and the feet shoulder width apart and staggered heel to toe. The player's body leans slightly opposite the direction of stopping.

With the weight over the midline of the body, the player should stop while pushing on the inside edge of the lead skate and pushing with more strength on the outside edge of the trailing skate. As the player slows, body weight should transfer to the trailing skate as the lead skate is lifted off the ice to begin the movement in the opposite direction.

The player can change directions quickly by immediately positioning the stick blade on the ice in the new, intended direction and stepping over the top of the trailing skate with the lead foot.

By extending the leg of the trailing skate, the player generates the power to push back in the opposite direction as the lead skate returns to the ice to begin striding again.

and provide balance. The body leans backward slightly, and the feet are shoulder width apart and staggered heel to toe.

While stopping, the player's weight should be distributed over the midline of the body to maintain balance. Edge control becomes a vital factor in the next step. The player must be able to stop using the inside edge of the front skate and the outside edge of the trailing skate. This is especially important when the skater needs to change directions quickly. Having the feet staggered makes it easier to change direction because the front stopping skate can immediately step over the top of the trailing leg to begin skating in the opposite direction. Explain to players that they'll need to stop while facing in different directions many times during an actual game so they must practice stopping correctly in both directions. The most common mistakes made are failing to bend the knees enough and having the skates too close together or too far apart.

Turning

It's important for hockey players to know how to turn quickly because they'll use this skill many times during practices and games. When your players need to change directions quickly, it's often more efficient for them to use a glide turn or forward crossover to maintain speed rather than stopping and starting again.

While gliding to change direction but maintain speed, the player's knees are again bent, and the body is in the athletic hockey position. The player's feet are staggered, shoulder width apart and solidly in contact with the ice. Remind the player to feel centered over the skate blades to maintain balance while turning; however, slightly more body weight is on the inside skate. The player's stick leads into the turn. This enables the player to turn with greater ease while maintaining the ability to receive a pass both during and at the conclusion of the turn. The inside skate follows, gliding on its outside edge and with the knee bent over the toe. To finish, the outside skate thrusts as the player pushes off the inside edge while rotating the hips to complete the turn. The most common mistakes made during glide turns are failure to position oneself on the outside edge of the lead skate, inadequate knee bend over the inside skate, and failure to lead with the stick.

For forward crossovers, again explain that the player needs to be on the outside edge of the inside skate and the inside edge of the outside skate. The crossover begins when the outside skate crosses completely over the inside skate. The player must lift and reach with the outside leg, not just step over, and should be leaning into the turn on the outside edge of the inside skate, fully extending the inside leg out with a good snap at the end of the stride and finishing on the toe. For the recovery, the player's weight should stay completely over the midline of the body on the crossover (outside) skate as the player lifts the inside skate slightly, returning it to the starting position under the inside shoulder. Now the player can begin to crossover again. The

Principles of the Glide Turn

1. Knees are bent, with body in good athletic hockey position
2. Feet are staggered, shoulder width apart
3. The stick leads through the turn with the inside skate next, followed by the trailing skate
4. The player should feel centered over the skate blades for balance but maintain slightly more weight on the inside skate

Drills

- Glide Turns (also a good warm-up) F4
- Continuous Glide Turns F5
- Continuous Inside-Outs F12
- Stickhandling Turnbacks F34

Principles of the Forward Crossover

1. Knees are bent, with the body in good athletic hockey position
2. The stick is on the ice, leading through the turn
3. Body weight is on the outside edge of the inside skate and the inside edge of the outside skate
4. The player leans slightly into the turn with the inside knee bent over the toe of the skate
5. The outside skate lifts completely over the inside skate
6. The inside leg extends fully, finishing on the toe
7. Body weight stays over the midline of the body on the crossover (outside) skate as the inside skate is lifted slightly to recover

Drills

- Forward Crossovers F8
- Tops and Bottoms F10
- Transition Moves (Mohawk Turns) F11
- Crossover, Follow Your Pass F21

The glide turn is used to change direction quickly while maintaining speed. The skater must position himself on the outside edge of the lead skate and the inside edge of the trailing skate, leading himself through the turn with his stick.

A forward crossover allows the skater to gain speed while turning. The player must lift and reach the outside leg while leaning into the turn.

most common mistakes made when attempting to do crossovers are failure to cross completely over with the outside skate and not enough knee bend in the inside leg.

Remember when executing either a glide (tight) turn or a crossover turn to carefully shift the body toward the direction of the turn. Shifting too much body weight or shifting too suddenly will cause players to lose their balance. Players who can master good body positioning and edge control while maintaining speed will be in a perfect position to receive a pass on their stick. It might sound difficult, but with practice your players will catch on. Don't forget to practice turning in both directions, because hockey is a transition game; all players need to be able to move quickly from defense to offense or vice versa.

Backward Skating

And you thought stopping and turning were hard to teach? Backward skating is the hardest type of skating for young kids to learn. In backward skating the overall body position is the same as in forward skating. Show your players how to use a good athletic posture where their heads and chest are erect, but their knees are properly flexed (like sitting in a chair). Teach backward skating the same way you would teach forward skating.

When children first learn to skate backward, they have a tendency to look down at their toes. This puts too much weight over the front of the skates, so the children lose their balance and fall forward. Good balance can be attained when body weight is evenly distributed over the middle of the skate blades and the knees are properly bent. Tell your players to concentrate hard on keeping their head and eyes up. They now need to thrust hard outward and backward at a 45-degree angle in a C-like motion with the inside edge of one skate. Remind them to begin carving with the heel, extending the leg fully, and pulling back in with the toe to recover. Once the C cuts have been mastered, it's time to teach the backward crossunder, which is taught much like the forward crossover.

As with all skating, balance becomes a big factor in mastering *backward crossunder* skating. The player should start in a good athletic hockey position with bent knees and with head, chest, and eyes up. The backward crossunder starts with most of the power coming from the strong push off the inside edge of the outside skate. While the outside skate thrusts into full extension, body weight is transferred to the inside leg. There should be a gradual shift in weight toward the inside when doing backward crossunders. (Players who shift too much of their weight will find themselves lying rather uncomfortably on the ice.) The heel of the outside skate then crosses in front of the inside skate while the inside leg pulls underneath it, also to full extension. Emphasize to players that when each leg is fully extended, there should be a distinct snapping motion of the ankle. To recover, the player keeps the body weight completely over the outside skate, lifting the inside

Principles of Basic Backward Skating

1. Knees are bent, with body in good athletic hockey position
2. Head and eyes are up; focus is away from the feet
3. Body weight remains evenly distributed over both skate blades
4. The player thrusts hard outward and backward at a 45-degree angle, imitating a C movement on the inside edge of one skate
5. The same leg is extended fully and then pulled back in to recover underneath the body

Drills

- Backward Skating C Cuts **F2**
- Pivoting **F6**
- Poke Check **F49**
- Successive One-on-Ones **F51**

Principles of the Backward Crossunder

1. Knees are bent, with the body in good athletic hockey position
2. Head and eyes are up; focus is away from the feet
3. The outside skate pushes off the inside edge to full extension
4. Body weight transfers to the inside leg with the knee bent
5. The heel of the outside skate crosses in front of the inside skate, while the inside skate pushes off underneath the outside skate to full extension
6. The player slightly lifts and brings the inside skate back to the starting position to recover

Drills

- Backward Crossunders F9
- Tops and Bottoms F10
- Transition Moves (Mohawk Turns) F11

It's best to practice backward crossunders while skating around a circle. Maintain a good hockey stance, keeping the head up and eyes forward. Here the player starts the crossunder with the outside leg striding to full extension as the body weight is transferred over a bent-knee inside skate.

The heel of the outside skate crosses in front of the inside skate. At the same time, the inside skate pushes off underneath the outside skate to full extension. The player lifts the inside skate slightly, returning it to the starting position to recover.

skate slightly before returning it to the starting position. Now the next crossunder can begin.

Backward crossunder skating is a difficult skill to master, but like everything else, it can be achieved with practice using the proper technique.

Pivoting

Pivoting from forward to backward skating and vice versa is not just a defenseman's maneuver. Forwards need to pivot when backchecking to present themselves for a pass before they transition to offense.

The next challenge involves pivoting from forward to backward without losing speed. When pivoting, players should keep their knees bent, their back straight, and their head and eyes up. To begin the pivot, players turn their hips 90 degrees, keeping both skates turning in the same direction. It's important that they stay low. If their upper body stays over the skates, they can balance perfectly and maintain speed during the pivot. As the players' hips move toward the 90-degree angle, their trailing leg should be bent firmly on the inside skate edge to achieve a hard stride, and they push their body through the pivot. At the same time, the opposite skate turns quickly from forward to backward, landing on the outside edge of the skate. This leg will straighten out players going backward if they pull the skate back beneath their body by grabbing the ice on the outside edge to recover. When these steps are followed, players will pivot 180 degrees.

Defensemen often pivot from backward to forward to play an opposing

The player's knees should be bent while maintaining a straight back. The head should be kept erect and the eyes kept facing forward. Both skates should be brought close together in a T position before the pivot begins. The pivoting shoulder leads the body through the turn.

The player's trailing skate strides to full extension as the body weight is transferred to the planting foot.

With the planting foot pointing in the direction of travel, the trailing skate is lifted off the ice to continue its movement in the new direction.

The trailing skate crosses over the planting foot and lands back on the ice to begin its first stride in the new direction. Notice how the planting foot finishes with an ankle snap.

Principles of Pivoting Forward to Backward

1. Knees are bent deeply, with the back straight and the head and eyes up
2. The player rotates the hips 90 degrees, with both skates turned in the same direction
3. The upper body is centered over the skates
4. The trailing leg is bent firmly on the inside edge of the skate to make a strong push-off to full extension
5. The opposite (landing) leg turns quickly, landing on the outside edge under the body, and pulls back beneath the body on the outside edge

Drills

- Pivoting F6
- Give-and-Go Mohawks F27
- Mohawk Shooting F46

forward or chase down a loose puck. Remind your players to keep their knees bent deeply, their back straight, and their head and eyes up. Both skates should come together more closely before the pivot begins. Lead into the pivot with the shoulder turning in the direction of the pivot and with the hips swiveling as well. Most of the players' weight should be over the trailing (pushing) skate. As players' hips move toward a 90-degree angle, their trailing leg should be firmly bent on the inside edge to achieve a hard stride, extending fully to push their body through the pivot. At the same time, the opposite (landing) skate turns quickly from backward to forward, planting beneath the body on the outside edge. Skaters are now at an approximately

Principles of Pivoting Backward to Forward

1. Knees are bent deeply, with the back straight and the head and eyes up
2. Both skates are brought closely together before the pivot begins
3. The shoulder on the pivoting side leads
4. Body weight is over the trailing (pushing) skate
5. The trailing leg is bent firmly on the inside edge of the skate to make a strong push-off to full extension
6. The opposite (landing) skate turns quickly, planting beneath the body about 135 degrees from the forward-facing position
7. The trailing skate finishes by crossing over the landing skate to recover

135-degree angle from the direction they previously faced. The trailing skate finishes by crossing over the landing skate, grabbing for the next stride and finishing 180 degrees from the original position. The most common mistake made in pivoting backward to forward is a failure to bring the landing skate beneath the body when beginning the pivot. Players can maintain their speed and retain their full extension if they concentrate on keeping their feet close together when they begin their pivot.

Transition Moves (Mohawk Turns)

Transition moves (Mohawk turns) are used often in ice hockey. Transition moves differ from pivots because while doing a transition, players are always facing the same direction. All players use transition moves, but for differing reasons. For example, forwards sometimes use them to put themselves in a better shooting position or while killing penalties. Defensemen use them to move quickly from defense to offense (or vice versa) while "closing the gap" on the opponent and when "stepping up," anticipating taking away an opponent's pass.

To transition from forward to backward, a player must start in good athletic hockey position, with the knees bent deeply over the toes. The head and eyes are up, with the back straight to provide good balance. To begin the transition from forward to backward, the hips swivel 90 degrees away from the direction in which the player was traveling. With skates turned in the same direction and body weight centered over both skates, the player now begins moving from forward to backward without taking her eyes off the puck or the play. Remember, while transitioning, the player always faces in the same direction. The lead skate is planted firmly on the inside edge and pushes deeply to cut a C into the ice. The trailing skate follows, with body weight on the outside edge pulling back beneath the body to help straighten out to backward skating.

The most common mistake made when transitioning from forward to backward is beginning the transition with the hips and skates turning in the wrong direction. When players turn their skates 90 degrees in the wrong direction, a second 180-degree swivel is needed for them to begin skating in the proper direction.

To transition from backward to forward, players must also begin in good athletic hockey position, with their knees bent deeply over their toes. Again, head and eyes are up, and the back is straight to provide good balance. Players who are skating backward and want to transition quickly to forward must first transfer all their weight over the pushing skate and plant firmly on its inside edge. With the knee bent, they should lift the opposite (landing) skate slightly off the ice and take a step, planting their landing skate directly beneath the body to form a V shape with both skates. As they push off, they stride strongly on the inside edge of the pushing skate, with all their weight transferring to the new direction onto the landing skate.

Principles of Transitioning from Backward to Forward (Mohawk Turn)
1. Knees are bent deeply over the toes, with the body in a good athletic hockey position
2. Head and eyes are up; back is straight
3. While skating backward, the player transfers all weight over the pushing skate and plants firmly on the inside edge
4. With one knee bent, the player steps with the opposite (landing) skate slightly off the ice, planting it directly under the body (forming a V shape)
5. Body weight transfers to the landing skate as the player pushes off, powerfully thrusting forward on the inside edge of the pushing skate

The most common mistakes made when transitioning from backward to forward are turning both skates in the new direction, instead of planting and stepping forward, and opening up the hips too much, which forces the player to move sideways, thus losing forward momentum.

Passing

Passing is a crucial skill. The puck can travel much faster than anyone can skate, so by moving or passing the puck quickly and accurately, your team will have a better opportunity to score goals and win games. Players should learn how to pass and receive the puck at the same time. To teach this most effectively, pair up your players 10 to 15 feet away from each other and instruct them to pass the puck to their partner while standing still. Stress the importance of players passing the puck as accurately to a teammate as they would want the puck passed to them in return. Or as coach Tom McVie used to bark, "Pass from the heart!" In an NHL game, you'll often see players make a 90-foot "tape to tape" (stick to stick) pass to a player at center ice, but this kind of accuracy takes years of practice.

There are three types of passing: forehand, backhand, and flip (or saucer). The same basic principles (with some modifications as indicated below) apply to each.

Forehand Passing

When teaching forehand passing and receiving the puck, make sure your players see the demonstration from two angles: straight on and from the side. When passing, players should keep their hands out, away from their body. Players should maintain good athletic hockey position, and the puck should be in the middle of the stick blade, just behind the back leg.

Show your players how to cup the stick around the puck for better control, keeping more of their weight on their back leg. Their head should be up, with their eyes focused on the target. To pass the puck forward, they pull their top hand and push their bottom hand by sweeping the puck to a target, remembering to transfer their weight from the back leg to the front

Principles of Transitioning from Forward to Backward (Mohawk Turn)
1. Knees are bent deeply over the toes, with the body in a good athletic hockey position
2. Head and eyes are up; back is straight
3. The hips swivel 90 degrees away from the direction of travel
4. Skates are turned in the same direction, with body weight centered over both skates
5. The lead skate plants firmly on the inside edge, pushing deeply in a C-cut motion
6. The trailing skate is on the outside edge, pulling back beneath the body

Drills
- Transition Moves (Mohawk Turns) F11
- Continuous Mohawk Turns F13
- Give-and-Go Mohawks F27
- Mohawk Shooting F46

Principles of Forehand Passing

1. Both hands are kept away from the body
2. The puck is centered in the middle of the stick blade
3. The player cups the stick around the puck
4. The stick blade is positioned behind the back skate
5. Body weight is slightly back
6. The player sweeps the puck to the target by pulling the top hand and pushing the bottom hand while transferring the weight forward
7. The stick blade finishes no more than 2 feet off the ice, pointing at the target

Drills

A good coach demonstrates proper form by showing players how it's done. If you're not able to demonstrate the skill yourself, utilize your most skilled player. You can point out what the player is doing correctly and incorrectly. It's always a good idea to have your players watch skill demonstrations from different angles.

leg. The stick blade and their hands should follow through and finish with the end of the stick blade pointed directly at the target. The most common mistakes players make when passing are inaccurate puck or stick position when starting the pass, poor transference of weight, and inaccurate stick position when finishing.

Backhand Pass

The principles for teaching the backhand pass are identical except for principle number three. When cupping the puck on the backhand, the wrists are not as flexible at bending backward, so players need to dip their front shoulder down toward the ice to keep control of the puck in the starting position. (See photos, opposite.)

Flip or Saucer Pass

The flip or saucer pass is the most difficult pass to master. This pass is used when the stick blade of an opponent blocks the passing lane, forcing the player to pass the puck over the stick. A good way to teach this skill begins with pairing up your players and positioning them about 10 feet away from their partner with a stick placed on the ice between them. The goal of this drill is to elevate the puck over the stick so that it lands flat on the ice, directly on the stick blade of their partner.

Begin with the same principles as the forehand pass. Have players keep their hands away from their bodies, with the majority of their body weight beginning in the back and then transferring forward. The puck should be positioned in the middle of the stick blade, with the stick cupped

Top left: Stationary partner passing works well when teaching the backhand pass. Stick blade, hand, and puck position are key. The stick blade should be cupped for control, and the hands should be away from the body, with the puck positioned in the middle of the stick blade and back.

Top right: The player's hands and weight move forward with the stick blade still cupped and the puck in the middle of the stick.

Left: The hands follow through to ensure that the stick blade points directly at the intended target.

Principles of the Flip or Saucer Pass

1. Both hands are kept away from the body
2. The puck is centered in the middle of the stick blade
3. The stick blade cups the puck and is positioned behind the back skate
4. Body weight is slightly back
5. To elevate the puck, the player snaps the lower wrist abruptly upward while pulling with the top hand
6. The stick blade finishes by pointing at the target no more than 2 feet off the ice

around the puck. The stick blade begins behind the player's side. The thrust of the flip pass depends on the force of the abrupt upward snap used in the lower wrist while pulling the stick's shaft with the top hand. The stick blade follows through but is not lifted higher than 2 feet off the ice. How high the puck travels is determined by the height of the follow-through. Wrist strength determines how far the puck will go. Properly mastering the flip pass requires a great deal of practice and patience. The most common mistakes players make when trying the flip pass are poor stick position (in other words, players have the puck too far in front of their bodies) and failing to snap the wrist abruptly when attempting to elevate the puck.

Receiving a Pass

It's critical for players to be ready to receive a pass at all times. To ensure this readiness, remind everyone to skate with their head up and to know where the puck is at all times. Teach your players that if they have their sticks on the ice, they're "presenting a target" for a teammate who's ready to pass.

Principles of Receiving a Pass

1. The stick is on the ice to present a target
2. The player makes eye contact with the passer
3. The player moves the stick blade squarely toward the passer
4. The stick blade cups and cushions the puck on contact
5. The player, with soft hands, allows the puck's momentum to push the stick back to the passing or shooting position

Drills

- Partner Passing and Receiving a Pass F14
- Center-Ice Crossover and Go F18
- Blue Line Cross Pass F19
- Four-Player Breakout F20
- Blue Line Three Pass F29

Stationary partner passing is a great way to teach both passing and pass receiving.

When receiving a pass, the player's eyes are locked on the passer, with the hands away from the body and the stick blade square to the puck

The player now cups the stick, receiving the pass in the middle of the blade and in front of the body.

Cushioning the pass will allow the player to control a hard pass. Note that the stick remains cupped, and the hands have moved in a backward motion to help absorb the pass.

They should make eye contact with the passer and watch the puck as the pass is made. Instruct them to move the stick blade to a position in front of their body, squaring it up to the passer. As the puck arrives, players should cup their stick to cushion the pass with soft hands and wrists, letting the momentum of the pass push the puck to a position of control. By doing this, players will be in a good position to shoot, stickhandle, or pass the puck. The most common mistakes that players make when receiving a pass are not squaring the stick up to the passer and not cushioning the pass.

The principles of receiving passes on the backhand are identical to the forehand except that players will be catching the pass on the backhand side of the stick and will need to slightly dip that shoulder. It's much more difficult to receive a pass on the backhand because of a number of factors. First, most hockey stick blades are curved, so the puck has a tendency to roll off the end of the stick. Also, because of body mechanics, there's less flexibility in a backward wrist flex; thus, it becomes more difficult to cushion the pass.

Stickhandling

Stickhandling is the ability to control the puck while moving it back and forth on the stick blade from the forehand to the backhand side. It's a vital skill in hockey. Good stickhandlers can create offensive attacks to score goals and are thus a great asset to their team. The term *soft hands* refers to players' ability to develop the proper feel for the puck on their stick, enabling them to stickhandle with agility. As important as stickhandling is, your players need to learn when to stickhandle with the puck and when to "head-man" or pass the puck forward to an unchecked teammate.

This is part of what is known as hockey sense, developed through play, observation, and the quick decision drills in practice.

Proper stick length is important to players' stickhandling skills. With the stick held in an upright position with the toe of the blade (the end of the blade) on the ice, the end or knob of the stick should come between the chin and nose of players when they're wearing skates.

When your players are learning to stickhandle, remind them to retain a good hockey position, keeping hands 6 to 12 inches apart on the stick. As before, have players watch you from two angles when you demonstrate the drill. Permit young players to look at the puck when they're first learning; however, as they progress, your players should be able to feel the puck on their stick. Only the lower line of their vision should remain on the puck; their head and eyes must remain erect. Players may need to move their

Principles of Stickhandling

1. Knees are bent, with the body in a good athletic hockey position: head, eyes, and chest are up
2. Hands are placed 6 to 12 inches apart on the stick
3. The stick is held in front of the body with elbows and arms away from the body
4. The puck is cupped on the stick
5. The wrists are rolled while moving the puck from side to side

Drills

- Stickhandling While Skating **F32**
- Stickhandling While Turning toward the Boards **F33**
- Skating Figure-Eight Stickhandling **F36**

It's always important to work on essential skills in practice. Here players are working on the advanced drill called Stationary Figure-Eight Stickhandling **F37** around their own gloves.

Your players should try to use full range of motion while standing stationary, stickhandling back and forth. They'll need to reach away from their body with their bottom hand sliding up and down the shaft of the stick.

Your players should have their heads up and eyes forward, using the lower part of their vision to see the puck on their stick. They'll learn to feel the puck on their stick blade and be able to cup the puck with the blade by rolling their wrists for control. To keep their eyes up, have them count the number of fingers you're holding up while they stickhandle.

bottom hand up and down the stick shaft for more control, depending on how far they can reach and how great their control of the puck. Remember that the stick is always held in front of and away from the body. As with passing and shooting, players cup the stick and roll the wrists while moving the puck from forehand to the backhand side of the stick blade. Proper positioning helps your players have greater puck control.

The European hockey philosophy incorporates stickhandling into many of their practice drills. There's a great need for North American hockey players to improve their stickhandling skills to the level of the Europeans players, who are constantly improving their puck-handling skills both on and off the ice.

Shooting

Not surprisingly, kids want to work on shooting more than anything else. Since winning hockey games requires scoring goals, shooting is obviously an essential fundamental. Although most kids are excited by the prospect of mastering the slap shot, the most used and most important shot is the wrist shot. In fact, you should explain to your players that they have a much better chance to score a goal by using an accurate wrist shot than an inaccurate slap shot. The wrist shot is the shot most used in hockey because it's quick and accurate. Because the element of surprise is so important, it's a distinct advantage to get off a wrist shot before a defender or goaltender knows it's coming.

When you demonstrate any type of shot, make certain your players can watch your motions from the side and from behind. After your demonstration, have each player shoot pucks at the side boards while standing about 15 feet away. That way, they can work on their shots while the techniques are still fresh in their minds. This is an ideal time for your assistant coaches to move from player to player with corrections and suggestions. Since repetition is the key to improved shooting, players should be encouraged to practice shooting skills off the ice as well as on. They can use the outside wall of their home or an area in an unfinished basement as long as they take great care to avoid the windows.

Wrist Shot

The body position for a wrist shot is the same as in a forward pass, meaning players' knees are bent and their body is in a good athletic hockey position. Some coaches don't teach their players to look at the target; however, I've found it's important for skaters to give a quick glance at the target so they know where they want to shoot the puck. The surprise element in hockey is important, so keeping the glance brief will keep the goalie unsure of where the player intends to shoot. Although goalkeepers are taught to focus on the puck, skilled goalies can also "read" where the player is going to shoot.

The shooters' body should be squared up toward the net. Players cup the puck in the middle of the stick blade and then pull the puck toward the back leg. To ensure a more powerful shot, the body weight is slightly shifted back, with the bottom hand down the stick shaft. As the puck is swept forward with the bottom hand pushing and the top hand pulling, players move the puck from the middle of the blade to the heel, transferring his weight onto the front foot. While the stick moves across the body, players rotate the shoulders square to the target. Remind them to keep the front leg bent and point the foot, gliding in the direction of the shot. Right before the shot is taken, players snap the wrists from an open to a closed position, generating power for an accurate shot by snapping the bottom hand slightly toward the body and pulling the top hand in close. Follow-through is very important because the final position of the body determines whether the shot stays low or hits the top corner of the net. In the follow-through, the trailing leg comes off the ice. The most common mistakes made when practicing the wrist shot are beginning with the puck on the toe of the stick and positioning the stick in the front of the body when starting the shot. (See photos next page.)

Backhand Shot

The backhand shot is particularly useful when a player is close to the net and doesn't have the time or opportunity to move the puck to the forehand. In addition, a skater who is near the net often finds it easier to get the puck high into the top corner of the net using the backhand. Although it isn't usually a powerful shot, it can be accurate and cause the goalkeeper a great deal of trouble.

Drills

- Four-Player Breakout F20
- Three-Lane Shooting F38
- Three-Line Shooting F39
- Half-Ice Horseshoe F40
- Full-Ice Horseshoe F41
- Umbrella Shooting F42
- Wrist Shots, Backhand Shots, Snap Shots, and Slap Shots F43
- Curl-Out Shooting F45

Principles of the Wrist Shot

1. Eyes are on the target, with the body square to the net
2. Body weight, puck, and stick are back
3. As the puck is swept forward, body weight transfers to the front foot
4. The player squares the shoulders and front foot up to the net
5. Just before the shot is released, the player snaps both wrists
6. The follow-through determines the height of the shot

Top left: Quickness is the key when performing the wrist shot. Body weight, stick, and puck position are back. The puck is cupped on the heel of the stick. Be square to the net and feel the puck on your stick blade.

Top right: With the player's eyes on the target, the hands pull the puck forward. Body weight moves forward as the shoulders and front foot turn to point toward the net. The puck is released with the wrists snapping through the shot; the puck then rolls off the toe of the stick.

Bottom: The player must follow through with the stick blade pointed at the target, rolling the wrists over to feel that snapping motion.

To perform a backhand shot, players glance at their target, keeping their body squared up toward the net. The bottom hand slides down the stick shaft, and the puck is stickhandled from forehand to backhand. Players cup the puck in the middle of the stick, transferring their body weight toward the back foot. To retain puck control, players dip their front shoulder slightly. As their hands begin to move forward, players get their entire body into the shot by shifting their body forward. Players abruptly snap their bottom hand outward, square their shoulders toward the target, and glide toward the net on the front leg. As in the wrist shot, the follow-through determines the height of the shot, and using the entire body, not just the arms, yields the maximum power from the shot.

Hand movement is important when taking a backhand shot. The puck is cupped on the heel of the backhand side of the stick. The player's eyes should be on the target, but the body weight and stick are toward the back foot.

The eyes remain on the target, and the hands pull the puck forward. The player's weight moves forward as the shoulders and front foot turn to point toward the net. With the front shoulder slightly dipped, the player uses forward body motion and abruptly snaps the bottom hand outward to release the shot.

Principles of the Backhand Shot

1. Eyes are on the target, with the body square to the net
2. The player's bottom hand slides down the stick shaft, and the puck is stickhandled from forehand to backhand
3. The puck is cupped in the middle of the stick, and body weight transfers toward the back leg
4. The front shoulder dips slightly, and the body shifts forward
5. The player snaps the bottom hand outward, squares the shoulders, and glides toward the net on the front leg
6. The follow-through determines the height of the shot

The player should follow through with the stick blade and hands pointing at the target.

Snap Shot

The snap shot is like a wrist shot that has acquired some technique from the slap shot. Properly developed, the snap shot can be more powerful than the wrist shot and just as accurate. Many goaltenders are caught off guard by a snap shot because it's the quickest shot in a player's arsenal.

Principles of the Snap Shot

1. Eyes are on the target, with the body square to the net
2. The player keeps the puck and stick back
3. Body weight shifts forward as the puck is pulled toward the front foot, the stick is lifted slightly off the ice, and the puck slides ahead of the stick
4. The player firmly forces the stick blade down on the ice behind the puck
5. The player contacts the puck in the middle of the stick blade and snaps the wrists

Left: The snap shot is a quick-release shot that's often used to surprise the goaltender. A snap shot taken when shooting directly off a pass is known as a one-timer. Unlike the wrist shot, where the puck stays in constant contact with the stick blade until release, the snap shot is delivered with the stick blade contacting the ice in a downward motion a few inches behind the puck. The key to surprising the goaltender is in the length of the back swing. The stick blade should never be more than a few inches off the ice before making contact.

Right: The finish position for the snap shot is the same as with all shots. The body weight moves forward as the player's shoulders, head, and eyes square up to the target. The toe of the front skate and the stick blade follow through, pointing at the intended target. The stick blade should finish no higher than shoulder height on the follow-through.

All the initial mechanics of the snap and wrist shots are identical. However, during a snap shot, the puck separates from the stick as it moves from the back to the front leg. Again, players begin in a good athletic hockey position with the stick behind the back leg and the puck in the middle of the stick. They look at the target. Body weight shifts forward as the puck is pulled toward the front foot. The puck should leave the stick blade and actually be 6 to 8 inches in front of it, very close to the heel of the front foot. To shoot, the stick blade is lifted slightly and then brought down firmly on the ice 1 to 2 inches behind the puck. Using a downward, forceful motion, players bring the stick into contact with the puck at the middle of the blade, keeping the follow-through short and low. The snap shot's power comes from both wrists snapping through the shot. Many players use this technique, also called a "one timer," to take an immediate shot off a pass.

Slap Shot

Every kid wants to learn how to take a slap shot. They love the sound of the stick hitting the puck, followed by the even louder sound of the puck hitting the boards or glass. This is exactly the problem. More often than not, the puck ends up missing the net but finds the glass or boards. Although the slap shot is the most powerful shot in hockey, it's also the least accurate. More-

The slap shot is used most effectively when a defenseman shoots low to an awaiting teammate near a screened goalie.

Principles of the Slap Shot

1. The puck is behind the player's front foot
2. The player slides the bottom hand slightly farther down the stick
3. Eyes are on the puck, but the player also watches the net
4. The player lifts the stick back to shoulder height, keeping body weight back
5. The player quickly swings the stick down toward the puck and leans into the shot; body weight shifts forward
6. The stick blade hits the ice behind the puck
7. The player snaps the wrists, moving the stick to make contact with the puck
8. In the follow-through the player points the stick at the target

over, it's *not* the shot used by most professional players. I recommend delaying teaching this shot until Pee Wee level at the earliest. Even then, a player should have already mastered the wrist, backhand, and snap shots and be physically strong enough to bend the stick shaft before learning the slap shot.

A strong slap shot can beat a goaltender, but it's used most effectively when a defenseman shoots low toward a screened goalie so an awaiting teammate can deflect the puck on net. Most goalkeepers will stop a slap shot if they get a clear view of it, so the chances of scoring a goal increase considerably by using the element of surprise. Everyone in the arena, especially the goaltender, can tell when a player is about to unleash a slap shot.

As with the previous shots, demonstrate the slap shot so your players can watch from the side and behind. Have your players start with the puck a comfortable distance away from their body, about 6 inches behind their front foot. With their body square to the net, players slide their bottom hand slightly downward on the stick shaft, gripping the stick firmly. Remind players that while their eyes should be on the puck, they must maintain awareness of the location of the net.

In the next step, players lift the stick to shoulder height in a backward arc, with their weight on the back foot. The stick is then quickly brought toward the ice, pulling with the top hand and pushing with the bottom. Body weight moves forward so the entire body leans into the shot. The front foot and hips then turn toward the target. The stick blade makes contact with the ice 2 inches behind the puck, and with a snap of the wrists the stick strikes the puck. Again, the follow-through must conclude with the stick blade pointing directly at the target and the player's back leg finishing in the air. Using the proper technique ensures there is sufficient power behind the shot.

Keep in mind that timing is a big part of learning this shot, which is difficult to perfect. The most common mistakes made while learning the slap shot are contacting the puck beyond the front foot, contacting the puck

The STOP Program

In 1996, Kevin Stubbington of Windsor Minor Hockey developed the *Safety Toward Other Players* program (STOP) to raise awareness of the dangers of checking from behind in hockey. Five- to twelve-year-old youth hockey participants wear the STOP patch on the back of their jersey as a reminder to fellow players to exercise caution, especially when playing near the boards. Since 1999, over 385,000 patches have been distributed throughout Ontario, Newfoundland, and British Columbia, as well as parts of the United States.

The Fair Play component of the STOP program requires both parents and players to sign Fair Play Pledges. Parents commit to encourage their children to play by the rules without conflict, eliminate verbal abuse from the game, and support their children's coaches and game officials. Players promise to be true team players, control their tempers, be respectful of opponents, and accept the decisions of coaches and officials, remembering that "success is never final and failure is never fatal."

The STOP (Safety Toward Other Players) logo is worn on the back of a player's jersey to remind other players of the dangers of checking from behind.

Developed in 1996, the STOP program has spread throughout North America, and now includes over 385,000 participants.

Players and parents who agree to exercise self-control on and off the ice must sign the Fair Play component of the STOP program.

before the ice, and failing to snap the wrists through the shot. Many players think if they open up their blade on contact, the puck will rise. In reality, the blade must be squared and cupped toward the target, or the shot will fade ineffectively toward the toe of the stick. When practicing any shot, the most important element to master first is accuracy; power will come with repetition and increased strength.

Checking

Checking skills are used to prevent the opposing team from effectively controlling the puck. When people hear the term *checking*, many think only of body contact. Actually, there are body checks that involve contact (shoulder checking and hip checking) and noncontact (angle checking) as well as several types of stick checking (poke check, hook check, sweep check, stick lift, and stick press). Checking skills are used not only by defensemen but also by forwards while forechecking or backchecking after the puck has been turned over to the opponent. Checking is a crucial component of defensive play. To determine which type of check to use, players must first ascertain the number of attacking opponents and where the opponents are positioned on the ice. They must also recognize and evaluate the opportunities of their opponent. By skating, a player can gain proper position and be successful in body checking an opponent. Any league that is USA Hockey sanctioned, along with most other leagues, recommends teaching body contact no earlier than the Pee Wee level.

Noncontact Checking

Before learning the body check, youth hockey players must learn to make an angle check. *Angle checking* requires good skating skills because the opponent is forced to go in the direction the *checker* determines. The checker approaches the puck carrier from an angle instead of in a straight line, significantly cutting down on the puck carrier's options.

As the offensive player skates down the boards and is angled off by the defensive player, players will get the feel of this check. Remind defensive players to keep their stick on the ice when approaching the offensive player and thus to take away the passing lane.

Body-Contact Checking

It's extremely important to teach youth hockey players the proper techniques of body checking. You cannot overemphasize the dangers of checking from behind or the importance of respecting other players by refraining from this practice. Equally as important is teaching the proper way to play and body-check near the boards. USA Hockey's Heads-Up Hockey instructs players on how to react when they are being hit or find themselves falling headfirst into the boards, which can cause serious and permanent neck or spinal injury. Players who are falling near the boards should keep their head up and should also attempt to extend their arms over their head or turn sideways so their arms and shoulder pads take the brunt of the impact. Hockey equipment that's in good condition and that fits properly is essential for eliminating injuries while body checking and receiving checks.

Most kids have the wrong perspective about body checking. Coaches must convey that there's no room for a killer instinct in youth hockey. I have witnessed too many players who become overly excited when they are first permitted to body-check because they think it's a type of demolition derby on ice. Nothing could be further from the truth. Body checking is a useful technique for separating the puck from an opponent, but never at the expense of causing injury.

Principles of the Angle Check
1. The player's position separates the opponent from the puck
2. The player limits the opponent's options by forcing a hasty decision
3. The stick is kept on the ice in the passing lane
4. The player angles toward the boards to limit the opponent's options
5. The player lifts or squeezes the opponent's stick into the boards to gain control of the puck

Drill
- Angle Checking   F48

Drill
- Giving and Receiving Shoulder Checks, Body Checks, and Hip Checks   F50

Principles of Receiving a Body Check

1. The head is up, and eyes survey the ice
2. The player anticipates when contact will occur and tries to make the proper pass or shot before contact occurs
3. The player receives the check with knees bent and feet shoulder width apart
4. The stick and elbows are kept down
5. The upper arm (side of the shoulder pad) or hip pads absorb the impact of the check
6. The player avoids turning the back to an opponent when near the boards

Drill

- Giving and Receiving Shoulder Checks, Body Checks, and Hip Checks
  F50

Teach players the differences between legal and illegal plays. It's illegal to hit an opponent from behind when that player is facing the boards. However, an opposing player in possession of the puck near the boards can be body-checked from the side. Players can remove an opponent from the play in hockey, but they cannot go after their opponent in a reckless fashion. Remind players that body checking without regard to rules can bring injury to both the checker and the receiver of the check. Attempts to body-check an opponent by taking reckless runs at the other player are not only dangerous—it isn't smart hockey because instead of reading and reacting to the play, these reckless checkers are actually taking themselves out of it.

And finally, teach your players to recognize when an opponent is defenseless and to avoid further contact.

It's extremely important to teach your players how to protect themselves on the ice as soon as they begin learning to body-check. Vision becomes their most important tool in determining when body contact will occur. Tell your players to keep their head up at all times while skating, constantly surveying the ice. If possible, players should make the right pass or shot before contact with an opponent occurs. They should have both knees bent with their feet shoulder width apart and their weight over the midline of their body before body contact with an opponent. It's also important that they keep their sticks and elbows down to avoid injuring the contacting player. This will also prevent them from receiving a needless penalty.

Shoulder Check

To receive a shoulder check, the players' knees should be bent, with the body leaning slightly in the direction of contact. They should absorb the hit with their upper arm (side of the shoulder pad) or the side of the body, including the hip pad. Players are most vulnerable when they are 3 to 8 feet from the boards. They should never turn their back on an opponent to face the boards! Nor should they ever put themselves in a position that will cause injury. Players who are facing the boards before a potential body check should attempt to move laterally to avoid the check or absorb the check, or they should turn to absorb the check with the side of the body. At worst, they should keep both hands on their stick, raising their forearms and gloves onto the glass on top of the boards, thereby cushioning the blow. They should lean in slightly toward the boards, keeping their skates about a foot from the boards and planted solidly on the ice. Having their feet too close to the boards increases the risk of losing their balance on contact. Players who are hit against the boards should attempt to take the check with their shoulder, side, and hip together instead of the point of their shoulder, chest, or head. Remind players to have a strong base by keeping their feet shoulder width apart and knees bent when receiving a check. Most concussions occur in the NHL when a player's head is the first part of the body to make contact. Again, the best way to avoid being hit is by constantly surveying the ice. In

The Coach's Safety PAGE

Prevention: Prevent injuries by instructing your players to keep their head up and maintain readiness

Assessment: If your player is injured, assess the type and extent of injury

Get Help: Solicit help from a trainer or emergency medical personnel

Ensure: Ensure follow-up care

Principles of the Shoulder Check

1. The player reads the play and knows when to hit
2. The player utilizes gap control by gauging the opponent's speed
3. Eyes are focused on the opponent's chest, and the player's shoulder is aimed there as well
4. A good firm base is maintained, with weight on the inside skate edges and the body ready to make contact
5. The shoulder and side of the body make contact with the opponent
6. With knees bent, the player drives upward, extending the legs during contact

addition to teaching your players to take care of themselves, you cannot overemphasize the important of respecting other players by refraining from checking from behind.

To teach this technique properly, demonstrate correct body position and how to place the opponent into a position to be hit. Don't forget to first teach your players how to take a check and play near the boards.

When you first begin instructing players how to make a shoulder check, don't allow the player with the puck to cut back to the middle of the ice. Tell defensive players to angle the puck carrier toward the boards (remember: knees bent, back straight, head and eyes up), aiming their shoulder at the opponent's chest. With the body weight positioned on the inside edges of both skates, defensive players drive their shoulder along with the entire side of their body into the opponent's chest.

The key to retaining balance is extending both legs from the bent position after making the initial contact and then driving upward to a full extension. To avoid injuring the other player and receiving a penalty, players should keep the elbows and stick down. The biggest mistakes made when body checking are failing to time the hit properly, leading with the head,

It's important to teach young hockey players to respect their opponents. Never body-check an opponent from behind or when the player is in a vulnerable position. Serious injury may occur. Teach your players to body-check with a strong, athletic hockey base to maintain balance.

Principles of the Hip Check

1. The hip check is usually a defenseman's check, used while skating backward
2. The player reads the play and knows when to hit
3. The player utilizes gap control and gauges the opponent's speed
4. Knees are bent, with the body in a good hockey position: head, chest, and eyes are up
5. The player maintains a good firm base by bending slightly forward at the waist and keeping body weight over the skates
6. The player pushes off on the outside skate and then drives the hip into the thighs of the opponent
7. Legs are extended beginning at the moment of contact

checking from behind, and straightening the legs to a full extension too early.

Hip Check

A hip check is more difficult to make and deliver than the shoulder check. It's also easy for players to lose their balance after making the hit. A properly executed hip check uses the element of surprise because most players are anticipating a shoulder check. Defensemen who can anticipate a potential pass from one opponent to another can effectively neutralize the pass after it is received by using a hip check.

Remind your players that the checking hip must contact the opponent's thigh area. Throwing a hip check lower than the thighs could injure the opponent's knees. Delivering a hip check that is too high can result in the offensive player's stick injuring the defensive player's rib cage. The biggest mistake made when delivering a hip check is bending from the waist too early, thereby eliminating the element of surprise. An offensive player who knows when a hip check is coming can usually avoid it and continue with the offensive opportunity.

Stick Checking

Stick checking includes the poke check, hook check, sweep check, stick lift, and stick press. In all situations, a player must control his stick while performing any of these checks to avoid injuring another player. Performing any stick check incorrectly can also lead to hooking or tripping penalties that result in power plays for the opposing team.

Poke Check

The poke check is used most often by a defenseman skating backward against an attacking opponent. Defensemen must retain proper balance while skating backward, with the knees bent and the head, chest, and eyes up. The distance between defensemen and their opponent is especially crucial; smart defensemen always try to lure attackers into thinking they have enough room to attempt an offensive maneuver. Defensemen should concentrate on their opponent's midsection while watching the puck with their peripheral vision. Defensemen keep only the top hand on the stick, resting in front of them. That arm should be flexed, with the hand by the side of his hip. When an opponent comes into range, defensemen quickly extend that arm to knock the puck off the attacker's stick. Extending only that arm allows defensemen to keep themselves in good body position to continue defending the attacker if the poke check fails.

The biggest mistakes made when attempting a poke check are extending the stick too quickly and lunging at the puck, causing prospective poke-checkers to lose their balance. Remind players that a forward-skating defender can use the poke check as well to separate the puck from the opponent.

Minor Injuries? Think RICE

For any injury that is not a fracture (like strains and sprains), think RICE:

- **R**est the area to avoid further injury. Avoid activities that exacerbate the injury, but continue to move the injured area gently. Early gentle movement promotes healing.

- **I**ce the area to reduce swelling. Apply ice to the affected area for 20 minutes and then leave it off for half an hour. *Note:* Don't use ice on a player who has circulatory problems.

- **C**ompress the area with an elastic wrap (when icing, secure the ice bag under the wrap). Compression creates a pressure gradient that reduces swelling and promotes healing. An elastic bandage provides a moderate amount of pressure that will help discourage swelling.

- **E**levate the injured area above the level of the heart. Elevation is especially effective when used in conjunction with compression. Elevation provides a pressure gradient. The higher the injured body part is raised, the more fluid is pulled away from the injury site via gravity. Elevate the injury as high above the heart as comfortable. Continue to elevate intermittently until swelling is gone.

Hook Check

The hook check is used most often to attempt to gain puck possession when chasing an opponent from behind. Defenders should hold their stick with the top hand only, extending the shaft close to the ice. While maintaining their balance, hook-checkers should get as low as possible by bending one knee. Their stick blade should be lying flat on the ice, pointing in the direction of the puck. The hook check is so named because defenders attempt to extend their stick and gain possession of the puck by hooking it away from the opponent. This is considered a risky check to attempt because unsuccessful players will find their body in a poor position to recover quickly. As a last resort, players can attempt a hook check while diving flat out on their stomach. However, make it clear to your players that a penalty may be called if they leave their feet and in any way cause their opponent to fall because of contact with the prone player's stick or body.

Principles of the Poke Check

1. The stick is used to separate the puck from the opponent
2. Good balance and proper body position are maintained
3. Focus is on the opponent's midsection
4. The player uses peripheral vision to keep the puck in view
5. The player's top hand waits near the hip and holds the stick forward with the arm flexed
6. Only the player's arm extends to poke the puck away
7. If the poke check fails, the player must be positioned to continue to defend the opponent

Drill
- Poke Check   F49

Principles of the Hook Check

1. The hook check is used to stick-check the puck from behind an opponent
2. The player completely bends one knee while remaining in balance
3. The player extends the stick with the shaft low and the stick blade lying flat on the ice and pointing toward the puck
4. The puck is hooked toward the defender and away from the opponent's stick

Drill
- Hook Check and Sweep Check   F52

Principles of the Sweep Check

1. The sweep check is used to stick-check the puck from behind an opponent or from his side
2. The player extends the stick with the shaft low and the stick blade lying flat on the ice and pointing toward the puck
3. The player keeps his body low or sprawls flat on his stomach and uses his stick to make a sweeping motion toward his opponent; hopefully this will cause him to lose control of the puck

Drill

- Hook Check and Sweep Check F52

Stick Skills: A Defenseman's Best Friend

I remember being cut from a AA travel team when I was thirteen years old. Although I'd already played AA for four years, my coaches suddenly decided I was too small to play at that level. Fortunately, my parents were willing to drive me to another team located forty-five minutes from home. I was also lucky that my father was a coach. He taught me subtle defensive maneuvers using my stick that helped me throughout my entire NHL career. Although I was one of the smaller defensemen in the league, I had learned to use my stick as leverage, especially against guys who were a lot bigger and stronger than I was.

Sweep Check

The sweep check is similar to the poke check in the standing position and much like the hook check in the bent position. It should only be attempted from the side of the puck carrier. Players attempting a sweep check in front of their opponent run a greater chance that their shoulders and body momentum will turn, thereby opening an opportunity for their opponent to cut back and beat them. Although the technique used is similar to the hook check, it isn't used to gain possession of the puck, but rather to sweep it away from an opponent. Remind your players not to overcommit to the opponent's body and miss the puck completely because they need to maintain a good defensive position.

Stick Lift

Lifting the stick is used for two reasons: to gain puck possession and to eliminate an opponent's chances of receiving a pass or redirecting a puck on goal. In both cases, it's vital to retain good body position in relation to one's opponent. Advise players to take an inside position, staying between the opponent and their own net. They need to know where the puck is at all times, especially when the puck approaches the player they're covering. At that point, they can lift the opponent's stick near the heel of the blade to eliminate the offensive play. Remember that when defensemen are playing in front of the net, they can't overcommit to guarding one player. If a teammate loses the check, the defenseman in front of the net must react by covering two players at once but must know which player is the most dangerous.

Principles of the Stick Lift

1. Strength comes from a strong, athletic hockey base
2. The player skates into a firm position in front of the opponent
3. The player uses the stick to lift the heel of the opponent's stick off the ice
4. The player gains control of the puck or eliminates a scoring chance from a pass or shot

Drills

- One-on-One Battle (Stick Lift and Stick Press) F47
- One-on-One Battle GS3

Players need a strong, athletic hockey base when using the stick lift technique to gain possession of the puck and to prevent an opponent from shooting on net or receiving a pass from a teammate.

Lifting the opponent's stick blade off the ice also prevents the player from deflecting a shot or recovering a loose rebound.

Principles of the Stick Press

1. Strength comes from a strong, athletic hockey base
2. The player skates into a firm position in front of the opponent
3. The player's body weight presses down on the lower shaft of an opponent's stick
4. The player gains control of the puck or eliminates a scoring chance from a pass or shot

Drills
- One-on-One Battle (Stick Lift and Stick Press) F47
- One-on-One Battle GS3

Stick Press

The stick press is used in much the same manner as the stick lift. Defensive players press down hard on the top of the lower shaft of an opponent's stick to eliminate the possibility of an offensive play. However, if possible, the lift should be used instead of the press because it's much more difficult for players to score a goal if their stick is lifted completely off the ice. The body muscles are also stronger when using the stick lift as opposed to the stick press.

CHAPTER 5

Goaltending

The Last Line of Defense

The goaltender, the last line of defense, has the last chance to prevent the puck from entering the net. But because hockey is a team sport, it's important to explain to everyone on your team that no matter how the game is progressing, they must be supportive of their goaltender. Everyone should understand that when a goal is scored, usually more than one mistake has been made.

Since goaltending is often an overlooked position, coaches need to gather as much information as possible to help a goaltender progress. Speak with the team officials in your organization to see if goaltending coaches or older kids who play goal would be willing to donate some of their time and assistance. I encourage goaltenders to get instruction from a goalie coach. Most youth teams don't have such a position, so parents will need to sign up their child at separate clinics.

Goaltender-specific equipment is discussed in the equipment section of Chapter 3.

Goalie Psychology

You'll quickly learn when you have players who want to be a goaltender. They'll have a glimmer in their eye and the passion to play this difficult position. They must possess a good attitude, a positive mindset, and the right temperament, including the confidence to believe they can stop shots. Because of this, goaltenders cannot have any fear of the puck. Goalies must understand that they can never stop every shot and that they'll let in a weak goal once in a while. But the best goaltenders never allow a bad goal to affect their play. They learn to block out the negative thoughts so they can refocus and concentrate on the next shot. Although this position is clearly the most pressure packed, it's highly rewarding as well.

Goaltending Attributes

1. Good vision, including good peripheral vision, is one of the most important attributes of a goaltender.
2. Good athletes usually have the ability to transfer their talents to good net minding.
3. Great skating skills are essential; in fact, there's an old saying that the goaltender needs to be the best skater on the team. You'll see the truth in this statement when you watch a great goaltender move laterally with ease while wearing up to forty pounds of equipment.
4. Agility is key. Goalies must develop the quickness to move from post to post, drop to their knees and get up quickly, and move out toward the shooter and then back toward the net with agility and precise timing.
5. Overall dexterity, including eye-hand coordination, is a must. Smooth movements help the goalie stop the puck and direct rebounds out of harm's way. Good coordination usually develops as the child grows.
6. Lightning-quick reflexes enable goalies to catch or block shots.
7. Flexibility is a must. There are many stretching exercises that can be used at any age to help goalies become more flexible.
8. Concentration is an important part of this position. Most goaltenders play the entire game, so they must be able to keep their focus and concentration for long periods of time.
9. It's important for goaltenders to play other sports to attain body control and coordination. Off-ice training programs that include jumping, balancing, and speed work are great ways to improve.

A Goaltender's World

The goalie is usually the only team member who plays the entire game. If a team has two goaltenders, it's the coach's responsibility to speak with both and decide what's best for their personal development as well as best for the team. Some coaches alternate their net minders on a game-by-game basis while others have each goaltender play half of every game. Talk to your goalies and see what they prefer. Remember that your main objective is that your players have fun.

Goalie Fundamentals

Goalies must concentrate on the puck, not the body or stick position of the opponent with the puck. They should watch the puck when making a save, training their eyes to remain on it when it makes contact with their equipment. They always need to know the location of all the opposing players on the ice.

Goaltenders can see almost the entire ice surface from the goal crease; in other words, they have the best vantage point on the ice. By being constantly aware of the location of opposing players on the ice, goalies can spot any outnumbered situations. This will allow them to know whether to expect a shot, a pass, or the potential of both. Their overriding responsibility, however, is to stop the puck or direct any rebounds out of harm's way and into the corners.

Goaltenders are the only players on the ice who are permitted to close their hand on the puck and hold onto it. Other players may use their hand to knock a puck out of the air, but they risk drawing a penalty if they close their hand on the puck.

Only goaltenders can cover (freeze) the puck in the goal crease to stop play. Teammates may *push* the puck out of the goal crease in any manner including using their hands, but a penalty shot will be awarded to the other team if they cover the puck.

Stance and Movement

Stance. The basic stance for goaltenders is to have their feet shoulder width apart, with their knees bent as if sitting in a chair. Their skates are parallel, with weight on the inside edges. Body weight is slightly forward, but the chest and back are straight. The shoulders and knees are positioned over the toes. Their head is up, and the neck is relaxed. Both hands are out in front of the body, but outside the leg pads. The catching glove is open and facing forward at the same height as the blocker. The stick is held firmly with the blade positioned on the ice at a slight angle toward the leg pads and about 6 inches in front of the skates.

The most common stance errors for goaltenders are bending from the waist instead of the knees; positioning the hands at the side of the body instead of the front; holding the catching glove closed or not facing forward; and keeping the stick blade either off the ice or against the skates.

While maintaining the basic stance, goalies can move as follows:

Parallel shuffle. In the parallel shuffle, goalies take short, lateral side steps, pushing with the inside edge of the trailing leg. The trailing pad is brought back to meet the lead pad. The stick moves with the lead pad to cover the space between the legs. Body weight is on the balls of the feet.

It's important to have someone knowledgeable in goaltending to work with your net minders. Here we're working on the goaltender's basic stance.

Lateral T-glide. Here goalies make quick movements over longer distances. They push off the trailing skate, gliding on the lead skate to form a T. The stick moves with the lead pad, covering the space between the skates; the inside edges of both skates are used for stopping.

Pivot. This is the movement from the post across (across the crease) to square up to the shooter. Goaltenders swivel their hips and shoulders, pushing off the inside edge of the trailing skate and moving across so their skates face in the same direction. They can also employ the parallel shuffle to stay with the shooter.

Forward and backward skating. Goalies use forward and backward movements to move from the post out toward the shooter and back toward the post. They push off the inside skate edges, making short, quick C cuts. A snowplow on the inside skate edges is used for stopping.

The most common goaltending errors are straightening up too much while coming out of the stance; failing to keep the knees together; raising the stick off the ice or positioning it to keep the space between the skates covered; failing to remain square to the shooter; and losing the angle, which is where the net is in relation to the shooter.

The Five Spots that Players Shoot For

The *one hole* is the area located low to the goaltender's stick side. In competitive play, most goals are scored here. When a puck is shot at the one hole, the goaltender attempts to make saves by using the blocker to direct the puck to the corner or a leg pad (butterfly save); if the shot is on the ice, the goaltender will often make a stick or skate save.

The *two hole* is the area located low to the goaltender's catching glove side. Good flexibility is needed to reach these low shots. It's easier to stop a puck shot on the ice to the glove side by making a leg-pad (butterfly), stick, or skate save rather than using the catching glove.

The *three hole* is the area located high to the goaltender's catching glove side. It's easier to make a catching glove save on pucks shot to this spot from the stand-up position (basic stance).

The *four hole* is the area located high to the goaltender's blocker (stick) side. Although fewer goals are scored here, it's harder to protect this area with the blocker when a goaltender drops to the butterfly position.

The *five hole* (the space between the legs) is the fifth target. It is the most vulnerable spot for a goaltender because it is more difficult to cover when moving side to side or when dropping into the butterfly position.

The five spots players shoot for.

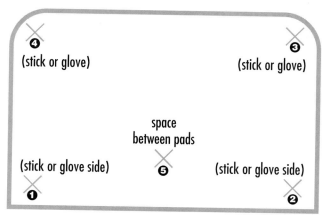

When the goaltender catches left-handed, players aim for the top left corner of the net high on the blocker side, the top right corner high on the glove side, the bottom left corner low on the stick side, or the bottom right corner low on the glove side.

At the beginner level, most goals are scored on the ice for two reasons. First, beginning goaltenders are not experienced with their lateral or up-and-down movements; second, many beginning shooters can't raise the puck off the ice. It takes a lot of practice to become accomplished at saving low shots.

As goaltenders progress and shooters are able to raise the puck, the top corners of the net become more difficult to cover. This is only because young goaltenders are not tall enough to cover the upper portions of the net.

By Bantam age, most of the goals are scored below the knees as shooters find less room to shoot up high.

Ways to Make a Save

From the stand-up position, goaltenders can make a stick, skate, or leg-pad save when shots come low. High shots are stopped with the catching glove, blocker, or any other part of the body. The butterfly position helps goaltenders cover all five spots a shooter looks for, but lateral movements become more difficult. In the butterfly position, goaltenders will make low saves with their leg pads or stick. Skate saves are made from the stand-up position to direct pucks toward the corners of the rink. Stick saves are made in any position to direct pucks to the corners or to cover up any rebounds. Stacking the pads to make a save should only be used on passes and plays that occur in close to the net while moving laterally.

Stand-up save. Using the basic stance, the goalie moves forward to the top of the crease to challenge the shooter, which reduces the amount of net the shooter is able to see. The goalie skates to square up to the puck, keeping the proper angle in relationship to the net. Any rebounds are covered with the stick and catching glove. This position is used to play the angles and force a shot to miss the net. Goalies may need to use their stick, skate, or blocker to deflect shots to the corners or their catching glove to trap the puck.

Butterfly save. In the basic stance, the goalie moves forward to the top of the crease to challenge the shooter, cutting down on the amount of net the shooter can see. As the player releases the shot, the goalie squares up to the puck by keeping the chest and upper body in line with it. Then the goalie descends to the butterfly position, dropping to the inside of the knees and legs with the feet fanned out and toes pointed toward the posts. The stick stays on the ice covering the area between the pads; it is used along with the catching glove to cover rebounds.

The butterfly save is used primarily for low shots in order to cover the greatest area. Many of today's goaltenders use it as their primary method of stopping pucks. The half butterfly is frequently used to stop low shots taken

Make sure your goaltenders use proper form for the butterfly save. Their body and stick position will allow them to direct shots to the corners or prevent rebounds by covering up the puck.

to one side of the net. In this position, the "saving" leg stretches out toward the post while the opposite leg lies flat on the ice.

Skate save. In the basic stance, the goalie moves forward to the top of the crease to challenge the shooter, cutting down on the amount of net the shooter can see. The goaltender squares up to the puck, pushing off on the inside edge of the skate opposite the "saving" skate. The "saving" skate blade turns in an arcing motion toward the corner, remaining flat on the ice to deflect the puck to the corner. At the same time, the opposite pad drops to the ice for support. The chest and catching glove are up; the stick follows across in an arcing motion to cover the space between the legs. Skate saves are made when goalies can't reach the shot by staying on their feet.

Stacking the pads. To stack the pads, the goalie pushes off the inside edge of one skate and slides across the crease while allowing momentum to help kick out the bottom leg so it can lie flat on the ice. As the top leg extends, the bottom leg curls underneath and behind, becoming a "scoop" along the ice. The pads stay together by remaining stacked as the goalie's hip also lands on the ice. One leg must kick hard to achieve the necessary pad-on-pad results. As the goaltender straightens out her legs, her body is bent at the hips with her shoulders facing slightly downward. This is extremely important, or both her feet will rise off the ice, and she'll end up on her back. The goalie must keep the glove on the stacking side just above the pads and the opposite arm flat on the ice, stretched out as long as possible in the other direction.

Pad stacking is used as a desperation move when the puck is within 5 feet of the net. It's employed only when an attacking player is cutting sharply toward the net or when the goalie is moving quickly across the crease to stop a shot off a lateral pass.

Goalie Warm-Ups

1. General skating around the ice or skating from side boards to side boards.
2. Parallel shuffles to center ice, staying near the boards and then turning and changing direction.
3. Moving in goal from side to side, either doing the parallel shuffle or the T-glide from post to post.
4. Moving forward from the post, pushing forward on the inside skate edge to a snowplow stop, moving back to the post, and then repeating from the opposite side.
5. Making the butterfly save movement while sliding side to side moving outward and then popping quickly back to the feet.

Rebound control. This is used when the goalie cannot deflect a shot to the corner or other specific area. Rebounds are easy to control on high shots because they can usually be caught with the glove, deflected to the corner using the blocker, or absorbed into the pants or chest or arm pads. Low shots, however, present rebound problems. Control is greatly increased by keeping the stick positioned 6 inches in front of the pads and angled slightly back. When a puck hits the pads, the goaltender bends the knees forward in an exaggerated position to help deflect the puck downward and then quickly cover it with the catching glove. Pucks that hit the pads rebounding outward can sometimes be brought back in with the stick.

Goalie Drills

Y Drill G1 ⬤

Purpose: To improve goaltenders' lateral movements and edge control and help them better understand their angles.

1. The goalie assumes the basic goaltender's stance.
2. He pushes forward from the middle of the net to outside of the crease area, stops, and glides backward to the top of the crease.
3. He pivots to a 45-degree angle and then does parallel shuffles back to the post.
4. Repeat on the opposite side.

Common errors during this drill are bending too much at the waist and failing to have the stick covering the area between the legs.

X Drill G2 ●

Purpose: To improve goaltenders' lateral movements and skating skills and teach them how to track the puck.

1. The goalie assumes the basic goaltender's stance.
2. She pushes forward from one post diagonally across the crease to the opposite angle, stops, and glides backward to the top of the crease.
3. She pivots to a 45-degree angle and then does parallel shuffles back to the beginning post.
4. Repeat drill beginning on the opposite post.

Common errors during this drill are failure to maintain the basic goaltender's stance and making more than one push off the post.

Butterfly Drill G3 ●●

Purpose: To develop proficiency at dropping to and recovering from the butterfly position.

1. The goalie assumes the basic goaltender's stance.
2. He pushes forward off one post, pivots to a 45-degree angle, drops into a butterfly position, and then returns quickly to his feet to begin a backward push to the same post.
3. He slides sideways using the parallel shuffle and then repeats from the opposite post.

Common errors are losing stick position, losing the catching glove position, and failing to remain square on the angle.

CHAPTER 6

Offense and Defense

Now that the essential skills have been covered, let's discuss the two basic concepts of the game: playing hockey on offense and playing hockey on defense. Unlike football, which has an offensive team and a defensive team, hockey players must be able to transition from defense to offense and back very quickly. All players on the ice must know when their team has possession of the puck and is trying to score a goal. But they must also know when the opponent has the puck, and their team must try to stop a goal from being scored.

It's very important for young players to play the game for fun without being burdened with learning difficult concepts. However, even Mite-level players can be taught to recognize when they're in an offensive or defensive position. For example, when a team goes on offense, all five skaters should be thinking about how they can help their team score a goal. Generally speaking, defensemen don't rush the puck up ice even though they're allowed to do so. Their focus should be on helping their team score a goal by making good passes and, as it's known in hockey, supporting the rush. In addition, it's their responsibility to keep the puck in the zone at the offensive blue line. When the team is on defense, all five players must work together to stop their opponents from scoring. Of course, the goaltender's job is to prevent the puck from entering the net, but the goalie cannot be expected to perform this responsibility alone. Hockey is called a team sport because all players must work together on both offense and defense.

Offensive Fundamentals

Hockey players generally receive the greatest recognition because of their offensive skills such as skating, shooting, passing, and stickhandling. When you teach offense, these four skills must be developed before working on team play.

Offense begins from the moment your team wins a face-off or when it gains possession of the puck from its opponent. All five skaters must know what to do when their team gets puck possession. The player with the puck should immediately look up and decide whether to start skating with the puck or pass it to an open teammate.

The offensive players without the puck should be looking to support the puck carrier or move to open ice to receive a pass. They must learn to make themselves available by having their stick on the ice, thereby presenting a good target to receive a pass. Everyone on the ice should move together in an offensive formation or rush up ice attempting to outnumber the opponent and score a goal. Generally, the three forwards lead the rush while the two defensemen support the attack from behind. Keep in mind, however, that it's not uncommon for a defenseman to join the rush as well.

Not all goals are scored on the rush or initial attack; many are scored during offensive zone plays. All coaches should encourage their players to be creative in producing scoring chances. Goals are often scored by winning a battle for the puck near the boards, in the corners, or behind the net. In this offensive zone area, three forwards work together to create scoring opportunities. Working together does not mean having all three forwards in the same corner trying to gain possession of the puck. One or two forwards should move to open ice in the offensive zone. This spreads out the opponent's defense and also helps create space for the offensive forwards to become open to receive a pass and, ideally, take a shot on goal.

Since most of the goals scored in the offensive zone come from a shot taken near the front of the net, it's a great idea to keep one forward situated in the slot. A player in the high slot area has the offensive potential of scoring a goal and the defensive capability of backchecking. Emphasize to your players that if their team should lose control of the puck, they must all transition to defense.

Offensive Face-Off

The player taking the face-off is the hockey equivalent of a football quarterback. Her responsibilities begin before the puck is even dropped. She should first assess the strength and weakness of the opponent and then position her teammates according to her own strengths and weaknesses. Before she moves in to take the face-off, she should make sure all players are in position and ready. Once her fellow players are properly positioned, she should anticipate when the linesman will actually drop the puck, thereby gaining an advantage over the opponent. Anticipation comes by watching the puck as it leaves the official's hand and reacting as quickly as possible. Smart players learn to confuse their opponents by varying their face-off techniques and patterns.

All players must be ready at every face-off. If your players work together, offensive zone face-offs can become great scoring chances. There are

---

Principles of Offensive Hockey
1. Understand the importance of skating, passing, stickhandling, and shooting
2. Utilize your teammates
3. When possible, create an outnumbered situation
4. Don't be a spectator when your teammate has the puck
5. Never give the puck away to an opponent

Drills
- Three-Player Cycle 04
- Three-Player Offensive Drive 07
- Three-on-Zero Rush, Return 010

Principles of the Offensive Zone Face-Off

1. To help win a face-off, be prepared to react quickly
2. Gain control of the puck, move to open ice, or screen the goalie
3. To create a scoring chance, skate with or pass the puck
4. Shoot with the following intentions: to score, get a deflection, set up a rebound, or get through a screen
5. If the face-off is lost, quickly force (pressure) the puck carrier

Drill

- Basic Offensive Zone Face-Off 08

varied alignments your players can use to create scoring chances, but none will work without puck possession. A good center who is quick and possesses great eye-hand coordination can win a high number of face-offs; however, he can't be expected to win every one by himself. But if he's adept at winning face-offs, he'll sometimes position one of his wingers directly behind him on the edge of the face-off circle. This gives the winger the opportunity to take a quick shot on goal. There are times when an offensive zone face-off is won with help from a winger. When this occurs, the winger will immediately react by stepping in front of and blocking out an opponent and by pushing the puck back to his defenseman. This often provides just enough time for a teammate to take a shot on goal.

If the face-off is won, the forwards must get open for a pass, screen the goalie, or drive to the net for a rebound. If the team loses the face-off, players must move quickly to regain possession of the puck. Generally speaking, two forwards attempt to force a turnover; one heads toward the puck, the other one reads the play. The third forward moves toward the high slot area to be in position for a scoring chance if the puck is turned over. If necessary, this forward will be in great position to backcheck from this area as well.

Nothing replaces practicing face-offs. As with every other skill in hockey, mastery can come only through repeated practice. Remember, puck possession is an important part of the game. Though quickness and eye-hand coordination are often natural talents, most players can improve upon them with practice.

Breakout

A breakout occurs when your team gains possession of the puck in its defensive zone and then attempts to move the puck up ice. When a defensive player gains puck control in her own zone, her teammates should move to support her effort to create a breakout. More specifically, a breakout occurs when a defenseman recovers the puck in her own end zone corner with her left and right wingers moving toward each side board near the end zone face-off hash marks. The wingers provide a target for the passer by keeping their sticks on the ice in front of them. The center mirrors the puck carrier, searching for a good passing lane while staying within 15 feet of the carrier. A smart center times her movement by staying in front of the net long enough to allow her defenseman time to step out from behind the net. When the defenseman steps out, the center jumps into the passing lane, where she's in position to either receive the pass or cover the front of the net if her defenseman makes an errant pass, and her team loses puck possession. The other defensive player has two options: to get open for her partner behind the goal line on the opposite side of the ice or to remain as protection in front of her own goal. As coach, you must decide if your team's passing skills are strong enough to give the defenseman the first option. The defenseman with the puck should skate quickly but always explore her options, which depend upon the pressure from the opposition. Her best option is to pass the puck "stick to stick" to a teammate who is not being covered by an opponent. As that pass occurs, her teammates move to support the player who's receiving the puck. If your team has players who've mastered the difficult task of completing more than two passes in a row while moving, encourage them to be creative on their breakouts.

Offensive Rush

Teams capable of skating, controlling the puck, and passing well usually create scoring chances on the rush. Instruct your players to either skate or move the puck quickly. Players without the puck must fill the *passing lanes* (unobstructed pathways that allow passes between players), moving to open areas of the ice. Quite often, forwards should move laterally across the ice in the neutral zone to keep their speed, get open for a pass, or create a space for the puck carrier to skate toward. Defensemen must move as well, supporting the rush while the forwards attempt to create an outnumbered attack.

Principles of the Rush

1. *Head-man* the puck (pass the puck to an open teammate who is farther up the ice) or skate quickly with it
2. Don't be a spectator; if you don't have the puck, move to open ice
3. Forwards should fill the left, center, and right lanes
4. Defensemen should support the attack
5. Forwards should look to create an outnumbered attack
6. The puck carrier and one forward should drive to the net
7. The third forward or "late man" moves to the high slot area for a scoring chance

Drills

- Three-on-Zero Rush, Return O10
- All in One GS14

The forward carrying the puck controls the play upon entering the offensive zone. If your team is on a three-on-two rush (three forwards are facing two defensemen), the puck carrier should attempt to skate wide toward the net around one defenseman. Usually the forward who is closest to the puck drives straight at the other defenseman, backing him up toward his own net. The third forward then moves to the high slot area for a scoring chance. If your team has a two-on-two rush, both forwards should attempt to isolate one defenseman by moving to one side of the ice. Often, a crisscross passing play works well here. If your forwards have a two-on-one rush, the player with the puck should look to shoot if the defenseman provides enough room. If, however, the defenseman forces the puck carrier, he should pass to his teammate. In each of these situations, the players without

Principles of the Breakout

1. Recognize when your team gains possession of the puck
2. Don't be a spectator; move to support the puck carrier
3. Present your stick as a target for a pass or move to create open space for a teammate
4. Be ready to receive a pass and then to decide whether to skate with the puck or pass it to a supporting teammate

Drills

- Four-Player Breakout F20
- Double Breakout O6

the puck are extremely important because they help provide the opportunity for scoring on the rush. Their job is to move into the passing lane to create more than one scoring option for their team.

Power Play

A power play opportunity occurs for your team when the opponent takes a minor or major penalty that is not offset by one taken by your team at the same time. The opponent is required to play with one or two fewer players on the ice (depending on the number of penalties taken) for a period of two to five minutes. If your team is on the power play during a two-minute penalty infraction and scores a goal, the offending player may return to the ice surface. The opposing team is then permitted to play at full strength. Note that if the opposition has two, noncoincidental penalties, the player who entered the penalty box last must remain there after the goal is scored, so the opponent is still shorthanded. If a noncoincidental five-minute penalty is called on your opponent, then your team may score as many goals as possible during the power play while the entire five-minute penalty is served.

The breakout is a key ingredient to a successful power play. Your players will need to work on passing and skating skills to have success in breaking cleanly out of their zone with clear puck possession. With younger kids and less-skilled players, this is often the most difficult part of the power play. It's best to keep things simple on a breakout unless you're coaching players with tremendous puck handling and passing skills. Explain to your players that it's important to be ready to move to open ice to support the puck carrier on every breakout including those in a power play. Show your team how to fill all three lanes, rush up the ice with puck control, and support each other by moving to get open for a pass.

There are two ways to enter the offensive zone. One is with puck control; the other is by shooting the puck into the zone and then trying to retrieve it. Obviously, the first option is the one you would prefer your players to use because they maintain possession of the puck. Entering the offensive zone with puck control is vital to a good power play. Any time saved by entering the offensive zone with puck control can be used to set up a scoring chance. Teach your players to carry the puck to safe areas of the ice (deep in the offensive zone or behind the net) where they will have more time and space to make a good pass. It's equally as important for teammates to move to support the puck carrier in the offensive zone so she can make an easy pass if she's under pressure from an opponent.

If your team is pressured in the neutral zone and must shoot the puck into the offensive zone, it's imperative that players move quickly to recover the puck. The key to recovery is outnumbering the opponent during the attempted recovery. Instruct your players to shoot the puck into the offensive zone with the intention of recovering it. The best results are achieved when the puck is shot hard around the boards with two forwards skating quickly to

Principles of the Power Play

1. Make a clean breakout
2. Carry the puck into the offensive zone, or shoot it in
3. Set up a scoring chance

Drills

- Three-Player Offensive Drive **O7**
- Full-Ice Two-on-Zero Follow Your Pass **O11**
- Full-Ice Two-on-One **GS1**
- Breakout, Regroup Three-on-Two **GS16**

recover it on the opposite side of the ice. If your opponent has one player battling for the puck, then your team should have two. If the opponent has two players, your team needs three.

When your players are trying to set up a scoring chance, quick puck movement is the best way to relieve pressure from your opponent. The most effective way to score on the power play is by passing the puck to your defenseman at the point (blue line), creating traffic in front of the goaltender, shooting on goal, and outnumbering the opponent in front of the net. Teach your defensemen that the ideal shot is taken from the middle of the ice at the blue line so any rebound will remain in front of the net. Some coaches like to teach their players to use the area behind the net to set up passing plays. If your players are skilled passers, this is a good area for creating plays. However, remember that a blind pass from behind your opponent's net can end up on the opponent's stick, giving him the opportunity to shoot the puck easily out of his zone. It's important to establish your point shots with traffic in front of the opposing net. This will allow many additional passing options to open up on the power play.

Defensive Fundamentals

Because all players love to score goals, it's difficult for a coach to teach players the importance of playing good team defense. Coaches must instill the value of playing a disciplined game and taking pride in playing strong defense in every area of the ice, not just the defensive zone. Young children can learn these skills by learning the basics; they don't need to memorize elaborate systems. Part of "hockey basics" includes being in a good offensive position because it helps to transition quickly to defense when the team loses control of the puck. The defensemen and goaltender are responsible for keeping the puck out of the net, but they can't be expected to do that without the help of their forwards. A young player who understands her defensive responsibilities will become a better hockey player when she gets older.

Believe it or not, good defense begins while the team has possession of the puck. Explain to your players that they're not playing good hockey if all five skaters move recklessly on offense. They need to learn that even on offense, they should still be in good position (one player in the high slot area) to be able to transition to playing defense. The forwards should focus on either backchecking the puck carrier or backchecking the opponents who are away from the puck. The two defensemen need to "read" the rush and then react to what they see. Ideally, they should use one of the previously mentioned checking techniques (see Chapter 4) to stop the opponent. A well-played hockey game uses the element of surprise, but good hockey players also have a great deal of patience. Many times defensemen facing an outnumbered rush will need to bide time, waiting for the forwards to backcheck before they can attempt to check the puck off their opponent.

Principles of Defensive Hockey

1. Understand the system and be disciplined
2. Learn to play away from the puck
3. Use checking skills to stop the opponent
4. Take pride in playing well defensively
5. Do your assigned job, but be prepared to react if someone misses an assignment

Drills

- Three-on-Three Defensive Zone Coverage D3
- Two-Pass Three-on-Three GS13

Good teams often win because they know how to play good defensive hockey. This does not mean that to be successful, you need to teach an elaborate defensive system to youth hockey players. When you teach defensive zone coverage, it's vital to make your system sensitive to the age and ability of your players.

I first heard the term "beehive soccer" when my daughter began playing soccer at a very young age. It didn't matter if a player was supposed to be playing offense or defense; everyone gathered around the soccer ball like bees on honey. Quite often, you'll watch a Mite or Squirt game with "beehive hockey" players. Having all five players attack the puck carrier in their own end often works at the beginner level because their passing skills are not developed. Personally, I feel it's important to teach basic defensive responsibilities at the Squirt level.

I teach my players to play "man-on-man" in the defensive zone, but to always maintain an awareness of where the puck is. Realize that man-on-man doesn't mean chasing the player you're covering all over the defensive zone. The most important area to protect begins at the front of the net extending to a V shape at the top of the face-off circles. Most goals are scored in this area. Your left and right wingers are responsible for covering the opponent's two defensemen. The defensemen and center are responsible for playing in the corners and in front of their own net to cover the opponent's three forwards. If a breakdown occurs, allow the winger away from the puck (*weak side*) the freedom to leave his player at the blue line to help cover the front of the net. I encourage all defensive zone players to keep themselves between the player they're covering and their own net.

When the opponent has the puck in the corner, I tell the closest defenseman to force the puck carrier. The center gives support by playing near the next closest opponent but keeping his position between his player, the puck, and our net. The other defenseman should be covering and protecting any player in front of our net or in the slot area. Working a three-on-three drill from below the top of the face-off circles helps the center and defensemen understand their responsibilities and also allows the offensive players to use their creativity. Most players will find that playing on offense is more fun, but playing defense takes hard work.

Defensive Face-Offs

All players must be ready on every face-off. Defensive zone face-offs are possibly more important than those in the offensive zone because loss of the puck in a defensive zone face-off can result in a scoring chance or, even worse, a goal for the other team. A center cannot be expected to win every face-off by herself, although the good ones win many through quickness and great eye-hand coordination. As with most face-offs, the center tries to win the face-off back toward her defensemen. In any case, the center often doesn't win a defensive-zone face-off; her teammates do. To gain possession of the puck, every player must react the instant it's dropped. A forward or defenseman can often help win a face-off by quickly jumping into the face-off circle to recover a puck that's loose near the two centers.

All players must be ready to react in the face-off circle as the puck is being dropped. Wingers often help win face-offs by quickly jumping into the face-off circle after the puck is dropped. They should then attempt either to gain puck possession or to block an opponent out without taking an interference penalty. Sometimes a winger will flick his stick slightly to push the puck back to a defenseman. But most often the player taking the face-off will choose the easiest and strongest maneuver of simply tying up his opponent's stick and then drawing the puck back to his defenseman. Sometimes when facing a strong opponent, the center will just tie up the opponent's stick and get help from his teammates to win the face-off. If he's playing in the offensive zone, he may decide to take an immediate shot on goal. Another option for the face-off winner is moving the puck forward between his opponent's legs or hitting a breaking teammate. However, these two techniques are very dangerous to use in the defensive zone because there's always a strong possibility of pushing the puck forward to the opponent, who, in turn, may then get an immediate scoring chance.

Coaches often overlook their defensive zone face-off alignment. I always like to put my team in the best possible situation to prevent a scoring chance in the defensive zone. I firmly believe this can best be accomplished if each player on the ice has a responsibility. We've already talked about defensive zone coverage, so why not line up for defensive zone face-offs by putting your team in the best possible situation for coverage? I have the two defensemen line up on their respective hash marks directly beside the opponent's left and right wingers. Of course, the center lines up to win the face-off with the opponent's center. Both wingers should be lined up toward the front of the net. The outside winger is responsible for the weak side (the side of the ice farther away from the puck) defenseman; the other winger lines up directly beside the defenseman in front of the net, but on the edge of the face-off circle.

If your team loses the face-off, your center covers the opponent's center, your defensemen cover the closest winger, and the outside winger moves to cover the weak-side defenseman. The inside winger first looks for a loose puck near either center before moving diagonally through the face-off circle to cover the *strong side* (the side the puck is on) defenseman. If your players win the face-off, the wingers move to the breakout position. The center supports the defenseman who recovers the puck. The other defenseman has two options. As coach, you need to decide if your players pass the puck well enough to give that defenseman the freedom to become open for her partner behind the goal line on the opposite side of the ice. Teams who have not yet mastered adequate passing skills should use that defensive player to stay in front of the net, thereby protecting her goal.

Principles of the Defensive Zone Face-Off

1. To help win the face-off, be prepared to move
2. Gain control of the puck
3. Skate with the puck or pass it to break out of the defensive zone
4. If the face-off is won, move to breakout position to support the puck carrier
5. If the face-off is lost, move to cover the opponent you're covering

Drill

- Defensive Zone Face-Off D8

Principles of Winning Any Face-Off

1. Practice face-offs often
2. Use the proper technique to win
3. Formulate in advance where you want to draw the puck
4. Get help from your teammates

Principles of Forechecking

1. The most important skill when forechecking is skating
2. Recognize which player should force the opponent with the puck
3. Use quickness to keep your stick in any passing lane
4. Attempt to force a turnover or bad pass; if permitted, finish with a body check
5. Teammates must read and react to the actions of the first forechecker

Drills

- Two-One-Two Forecheck D6
- One-Two-Two Forecheck D7

Forechecking

Forechecking is a defensive skill, but it's primarily used in the offensive zone (especially if the puck is dumped in) to create turnovers, enabling the team to gain puck possession and create a scoring chance. The intent is to pressure the other team while it's trying to get the puck out of its zone. A team that works together on forechecking stands a better chance of gaining puck possession by creating turnovers in the corner or around the opponent's net. Teams with superior forechecking ability tend to have forwards who are always hustling and pressuring the opponent who has the puck. In addition, their defensemen are quick, aggressive, and smart in the offensive zone. When a team doesn't forecheck aggressively, its opponents have multiple opportunities for uncontested breakouts, and the team must then rely on backchecking to regain the puck. Successful teams strive to get and keep possession of the puck and always work to prevent their opponents from controlling the puck.

At the Mite and Squirt level, you may want to teach a forechecking system that shows players how to play body on body (without contact, of course) and stick on the puck. This concept is used when body checking is not permitted. While forechecking, young players can use any of the stick-checking skills described in Chapter 4. Teach your players that forecheckers must adjust their speed so they don't overskate the opponent, must skate quickly when necessary, and must stop quickly as well.

Since body contact is permitted at the Pee Wee level and above, many coaches teach the first (or closest) forechecker to "take the body," or separate the opponent from the puck. Note that at any level, the forechecker should approach her opponent with her stick on the ice to block any potential passing lane. Likewise, players at every level should force the puck carrier, leaving the other two forwards to read and react to where the puck ends up. Quite often the second forechecker will recover a bad pass around the boards or pick up a loose puck close to the area of the initial forecheck. The third forward should look to play in the high slot to capture a scoring chance or recover an errant pass. This is known as the one-two-two forecheck.

If the opposition has players who move the puck very well, you may want to institute a two-one-two forecheck. In this formation, the second forechecker becomes more aggressive by forcing from the opposite side of the ice. He'll move quickly to either eliminate the puck carrier or take away an opposing defenseman's opportunity to pass to his defensive partner behind the net. If the pass is completed and the defenseman tries to make a head-man pass to a forward, the third forward should move to gain possession of an errant pass while the first forechecker recovers, skating to the high slot area. In any system, defensemen should also move up quickly to the offensive blue line to keep the puck in the offensive zone or recover an errant pass.

Backchecking

Backchecking is transitioning from offense to defense to prevent the other team from scoring a goal. Skating is the most important skill used when backchecking. The moment a player stops skating and reaches out to hook an opponent with his stick, he'll usually be called for a penalty. A smart defensive player knows when to backcheck the puck carrier and when to backcheck to cover an open player. These decisions are sometimes determined by the coach's system, sometimes by communicating with teammates, but most often they're instinctive. If your defensemen are focusing on two out of three opposing players on an offensive rush by the other team, the smart play is to backcheck the third (open) player. I teach my forwards to backcheck the puck carrier until he reaches center ice. This often creates a turnover, thereby preventing the opponent from reaching the center ice line and dumping the puck into the offensive zone. If the puck carrier has already reached center ice, the forwards should backcheck to cover the open player. Explain to your forwards that when the rush is equal or your team has the advantage, it's sometimes best for them to backcheck the puck carrier if they can be the first to reach him. Generally, however, as the puck enters your team's defensive zone, it's best for the forwards to backcheck to cover the open player. Meanwhile, the defensemen will focus on the puck carrier and one other attacker.

When backchecking to cover the open opponent, the player should always skate to gain an inside position slightly ahead of and within one stick length of the opponent. This allows the defender to be positioned between the opponent and the net as well as the opponent and the puck. The backchecker must cover her player by keeping her stick on the ice to take away any passing lane. She must also keep on eye on the location of the puck. One reason she should stay no farther than a stick length away from her opponent is the difficulty of watching the puck and covering the opponent simultaneously. A second reason is that as a defender, she can react more quickly to take away a pass or lift the opponent's stick during an offensive chance.

When backchecking the puck carrier, the player needs to skate quickly to catch her opponent. She can then either angle-check the opposition or gain possession of the puck using one of the stick-checking techniques discussed in Chapter 4. Tell your players to skate first to avoid hooking or tripping their opponent. To eliminate any passing opportunity for the puck carrier, players must keep their sticks on the ice when approaching their opponent.

Covering

In hockey, covering means establishing a good defensive position between the opponent and your own net. Good defensive players learn to take an inside position when covering, always keeping themselves between the opponent and their own net while at the same time keeping an eye on the loca-

Principles of Backchecking

1. Concentrate on skating; never reach or hook with the stick
2. Determine whether to backcheck the puck carrier or the open player
3. Continue to skate to an inside position with your stick on the ice, always knowing the location of the puck and the player you're covering
4. Cover either the open player or check the opponent off the puck

Drills

- One-on-One Battle (Stick Lift and Stick Press) F47
- Giving and Receiving Shoulder Checks, Body Checks, and Hip Checks F50

Drill

- Angle Checking F48

Principles of Covering an Open Player

1. Establish body position within one stick length of the open player
2. Always know where the puck is
3. Learn to anticipate when the player is going to be a threat

Drills

- One-on-One Battle (Stick Lift and Stick Press) **F47**
- Three-on-Three Defensive Zone Coverage **D3**

Principles of Penalty Killing

1. Read the breakout
2. Force the rush
3. Recover any dumped-in pucks
4. Use force in the defensive zone
5. Protect the front of the net

tion of the puck. Using a number of tactics, players should also stay close enough to their opponent to eliminate the player from offensive play. These tactics include using body position (within one stick length) to cover the opponent, thus discouraging the opponent's teammates from passing to him, and using body position to lift or press down upon an opponent's stick when the puck is heading toward him.

Penalty Killing

Penalty killing is the defensive situation when the opponent is on the power play. Penalty killing has become much more aggressive than it was fifteen or twenty years ago, when players used a passive style of allowing the opponent to set up in the offensive zone. Generally, penalty killers would set up a stationary box formation, trying to keep the puck to the outside of the box. Recovering the puck only occurred when there was a shot on goal.

Today, penalty killers use a more aggressive style. You'll often see a forward pressure the puck carrier as she moves up the ice, trying to force the opponent into a turnover or shooting the puck into the zone rather than carrying it in under control. You'll also see a penalty-killing unit be more aggressive in their own defensive zone when the opponent doesn't have clear control of the puck or has only one passing option.

Penalty killing is like playing good, sound, defensive hockey. It takes intelligence and hard work. The first step in penalty killing is reading the opponent's breakout. Since only two forwards are on the ice, it's important to teach that one of them should attempt to force a turnover as the opponent begins to move the puck up ice. However, they should never chase behind the opponent's net. I like to teach my players to angle-check from the middle of the ice toward the boards. Instruct your forwards to play in an I-formation (the shape of an I) about 15 feet apart from one another, angle checking from the middle of the ice. Both forwards should have their sticks on the ice to block any potential passing lane for the opponent. It's a good idea to remind your forwards that an angle check should be used in this situation, not a big body check.

As the opponent begins skating up ice with the puck and nears the top of his defensive zone face-off circles, the first penalty-killing forward in the I-formation should begin to angle-check from the middle of the ice. He should force the puck carrier to make a pass toward the boards. The second forward should read where the pass is going, reacting quickly by angling toward the player receiving the puck. As this is happening, it's imperative that the first forward hustles back with his stick on the ice, skating back toward the middle. It's great if a turnover is created, but if not, the forward tries to force the opponent to shoot the puck into his offensive zone rather than gain the zone with puck control. This is known as a one-three neutral zone force; in other words, one forward tries to force a turnover with two defensemen back while the other forward moves back through the middle of the ice.

Determination and a will to win the battle are needed to recover any puck dumped into your defensive zone. When the puck is shot in, the first defenseman to reach it should attempt to recover it and then immediately shoot it down the length of the ice. Often, this defenseman will get plenty of resistance from two of the opposing forwards. In this case, the defender's teammates must quickly help out. Sometimes one of your forwards will need to skate down deep into the defensive zone to help gain puck possession. At other times a defense partner may release the puck behind her own net, communicating that she is able to receive a pass and get the puck out of the zone.

When killing a penalty, it's often difficult to know when to force and when to stay in a stationary box. This is all part of gaining hockey sense, which can be learned only through repetition and on-the-job training. Any time an opponent doesn't have clear control of the puck (such as when facing the boards or fumbling the puck) the defending player should look to force a turnover. Remind your players to attack the opponent with their stick on the ice to take away any passing lane. When in doubt, protect the front of the net. When killing a penalty, you never want two players below your own goal line unless you're 100 percent certain you're going to gain possession of the puck. All four players on the ice need to work together, communicate, and make frequent 5-foot passes to gain puck possession and shoot it out of the zone.

If the opponent gains possession of the puck and attempts to shoot on goal with players driving to the net, it's important that your defensemen work hard to fight for position in front. They should try to block out the opposing players, but they'll also need the defensive forwards to collapse toward the front of the net to help recover any loose pucks. The most effective way to get the puck out of the defensive zone and down the ice is by shooting it hard off the side boards.

CHAPTER 7

The Practice

Preparation and Cooperation

Always have a written plan for the practice prepared before you come to the rink. If possible, consult with your assistant coaches in advance. Not only does this put all of you on the same page, but your assistants can easily plan for the necessary drill setups of cones, extra pucks, and mini-obstacle courses. At the very least, you can discuss the practice plans while the players are getting dressed, so the coaches are all in agreement. While you are preparing at home, remember to include some alternative ideas for use when the initial drills aren't working. Some drills may look great on paper, but when you go to implement them, you find they're either more complex than you expected or involve a skill level that your players haven't yet reached. More often than not, you'll have to stop practice, bring your players in, and explain the drill in more detail. This will take time away from another drill, but it's more important that your players learn fewer drills correctly than attempting to cover a

During practice, you'll occasionally need to diagram a new or difficult drill while on the ice. Make sure that everyone can see and understand the drill. Don't forget to bring your coaching board and dry-erase markers with you on the ice.

specified number. Flexibility is essential. Include both a full-ice and a half-ice practice in case you're sharing the rink with another team.

What to Bring

Make certain you bring plenty of pucks, water bottles, a coach's whistle, your coaching board with dry-erase markers, and your own skates, gloves, and stick to all practices. You may also want to wear coaches' shin pads and a hockey helmet for your own protection, but these are usually not required. Have a first-aid kit along, but also be knowledgeable about handling emergency situations at the rink. Rinks are fully prepared for emergencies, but it's vital that you know whom to contact if you need additional first-aid equipment or if something happens that you can't handle on your own.

Shared Practices

The majority of your practices will be shared with another team. I've found it's always a good idea to speak with the other coach in advance, recommending that you combine both teams for skating warm-ups, some fundamental drills, and possibly a scrimmage at the end of practice. The kids can move their legs a lot more and benefit greatly from practicing on the same size surface as playing an actual game. If you are co-coaching during drills, decide who will lead the group through them. Most coaches find a partial joint session beneficial for all players, but we all want time to work with our players individually as well.

Arrive Early

Ask the parents to bring their children to every practice thirty minutes before the actual starting time or, at the very least, dressed and ready to go on the ice ten minutes early. Understand that with today's busy schedules this may be difficult, but because ice time costs money, you don't want to waste time explaining a drill on the ice that players should have already heard about in the locker room. You, too, should plan on arriving early, using this time to bond with your players while you supervise them in the locker room. This is the ideal time to explain your practice plan to the players, using your coaching board to diagram new or difficult drills.

Getting Your Players to Respond to You Immediately

Hopefully, you've already introduced yourself and explained your coaching philosophy at your first player/parent meeting before the start of the season. If you're coaching a town team, you can have the meeting at the town hall or another easy-to-find location. If that proves impossible, have the meeting at the ice rink before the first practice. Most rinks are good about letting you

Rink Check!

When you get to the rink, check the following:

    Are there ruts or holes in the ice that may lead to unsafe skating conditions?

    Do the doors leading to the players' benches close properly?

    Is the air quality poor because of exhaust fumes from the Zamboni?

    Are there rough edges on the goal cage?

    Is the lighting adequate?

    Is the Plexiglas secure?

It is the coach's responsibility to report and rectify any of these conditions before a practice or game.

use one of their rooms for a half hour or so. In this situation, make sure you keep the kids involved in the meeting because you don't want them running through the rink unsupervised while you meet with their parents. At your first practice, have each player introduce himself or herself and include a brief personal detail such as where he or she lives or the name of a favorite hockey team or player. Some kids may be a bit shy about speaking in front of others so keep it simple. In this way, each player will relate to fellow teammates and ease into speaking aloud.

It's very important for you (and fellow teammates) to learn each player's name early. Players will feel special, and a bond will be created between you. I've often made name stickers for players to attach to the front of their helmet; however, you should remove the tape as soon as you learn all their names.

Always Think Safety

Never permit your players on the ice until the Zamboni is back in its room with the doors shut. No player should be allowed on the ice unless a coach is present. This is another reason to have a locker room meeting ten minutes before practice time; it ensures that you and your players head for the ice as a unit. Of course, everyone must be wearing full equipment for every practice. When the ice is ready, have the kids get their blood flowing by skating around the rink for a few minutes while they become comfortable on their skates. They've probably been wearing sneakers all day, so you want them to get used to the feeling of being in skates. After surveying the ice for any dangerous skating conditions, make sure that all gates and players' bench doors are latched closed.

First Practice

If some children and parents were not at your preseason meeting, spend some time introducing newcomers and telling them what's expected of them. Have them introduce themselves to their teammates and coaches,

Practice Makes Perfect

I firmly believe that if you encourage your players to work hard in practice, it makes it easier for them to play in games. Encourage them to perform all drills accurately and as fast as they can; it's impossible for players to get to the next level if they cut corners. Remind them that practice is the place where mistakes can be made and corrected. They should work on the areas where they are least skilled, such as the backhand shot or backward skating.

stating their names and a personal tidbit such as their favorite hockey player. Remind parents of your coaching philosophy, what they can expect from you as a coach, and what you expect of them and their children.

When your team has completed a few laps, blow your whistle and use a verbal direction such as "Bring it in!" to gather them around you. At your first practice, compliment your players on how great they look in their practice jerseys, stressing that the upcoming season will be fun and instructional. Speak briefly about the value of ice time, good work habits, and the importance of responding quickly to your whistle. Help them understand that the more quickly they respond to your directions, the more time they'll have to enjoy the practice drills.

At the first practice, it's important to teach the fundamental skills of hockey. As each player runs through drills, you can assess individual ability levels.

Call your players in for a quick talk about the expectations for practice. Remember that ice time is valuable, so keep it brief. Provide words of encouragement and praise during the follow-up time in the locker room.

Planning the Practice

Before you can successfully budget practice time, find out how long you can be on the ice. Most practice times are going to be one hour. Generally, high school programs that have access to their own ice or high-level competitive teams may sometimes have ninety-minute or two-hour practices. Have a consistent format for every practice. Kids certainly respond better when they know what to expect; in addition, consistency helps the flow of practice. For example, do general skating warm-ups first, do a shooting drill to warm up the goalies next, follow with fundamental drills, offensive and defensive drills, and a game situation. Conclude with something enjoyable such as a scrimmage, competitive drill, or race. Of course, you need to be flexible within the format, but it's best for the structure to remain the same.

It's perfectly fine to sandwich fundamental drills around a systems drill because too often goaltenders become forgotten players. If your goalies aren't involved in an offensive or defensive drill, they'll be standing around with nothing to do. Your players may also be slowed down as you walk through a defensive zone coverage or face-off alignment. Though you'll want all your uninvolved players paying close attention to those teammates working with your systems drill, it's sometimes preferable to have them working with your assistant coaches on a fundamental skill in an open area of the ice. It's especially important to keep all younger players moving and interested as much as possible.

Don't forget to allow time for water breaks. I usually plan water breaks for when I gather my players around to explain the next drill. This also gives your assistant coaches time to gather and set up any items necessary for the next drill such as cones, sticks, or extra nets. If you have a longer ice slot, I recommend adjusting the segments according to your players' needs. Generally, with younger players at the Mite and Squirt level, you should spend more time on fundamental and fun drills. If your team is older or has a higher skill level, try the method I describe below in the Hydration section.

General Practice Format

The following practice plan is based on a seventy-five-minute session using full ice for sixty minutes.

Team Meeting (10 minutes)

Go over the practice plan in the locker room to save ice time. During this session, explain your plan for the practice. Diagram any new drills, and then talk about areas from the previous practice or game that need work. Don't forget to ask for questions.

Team-Building Exercises

As mentioned previously, ice time is costly, so your practices will often be shared with another team. Encourage the other coach to work with you for the warm-up and some of the drills so all the players have a chance to use the full length of the rink. Games are, of course, played on full ice so it's important to practice that way during a portion of each practice. Understandably, you'll also want to split the ice in half so you can work individually with your own team.

Following are some suggestions for getting your team warmed up and gathering them during practices.

Warming Up: Have players make six equal lines standing next to each other across the length of one goal line.

How low can you go? This drill can be worked into your warm-up when splitting up your players into five or six lines across one goal line and performing end-to-end skating drills. Any and all balance drills are great for learning how to feel the edges of the skates.

Explain that each time they hear the sound of your whistle, the first player in each line will start the drill. You can begin the season with a few drill changes and then add more as your players progress.

Use any combination of the following while they skate one length of the ice: skating using the proper stride; stopping and starting; single knee touches while skating; skating while balancing on one foot; hopping over the neutral ice lines; pivoting, then skating backward.

This drill has three purposes. Players must listen carefully to your initial directions and must also react to the coach's whistle. Each drill hones their skating skill without players even being aware of it. In addition, every practice must begin with exercises that warm up the muscles slowly. This is a perfect way to provide a warm-up that sharpens skills and concentration at the same time.

Last One In: When players hear your whistle signaling that you either want them to change a drill or gather around you for instruction, they must respond as quickly as they can. Blow your whistle at various times during a practice and give the "last one in" a small forfeit such as push-ups or one hard lap around the ice. Keep in mind, however, that a safe environment is one of the most important prerequisites in youth hockey. If your players are young and haven't yet mastered stopping skills, you don't want them skating at full speed toward each other (or you!) without the slightest idea of how they'll stop once they arrive.

This drill will help your players listen for your whistle at all times and will reinforce that they must react to your signal immediately.

Teamwork Hustle: Designate four teams of equal abilities and run relay races that are straight skating or involve a combination of skating, shooting, stickhandling, or passing. Begin by having the four teams line up at the goal line at one end of the ice. At the sound of your whistle, the first player on each team must skate, stickhandle a puck, and pass a puck to someone stationed at the far end or shoot on the goalie. Players then skate back to their team and tag the next person. Play continues until one entire team finishes.

An added challenge would be to set up two cones a few feet apart and place a stick across the cones, which players must dive under. You can also place a stick on the ice for players to jump over. The last-place team does push-ups or sit-ups.

Players must work together and encourage each other, two essentials of good teamwork and sportsmanship. Children will have fun taking part in these relays, which have the added bonus of being great skill development drills. Jumping over or diving under obstacles enhances agility and coordination.

Two-foot jumps over sticks are an enjoyable, advanced way to help your players learn about explosive movements, timing, body control, and cushioning the landing. Hockey is a bent-knee sport!

Practice Session Worksheet

Team meeting (10 min.):

_____

_____

_____

_____

_____

Warm-up (10 min.):

_____

_____

_____

_____

_____

_____

Fundamentals (20 min.):

_____

_____

_____

_____

_____

Offense, defense, and game situations (20 min.):

_____

_____

_____

_____

_____

Competition/fun drill (10 min.):

_____

_____

_____

_____

Wrap-up/doggy bag (5 min.):

_____

_____

_____

_____

Practice Session Worksheet

Team meeting (10 min.):

Get everyone's attention with an enthusiastic welcome.

Go over the practice plan in the locker room to save precious ice time.

Warm-up (10 min.):

Ease into practice — stretching, skating drills.
Demonstrate proper form for drills.

Fundamentals (20 min.):

Passing drills between partners: remind players to pass and receive on both the forehand and backhand.

Offense, defense, and game situations (20 min.):

Three-on-three mini-game — mimic situations that occur during games.

Use width of rink, not length.
Stop the game to help players understand positioning.

Competition/fun drill (10 min.):

Race around cones, battle for puck, attempt to score on goalie.

Provide a lot of vocal encouragement!

Wrap-up/doggy bag (5 min.):

Praise the positives from practice.

Select a skill that needs work for players to practice at home.

Be Prepared but Stay Flexible

A well-thought-out written format will ensure that your practices run smoothly and efficiently. Have a consistent format, but allow flexibility within each drill. Reinforce learned skills, teach new ones, and above all, have fun.

Warm-Ups (10 minutes)

All players need to stretch adequately because well-stretched muscles are less easily injured. It's important that your players warm up their muscles before stretching. A cold muscle won't stretch to its full range of motion. I always start warm-ups with a moderate skate. I recommend increasing stretching time beginning at the Pee Wee to Bantam levels. The best stretching exercises include balance, flexibility, and short drills that will elevate the heart rate such as V-Starts and Control Stops **F3** and Continuous Glide Turns **F5**.

Always do some light skating to warm up the muscles before stretching. Caution your players not to bounce while stretching. They should feel the muscle stretch and hold it for ten seconds.

A player leans comfortably into a hip flexor stretch while maintaining good form.

This player stretches the groin muscles while kneeling on the ice.

Players should stretch slowly and be careful not to overstretch the normal range of motion.

Fundamentals (20 minutes)

Hockey is a game based on the fundamentals of skating, passing, receiving a pass, stickhandling, shooting, and checking. Because a good hockey player needs a solid foundation in each of these skills, you'll want to do a lot of fundamental drills early on in the practice to be certain players are using proper technique. *Every* practice should emphasize skating skills, because in hockey smooth skating is as vital as running is in other sports. Because hockey is such a fast-paced game, you need to include a combination of fundamentals into your drills; for example, skating, stickhandling, passing, and shooting can all be addressed in one drill. I like using some drills that mimic something that actually occurs in a game, such as a two-on-one situation. Faced with such a situation, your players will be working on a combination of defensive backward skating, forward skating, stickhandling, passing, shooting, playing the proper position, and taking a player out. Players find these drills so enjoyable that they won't even realize how many skills they're improving at one time.

Offense, Defense, and Game Situations (20 minutes)

Offense, defense, and game situations encompass all the skills in a teaching system. It's important to adjust your teaching system based on the age and ability level of your players. It's not necessary to overload them with a lot of technical information, but they should learn the basics of playing offense and defense. If you keep the kids moving while making the drills competitive and game-like, you'll be amazed at how quickly they learn the drills, techniques, and skills needed to play a great game.

Competition/Fun Drills (10 minutes)

It's important to end your practice on a fun note. Your players have worked hard improving their skills and incorporating some complex concepts. Ending practice with a drill that's competitive, rewarding, and fun leaves everyone feeling upbeat and positive. Select a drill that touches on the skills you've just practiced. Combining skating and shooting in a competitive drill is always a good choice. As the season progresses and your players continue to improve, end with a fun scrimmage.

Wrap-Up/Doggy Bag (5 minutes)

Always conclude with a team meeting in the locker room immediately after practice. Give a brief summary of the skills your players worked on in practice. Praise them for what they did well and then explain what needs particular attention in the next game or practice.

Although most kids groan when they hear the term *homework*, they're very receptive to a doggy bag, something they can practice on their own. In addition to working on their skills away from the rink, I like to ask them to watch their favorite professional hockey team on television. I give them

Develop Skills away from the Rink

Encourage your players to practice their hockey skills on their own time, away from the rink.

Stickhandle with a tennis or golf ball in the driveway

Shoot pucks against a sheet of plywood, a concrete basement wall, or an outside brick house wall (don't hit any windows!)

Play street or roller hockey

In-line skate around a homemade obstacle course in the driveway

specifics to look for, such as watching a particular player during positional plays or game situations that they themselves are struggling with. Before the next practice, they report to me about what they've observed and, hopefully, learned. This is a great way to motivate your players to work on their areas of weakness as well as keeping them involved with hockey when they're away from the rink.

Practice Success
Listen and Learn

When you're speaking with your team, it's important to minimize the distractions. If you're sharing the ice with another team, position yourself and your assistants against the corner boards and have the players face you. That way, their focus will be on you, not whatever is happening at the other end of the ice. A good way to bring their concentration back to what you're saying is to simply stop talking and wait for eye contact. If a particular player isn't paying attention, use the player's name when describing a drill; for example, "Chris, this drill involves skating around the face-off circles." Another technique is asking one individual player a question that pertains to the situation or asking the player to demonstrate the next drill.

When you address one specific player, make sure everyone is listening. If a drill doesn't involve everyone or you're explaining a drill or teaching a technique, have your players in a one-knee, crouching position. But remember that because most kids have high energy, you need to keep them moving when you aren't addressing them. Whenever possible, avoid drills that use only a few participants. With younger kids, use mini-game situations early in the year. Kids love scrimmages, but they learn more through game situations and competitive drills that mimic games.

As coach, you wear many hats. You must be alert to problems that one or more players might be experiencing. Does a player appear out of sorts because she's ill? Do you sense that a player is frustrated with herself or a teammate? If so, encourage her to come to you so you can help her work out the problem.

Teaching versus Coaching

There are really two types of coaches: the teaching coach and the coaching coach. At the youth level, it's important to be a teaching coach. Younger players need work on skill development in shooting, stickhandling, skating, and passing. Teach them the skills to get to the next level and learn the way the game is played. In the Bantam, Midget, and high school years, you can introduce more team concepts and strategies.

Encourage Politeness

Players should know from the very beginning that when one person is speaking, everyone else should be listening. This is true whether the speaker is their coach or their teammate. Remind players that someone's question will probably involve something they need to know immediately or in the future. Information they learn now will undoubtedly become valuable when they're in a game and need to make a quick decision. Moreover, by requiring your players to listen attentively to others, you're teaching them to respect their teammates and, of course, their coaches.

Although it's important to encourage your players to ask you questions, this doesn't mean they have the right to question your choice of drills or instruction. You're there because you know the game and wish to pass your expertise on to your players. In order to do this, your role is to make the decisions; your players' role is to follow them.

Hydration

People who participate in sports lose water through sweating and exhaled air. Always make certain you provide clean, filled water bottles for your players. Cold water is ideal because it can be ingested rapidly. Some children bring their own water bottle to games and practices, which is fine, but you must be certain to provide for those who don't. Bring the team water bottles home after every game or practice and wash them in the dishwasher. Don't forget to give your players at least one water break for every twenty minutes of practice. If your practice involves a particularly high tempo, allow for more breaks.

CHAPTER 8

Sample Practices

You'll probably feel a mixture of emotions on your first day of the season. You'll be nervous about how the kids will respond to you, how to make your practices productive but fun, and how to map out each practice in advance. Relax. This chapter details everything you'll need for several practices ranging in difficulty level from basic to more advanced. The basic practice is for any level player. It introduces the fundamental skills of hockey that need reinforcement at every practice. Remember that skills are honed, never mastered. The more your team practices skating, shooting, stickhandling, and passing, the better they'll become at playing and enjoying the game.

These sample practices are designed as models that you can use for the entire season. They outline a basic lesson plan including approximate time allotments for each activity. As your players become accomplished skaters, you can cut the warm-up to five minutes by using only one skating drill because they'll get plenty of skating in the other areas of practice. Add the extra time to fundamental shooting, stickhandling, passing, offensive-defensive, or game situation drills. As your team progresses in skill and experience, you can replace the drills cited in this chapter with other drills given in Part Two of this book. You'll find fundamental drills in Chapter 11, offensive drills in Chapter 12, defensive drills in Chapter 13, and game situation drills in Chapter 14.

Basic Practice
Team Meeting (10 minutes)

After the first practice, your practice drills will vary, but remember that the structure should always remain the same. Some of the beginner-level fundamental drills you use at the first practice should also be used at each and every practice because players of all abilities need to work on the fundamentals. Diagram how the drills work in the locker room before you hit the ice. This prevents wasting valuable ice time. Don't forget that backup plan for a shared ice practice.

Warm-Up (10 minutes total)

These warm-up, fundamental skating drills are a good way to begin practice because they get the blood flowing. It's important, especially with older players, to ease into practice by using stretching and full range of motion skating drills to prevent muscle pulls. Be certain to demonstrate proper form before starting each fundamental skating drill. Remind your players to stay low in a good athletic hockey position with head and chest erect. Sticks should be on the ice in front of them. Players should feel their skate edges as they stride to full extension and then recover. Each drill should last take about two minutes.

- **Easy Skate.** Skating around the rink for a short time helps to get the blood flowing.

- **Forward Skating C Cuts.** Players make C cuts as they skate from one goal line to the other. **F1**

- **Backward Skating C Cuts.** Players make backward C cuts as they return from the farthest goal line to the closest. **F2**

- **V-Starts and Control Stops.** Players alternate V-starts and control stops from one goal line to the other. **F3**

- **Glide Turns.** Beginning at one corner, players perform glide turns around eight cones placed on the ice. **F4**

Performing single-leg knee touches is a great way to work on balance and also helps players improve their overall skating ability.

Fundamentals (20 minutes total)

A large portion of basic practices should be devoted to working on fundamental skills. In other words, skating, stickhandling, passing, and shooting drills should be included in every practice. It is critical that every coach take the time to give one-on-one instruction if a player is not using the correct form. It is equally as important to keep these drills up-tempo so players remain engaged as much as possible.

Passing. First demonstrate and review the principles of making and receiving a pass. Make sure that your players watch the demonstration from more than one angle so they can easily see the proper technique. Show your players the proper positioning of their hands, their stick, and the puck, followed by proper weight transfer and follow-through. Passing is a crucial skill to master because puck possession is a huge part of the game. Hockey is one of the fastest sports, but no player can skate faster than a good, hard pass. In the game of hockey, good passing and puck possession are vital in helping your team quickly move the puck up ice to create scoring chances. Each drill will take approximately five minutes.

- **Partner Passing and Receiving a Pass.** Two players stand 10 to 15 feet apart passing and receiving a pass on the forehand and backhand. Goalies should be working on passing as well. **F14**

Passing/Shooting. If you plan on progressing to a combination fundamental drill, demonstrate the new skill that you're adding. Here, we're combining shooting with passing the puck up ice. Explain the principles used to develop the shot on which you're working. Again, players should watch you demonstrate from more than one angle.

Remember that the first shooting drill your players will do should be a warm-up for your goalies, where they get a feel for the puck. Therefore, encourage your players to shoot the puck without emphasizing scoring. After the goalies have been warmed up, tell players to shoot to score.

- **Five-Foot Passing.** Players form two lines, one on either side of one net. Skating 5 feet apart, two players pass back and forth down the ice ten to fifteen times, make one pass inside the blue line, shoot on net, turn toward the boards, and then return. Remember to alternate goalies after approximately ten shots. **F15**

Stickhandling. As with any new skill you're demonstrating, it's important to talk about the principles of the skill. To stickhandle well, players must be in an athletic hockey stance with knees bent and head, eyes, and chest erect. The stick is held on the ice in front of the body with hands positioned 6 to 12 inches apart. Arms and elbows are held away from the body. The puck is cupped on the stick while the wrists are rolled to move the puck from the forehand to the backhand side of the stick. Stickhandling also plays a big part in puck possession; therefore, players who can control the puck help their team keep that valuable possession.

- **Stationary Stickhandling.** Each player finds a place on the ice and stickhandles a puck from side to side. **F31**

   Goalies should work on their own fundamental skills at this time. **G1–G3**

- **Stickhandling Slalom and Turnbacks.** Place two cones on one side of the ice, a slalom course on the other. This drill works on two different turn speeds, finishing with a scoring chance. **F35**

Offensive and Game Situations (20 minutes total)

Keep in mind that you'll probably not have enough time in any one practice to work on offense, defense, and game situations. As coach, you need to vary what drills to use in this segment of practice based on what your team's needs are. Often, I like to split up my practice by using one of these ten-minute drills earlier in practice, sandwiching a shooting drill in between. I do this to give my goalies as much action as possible and to keep the attention of players who might otherwise be standing around losing interest. Remember that the more young players are kept moving during practice, the faster their skills will improve.

   Here we're using one offensive drill, one game situation drill, and no defensive drills. Both drills in this practice will have players skating, passing, and shooting, so it's fine to leave the practice plan as is. Just remember that before practice begins, you should use your coaching board to diagram most drills of this type because they'll usually be slightly more difficult. Each drill will take approximately ten minutes.

   Offense. Here, we're trying to teach players simple positioning to break the puck out of the defensive zone to move on offense. While encouraging your kids to be creative in the offensive zone, you want to maintain structure in breaking the puck out of their own zone. As you can imagine, this is a great opportunity for teaching.

   This drill should be explained and diagrammed before practice so your players can best grasp their positioning as the drill is performed. I often send my players home with a diagram of our positioning during drills used in this segment of practice. Take-home diagrams include breakout position, face-off position, and defensive zone coverage position.

- **Double Breakout.** The first time you use this drill will require more teaching and less action. Have only two goalies, three forwards, and two defensemen on the ice. All other skaters should be on the players' bench. If you're coaching Mites or Squirts, one of your assistants should also be on the bench to make certain everyone is paying attention and to open the players' bench door. This drill consists of two breakouts, two rushes up the ice, and three scoring chances. The next five players will then perform the drill starting from the opposite end. **O6**

Game situation. I like to use game situation drills in every practice. It might be as simple as the two-on-one drill described here or a fun, competitive drill such as a three-on-three mini-game played across the ice. After fundamental skill development, game situations are the most helpful in preparing your players for the real game; in addition, most players greatly enjoy them. All drills in this segment of the practice should mimic situations that may occur during a game.

- **Full-Ice Two-on-One.** Use cones to diagonally separate the ice. Use three lines of two forwards, stationing one defenseman in opposing corners. Players skate two on one out of each corner the full length of the ice. **GS1**

Competition Drill (10 minutes)

It's always good to finish practice with a fun drill for your players. Kids enjoy this part of practice whether it involves a scrimmage, a mini-game, or a competition drill.

- **One-on-One Battle (Stick Lift and Stick Press)/One-on-One Battle.** This is a simple, competitive, and good conditioning drill. You can use one or both ends of the ice; just make certain that there are two lines, one on each side of the net, lined up on the goal line. Place one cone on each face-off dot outside the blue lines. On the whistle, the first player in each line races out and around the nearest cone, and then the two players battle for one puck in the slot area to score against the goalie, who is in net near the end where the action began. **F47 GS3**

Wrap-Up/Doggy Bag (5 minutes)

After practice, use the locker room to have a short meeting. Begin by telling your players how well they did in practice; then give them something to work on for the next practice. It's best to find something that the majority of players need to improve upon as away-from-the-rink "homework." If you can't find one particular item, it's always good to have them work on shooting, stickhandling, or passing.

Explain to your players that the first practice is typically the slowest because you have to show them drills for the first time. Tell them you expect them to learn and remember the drills so things will move more quickly in future practices. Finish with encouragement on a job well done and then announce the day and time of the next practice or game.

Intermediate Practice
Team Meeting (10 minutes)

Intermediate practices should be used when you feel your players are ready for drills that will challenge their ability level. For example, this practice emphasizes speed, passing, and shooting. If you're having a shared-ice practice, it's imperative that you speak with the coach of the other team to coordinate your practice plan. Make sure you have a backup plan for half-ice drills if necessary. Don't forget the importance of diagramming some of the more difficult drills in the locker room before you hit the ice. You should know every player's name by now, so you should be encouraging each player personally.

Warm-Up (10 minutes total)

Again, begin with a quick warm-up to stretch and loosen the muscles, instructing players to lengthen their strides using full range of motion and working up to faster speeds. Each drill should last about three minutes.

- **Easy Skating.** Have players skate around the rink for a few minutes to get the blood flowing. Tell your players to lengthen their strides between the blue lines or turn and skate backward instead. Make sure you have them change direction.

- **Two-Skate Power Stops.** Starting from the goal line at one end of the ice, players do two-skate power stops, working on quickness and explosiveness coming out of every stop. **F7**

- **Forward Crossovers and Backward Crossunders.** Four players at a time skate forward crossovers around the five face-off circles, finishing at the opposite end. If time permits, repeat using forward skating, beginning at the opposite end. If time is short, three players should skate backward crossunders around the five face-off circles beginning at the opposite end. **F8   F9**

    Goalies should do Parallel Shuffles the length of the ice, staying close to the boards.

Fundamentals (20 minutes total)

Every player from beginner to pro needs to work on the fundamentals. The drills in Chapter 11 will help your players work on all the skills necessary for them to excel as hockey players. Don't forget to be flexible; you may have to adjust a drill that is either too difficult or not challenging enough for your players. Each drill should last about five minutes.

- **Reverse Four Pass.** This drill also works out of both ends so the transition will be smooth. Encourage your players to "pass from the heart." They need to be thinking and moving quickly to keep the pace of this drill high. **F22**

- **Two Players, Two Shots, Long Pass.** Again, use the first shooting drill as a warm-up for the goalies. Encourage your players to shoot the puck so the goalies get a feel for it. This drill forces your players to concentrate on being ready to pass and follow directions. Players begin only on the coach's whistle. **F23**

- **Center-Ice Crossover Give-and-Go.** Encourage your players to use good form while carrying the puck around the center face-off circle, remembering to make good passes on the stick. Urge your players to explode when they break in on the goalie. **F24**

- **Mohawk Shooting.** This drill is done using both ends of the ice. Remind your players to use good form while performing Mohawk turns, make "stick to stick" passes, and, when changing lines, stay clear of the players involved in the drill. Remember to switch sides of the ice halfway through the time allotment, with goalies switching ends so they face all shooters. **F46**

Defense and Game Situation (20 minutes total)

Defense. Use this time to work with your players on the team-play situations that need improvement. I'm a big believer in "defense wins championships." Teach your players the foundations of playing good, positional hockey in all areas of the ice, especially when playing defense. Each drill should last about ten minutes.

- **Three-on-Three Defensive Zone Coverage.** Definitely diagram this ten-minute drill before practice. Depending on the ability level of your players, you may need more time, so be ready to adjust your practice. Your players will work three-on-three "man on man" while maintaining awareness of the puck position in a controlled situation. Teach proper positioning, and don't be afraid to stop play to correct mistakes. **D3**

Game situation. It's important to use game situation drills in every practice or your players won't have any idea how to perform in a game. Players enjoy game situation drills because they always mimic things that happen in a game. For example, the Continuous Two-on-One drill is a highly realistic game situation that improves each and every player.

- **Continuous Two-on-One.** This is a great full-ice drill that I like to use in nearly every practice. Two-on-one situations happen fairly often in youth hockey games, and this drill flows well because it keeps the players moving. Encourage good, low, point shots, "stick to stick" passing, speed through the neutral zone, shooting to score, going for rebounds, and battling for position in front of the net. That's a lot to accomplish in one drill! **GS8**

Competition Drill (10 minutes)

It's always a good idea to finish with an enjoyable drill for your players. Kids like this part of the practice so much that they'll leave the rink talking about how much fun it was, and they'll anxiously await their next practice.

- **Scrimmage.** Players love full-ice scrimmages, which are a great way to end practice. You can have them play five-on-five, four-on-four, three-on-three, two-on-two, or one-on-one. Vary your choice depending on the number of players, making certain you match up the ability levels of your players. If you find one side is stronger, join in on the scrimmage yourself and help the weaker team out for a few minutes. This keeps morale up and challenges the stronger team to work hard.

Wrap-Up/Doggy Bag (5 minutes)

Tell your players that practice had a great, up-tempo atmosphere, that you see them improving with every practice. Advise them to work on a skill that needs attention for the next practice. Remind them that it's easy to work on things they're already good at, but to truly become better hockey players, they should practice the skills they most need to improve. Remind your players of the date and time of the next practice or game.

Intermediate/Advanced Practice
Team Meeting (10 minutes)

Intermediate/Advanced practices should be run *only if* your players have become proficient at passing. Some of the drills in this type of practice will also challenge your players to think, read, react, and be extremely attentive. As with any practice, it's always important to make sure that you diagram the most difficult drills in the locker room beforehand. You'll probably need to walk through some of these drills slowly, patiently explaining each step. If your players' ability is high, they'll catch on and rise to the challenge. Again, you'll need the cooperation of any coach with whom you're sharing the ice for practice. Be prepared with a half-ice practice plan as well. Tell your players that today's practice will be challenging, but they'll do fine if they use their speed, make good passes, and think on their feet.

Warm-Up (10 minutes total)

Skating drills are the best way to have players warm up. Have them get the blood flowing by easing into the drills, remembering to stride using a full range of motion. Beginning slowly prevents injuries from muscle pulls. Each drill should last about three minutes.

- **Easy Skating.** Skate around the rink for a few minutes to get the blood flowing. Instruct your players to lengthen their strides between the blue lines or turn and skate backward instead. Make sure they change directions.

- **Continuous Inside-Outs.** Skaters must concentrate on doing four tight glide turns, always skating from the inside of each cone and turning toward the boards. Remind your players to explode out of the turn to maximize speed. **F12**

- **Stickhandling Turnbacks.** To challenge players who possess higher skill levels, have them perform more skating drills while carrying a puck. This drill will help your players improve their puck control skills during turns while also maintaining speed. They'll need to concentrate on making all turns either toward the players' bench or toward the penalty boxes to prevent collisions. **F34**

Fundamentals (20 minutes)

Fundamentals are the staple of every practice. As your players become more skilled, you will need to challenge them both physically and mentally. Drills that require players to complete more than one pass make them better hockey players. Remember Tom McVie's motto: "pass from the heart."

- **Blue Line Three Pass (5 to 7 min.).** This is definitely a thinking drill. Its difficulty lies in the absolute attention that each player at the front of each line must pay while remembering exactly what to do next. What's more, the role of each player at the front of the line is not always the same. Players need to make "stick to stick" passes, move their feet quickly, and present themselves for a return pass. **F29**

     If your players just can't perform this drill, move into the Blue Line Three-Pass Two-on-Zero instead. **O12**

- **Timing (8 to 10 min.).** Initially, you'll need more time for this drill because of the difficulty level. The first time you employ this drill, take extra time to demonstrate it and walk through it slowly. Stick with the drill, though, because it flows well and helps your players learn precise timing and angles while improving their thinking and passing skills. Make sure you change sides of the ice after about five minutes. **F30**

- **Blue Line Three-Pass Two-on-Zero (5 min.).** This drill will still test your players' ability to pass and focus, but it's a bit easier than the Blue Line Three

Pass. With two players skating at the same time, the drill becomes less complicated. **012**

Offense and Game Situations (20 minutes total)

Offense. Use this time to work with your players on the team-play situations that need improvement. You don't need to overwhelm players with a massive number of drills, but they need to learn the foundation of playing good, positional hockey. Expand a simple breakout drill by challenging your players to make a number of passes. This keeps the drill flowing and keeps players on their toes if they maintain speed and intensity throughout. Each drill should last about ten minutes.

- **Breakout, Regroup Three-on-Two.** This drill works on *gap control*; the gap is the space between defending defensemen and attacking forwards on an offensive rush. Only seven players are on the ice. Keep the drill moving by running it from alternating ends. Encourage everyone to make good passes and move their feet at top speed. This drill helps players learn about creating time and space, filling lanes, and attacking with speed. Defensemen learn to control the gap by playing closer to the opponent, working with their partner, and gauging the speed of the attacking forwards. **GS16**

  Game situation. It's important to use game situation drills in every practice so your players will be prepared for an actual game. Kids love these drills because they closely resemble game play. Don't forget to stop a game situation drill if you see something that needs immediate attention or correction.

- **All in One.** This drill combines six game situations: defensive zone coverage, a breakout, forechecking, two offensive zone plays, and a three-on-two. Only five players at a time are on the ice. To maximize what your players gain from this drill, encourage them to perform every aspect at top speed. Again, good passing is essential for this drill to work. **GS14**

Competition Drill (10 minutes)

Always use a fun drill at the end of practice. Your players will view it as a reward after working so hard and come away with a real sense of enjoyment and accomplishment.

- **Timed Three-on-Zero.** This is a fun way to conclude practice. For older players, this provides time for individual, cool-down stretching while they wait their turn on the ice. Encourage speed of attack, puck movement, and quickness while getting out of the zone. If time permits, you can give forfeits (additional skating laps around the rink, push-ups, or sit-ups) to the slower teams. **05**

Wrap-Up/Doggy Bag (5 minutes)

It's very important to encourage your players and tell them what a great job they did in practice, even if they had trouble with one or two drills. Make it clear that your job is to improve their skills and level of play, and that the only way to do this is by challenging them. Assure them that the next time they perform some of these advanced drills, they'll find the drills easier. Ask them to watch their favorite pro hockey team, paying close attention to one aspect of the game they worked on during today's practice. As always, announce the day and time of the next practice or game.

Questions and Answers

Q. I thought I had a great plan for the first day of practice, but some drills took so long to explain that we barely made it through half of them. Some kids seem to understand quickly, while others take more time to catch on. How can I better plan my practices? How do I keep the kids who catch on quickly from becoming restless?

A. The important thing about a practice plan is to make it flexible. Sometimes a plan that looks great on paper doesn't translate into a great practice. Before trying any new or difficult drill, you should utilize the locker-room time before practice to diagram drills with your coach's board. This gives players a chance to ask questions about anything they don't understand, and it doesn't take away from precious ice time. If your practice seems to be moving slowly, determine if the drills are simply too hard for your players or if you believe they'll catch on in the next practice. Sometimes a drill is too difficult for the skill level of the players you're instructing, but often you just need to give it time. If performing the skill seems to be the problem, you should consider using a different drill next time, but by repeating some of the new drills in the next practice you'll often see your players respond.

Understand that the best practice plans involve as many players as possible at one time. Nothing is worse than having parents complain about a practice because they feel their children were standing around doing nothing. Keep your practices upbeat and positive, quickly transitioning from drill to drill.

Kids who catch on quickly need to be challenged. It's important for them to understand that the basic skills need work at every practice. All your players will continue to improve their basic skills if they're willing to work hard. I always remind my players to work extra hard on the parts of their game that need improving. Anyone can work on a skill at which he or she is already adept, but becoming the best player one can be requires working hard on weaknesses. The best way to challenge all players is by utilizing competition drills. It's a simple fact that most kids get excited about competing in games and races.

Every team is going to have players at different skill levels, but this becomes less of a factor if you make sure you match up players who can challenge those of their own ability level.

Q. I'm coaching a group of younger players who spend the entire practice asking to scrimmage. They complain that the drills are boring. I want to make practices fun, but how can I teach them to play hockey if they don't like practicing the essential skills?

A. When you're teaching the game of hockey to younger players, the most important thing is that they have fun. Don't compromise this. If you find your players are bored, then you need to explain that if they work hard improving their skills, they'll be rewarded with a scrimmage or fun competition drill later in practice. If your players still complain, maybe you need to change your approach to practice. Almost all kids love to shoot the puck and compete, whether it's in a scrimmage, mini-game, or relay race. If your practice is stuck in first gear, give your players a fun relay race or competition drill that also requires them to work hard at the essential skills without their realization. When all else fails, understand they are kids and are playing hockey to have fun, so scrimmage away!

Q. We've started body checking, and some of the bigger kids are intimidating the smaller ones. Should I pair up only the kids who are the same weight and height?

A. First remember that when you begin teaching body checking, you must explain that it's not a license to hurt other players. Respect should be the first point you discuss. If some of your bigger kids are intimidating to the smaller ones, explain the objective for everyone. For example, it's essential that everyone learns how to take a check as well as give one. The old saying "every dog has his day" is important to remember here. Bigger kids must put themselves in the shoes (or, in this case, skates) of their smaller teammates because they may not always be the big kid.

   If you see the potential for intimidation, you must head it off before it happens. When teaching how to body-check, it's often a good idea to match up players who are approximately the same size and who have similar overall hockey abilities.

Q. How do I know when my team is ready to handle more complicated drills? If the majority of the team is doing well with a skill, but a few kids are still struggling, how do I address each player's needs?

A. Generally, your players will show you that they're ready for new, more demanding drills. As they progress, you need to keep challenging them. See how your players handle it when you increase the difficulty of a drill. Be patient. Sometimes this requires more time than you'd expect. Just remember that drill repetition often helps your team perform the drill properly.

If you have a few players who are still struggling with a skill, it's essential that you continue to involve them in a more complicated drill. Both you and their teammates should continue to provide encouragement. There's nothing more satisfying for a coach than watching players truly become a team by pulling for each other. In fact, you'll usually see great improvement when the players encourage each other in this manner. The best players improve not only themselves but also the players around them!

Sometimes kids who are struggling also need more individualized instructions; your assistant coaches can really be helpful in providing this one-on-one help.

Q. My team does very well when I give them specific instructions, but they have a difficult time reading and reacting. How do I teach my players to think quickly and adapt to different situations?

A. The most difficult part of coaching is teaching the mental aspect of the game. Reading a play in hockey, whether defensively or offensively, requires great vision. The best hockey players "see the ice" extremely well, actually anticipating and reacting beforehand to what will occur. Vision is something that can't be taught; it's a natural talent. However, you can improve the vision your players possess by always reminding them to skate with their heads up and on a swivel, looking around so they can see more of the ice. For example, your defensemen should always be counting the number of opponent jerseys they see on the ice in front of them. That way they'll know if someone on the other team is lurking out of their line of vision. The same technique can be used when facing an opponent's rush up the ice. I teach my defensemen to count how many opponents are involved in the rush while determining if they have teammates in position to help out. Offensively, forwards should be counting opponents to determine if they have an outnumbered rush and seeing if there's an open teammate available for a pass.

To help your players react quickly, they need to perform every drill at high speed. By using repetition and a lot of game situation drills in practice, you can give your players the tools needed to "see the ice" well and react quickly to the situation.

CHAPTER 9

The Game

Your team has practiced faithfully for many weeks, developing their skills and hockey sense. Now you've reached the time when those skills will be tested in a game. The first game always brings a combination of nervous anticipation and pent-up excitement. Everyone is anxious to do his or her best, and as coach, you might be tempted to judge the team and your coaching ability on the final score of the game. Keep in mind that you've always stressed that winning and losing is not the be all and end all. Your concern should focus on how the kids play, the amount of effort they exert, and their level of enjoyment in playing. Use the game to assess your team's strengths and weaknesses. Later, you can point out the game situations where they performed particularly well and offer advice to correct problems.

Set an Example

Once game time arrives, it's especially important that you continue the positive example you've set during practices and team meetings. You'll need to maintain control over your anxiety and excitement. Remember that you can talk all season long about good sportsmanship, but your actions carry the most weight. It's a good idea to review important points on which your players should focus during each game. Leave the locker room to enter the playing surface on an upbeat note. Remember to emphasize that, above all, your players should have fun!

Respect the Officials

Meet the officials before the game; shake their hands and show them the respect they deserve. If an official makes a bad call, don't dwell on it. Tell your players to move on and focus on the next play. If coaches and parents complain to each other or the officials, the kids pick up on the negativity and lose their concentration. Never question an official's call; it's best to use the

Game Day

Most game day preparation involves structured practices and, as players progress to higher levels, learning about how their opponents play. For example, when I played college hockey at Wisconsin, my coach, Bob Johnson, held a week of practice before each weekend series. We also had a team meeting to learn about our opponents and their playing style.

But every player has his or her own way of preparing for game day. Many hockey players are also a bit superstitious, so you might see a Bantam player wear the same "lucky" T-shirt to every game, or perhaps a seasoned NHL player who would never dream of lacing his left skate before his right. The best advice I can offer is to do what it takes to be prepared, calm, and focused.

opportunity to show your team that a good player perseveres through any setbacks. Tell them to concentrate on things they can control, such as their level of play. Don't permit any player to question an official's call. Stick to that rule, no matter what.

After the game, thank the officials for their time and effort and shake hands again. Most of them are volunteers or receive little pay for their efforts. They deserve to be acknowledged for what is often a thankless job. If you're dealing with young referees and feel that you could offer them some constructive help, wait until the game is over and then approach them in a quiet, nonconfrontational way. Keep in mind that immediate negative reactions to missed or poor calls by young referees could have extremely negative effects on their confidence. Deal with them as you would your players; "sandwich" a suggestion between two compliments. It's youth hockey, and it's supposed to be fun.

Be Ready

In addition to being prepared for every practice, you need a well-established game plan before you come to the rink on game day. Include your starting lineup, player positions, line rotations, and possible power play and penalty-killing units. Decide beforehand what you'll do if you're winning by a lot, or losing by a lot, or if the game is "on the line" in the final minutes. Be prepared to move players around to different positions if you're winning by a wide margin, and let some of your less talented offensive players play forward to avoid running up the score. Make sure you have everything you need on the bench at your disposal: pucks, water, first-aid kit, rulebook, lineup sheet, pen, dry-erase marker, and coach's board. You need to be well organized because your players will be nervous and looking to you for leadership.

You'll usually have about 3 to 8 minutes for a pregame warm-up. Use the following drill sequence as a possible warm-up template to loosen up your players:

Have players skate over to the side boards and back a few times to get the blood flowing.

Use Half-Ice Horseshoe or substitute Cross-Ice Follow Your Pass for most of your players, with a simultaneous Umbrella Shooting for about five of them. **F40** **F16** **F42**

If there's time, end the warm-up with Mad Dog Two-on-One to simulate a game setting involving a two-on-one. (In case you're wondering, when I came up with this drill, I was coaching a team called the Mad Dogs; the drill is named for them.) **GS6**

Game Overview
Opening Face-Off

The opening face-off takes place in the center-ice circle, with both teams' centers positioned across from each other. Both centers concentrate on the referee's hand and try to draw the puck back to their defensemen to gain puck possession. If your team wins the opening face-off, your players should try to move quickly on the offense. Defensemen generally look to pass the puck to one of the forwards to begin an offensive rush. If they're unable to pass, they should attempt to skate to center ice and dump the puck into the offensive zone, where the forechecking should begin. If your team loses the opening face-off, it's time to force a turnover to gain puck possession. Make certain you've explained to your players their specific responsibilities for a lost face-off. They should know where to skate and whom they need to cover in this situation.

Game Time

Hockey is a game of great speed, but it's often called a game of inches. Unlike basketball, it's difficult to slow down the action to set up an offensive play. Hockey requires creativity on offense and hard work on defense. The high speed of the game tends to cause players to make mistakes that frequently result in missed coverage assignments and goal-scoring opportunities. Coaches often tell their players that if they win the one-on-one battles, they'll win the game. That's usually true. The players that work together defensively by covering up for a teammate's mistake or missed assignment generally minimize scoring chances by their opponent. In turn, these players can transition quickly from defense to offense in an attempt to score a goal.

Explain Your Substitution Pattern

It's important that your players clearly understand the substitution plan before the game. It's equally important to ask your players what they'd like to do if the game is on the line. Ask them for input if you'll need a goal near the end of the game or if you're protecting a lead. They all like to win and

Game Day Checklist

Things to Bring

pucks for warm-up
first-aid kit
at least 6 large water bottles
rulebook
coaching board with dry-erase markers
pen and paper for notes
game plan, including lineup and positions
parent/emergency-contact list
cell phone

At the Rink

Arrive at the rink thirty minutes before the game.

Locate the locker room.

Check to see if the rink's schedule is on time (game times can change due to unforeseen circumstances).

Fill out a game sheet with player names, jersey numbers, and positions (usually supplied by the rink).

Meet the opposing coach (give him the game sheet to fill out and wish him good luck).

Meet with your players five to ten minutes before the warm-up (go over game plan).

Warm-Up

Bring all items on your "Things to Bring" list to the players' bench.

Greet the game officials during the warm-up.

At the end of the warm-up, bring your players in for a quick pep talk and any last-minute reminders.

will usually give you the green light to use the players you feel provide the best chance in the clutch. If you're coaching a house league or recreational team, you should rotate your lines, giving equal ice time to each line. If you're coaching a travel or highly competitive team, it's equally important to keep the playing time as balanced as possible, but understand that the expectations are a little higher at this level. It's OK to have power play and penalty-killing units, provided you give every player the opportunity to play on one during practices and early in the season. As the season progresses, you'll discover which kids are your go-to players in these and other clutch situations. Keep things in perspective! Remember these very young athletes are still playing the game for the fun of it.

Between Periods

When the Zamboni comes out to resurface the ice, it's called an *ice cut*. Most youth hockey games do not have an ice cut between periods; therefore, you only have a few minutes to speak quickly to your players about how the game is going. This is an ideal time to point out where they need to improve during the remainder of the game and to praise all the positives that you have seen.

When time allows and an ice cut *is* done, break times range from ten to fifteen minutes between periods. As coach, this allows you more time to address things that you'd like to change or see your players do in the next period. Make use of your coaching board to diagram player positioning or address situations that have occurred.

Player Lines and Changes

Although there is a starting lineup in youth hockey, that does not mean there are starters who play a lot and substitutes that play very little. Generally most teams consist of three or four forward lines and three sets of defensemen. Coaches should try to balance their forward lines and defensive pairings to benefit all players. You will find that the more-skilled players will help with the development of the less-skilled ones while playing on a line together.

In youth hockey, a player's shift should last somewhere between one and two minutes. Occasionally, beginner-level youth programs may implement a signal that halts play to allow all players on the ice to change every one and a half to two minutes. However, most leagues "change on the fly" while play continues. It is always a good idea to have the forwards at the end of the players' bench located closest to the opponent's goal and the defensemen at the end of the bench closest to their own goal. This allows for smoother changes and ensures that when your fresh players take to the ice, they are closer to the area where their responsibilities lie. It's important to make sure that one coach operates each player's gate to help with line changes. The coaches may have to remind a player on the ice that it's time to change and ensure that the correct replacement player takes the ice in his spot. In other words, right winger changes for right winger, left defenseman for left defenseman, etc.

Time-Outs

In youth hockey, each team is permitted only one time-out per game. They usually last one minute, but can vary by league. Generally, time-outs are called in the last minute of a close game. You should call a time-out if you need to rest your clutch players near the end of a game or if you have a key face-off late in a one-goal game. If a game is slipping away quickly, a coach sometimes calls a time-out. This may never happen, but if your team is floundering, it's time to bring the troops in and give them an encouraging pep talk. If the other team calls a time-out, use that time to calm your players, prepare them for the face-off, or explain what to do if the opponent pulls its goalie.

It's important to keep the playing time as even as possible, but keep in mind that all kids love to win. If the game is on the line in the final minutes, you should know what your team would like to do. To signal a time-out, make a T with your hands, giving the verbal command "Time-out!" You can also ask your captain or center to request a time-out from one of the officials. Once a time-out is called, all your players (including the goaltender) should skate quickly to the bench and form a tight semicircle around you. You must explain each player's responsibility on the ensuing face-off and then get the right players quickly onto the ice. It's vital that you go over these last-minute situations in practice so your players are familiar with what is expected of them.

Adjusting the Game Plan

A good coach makes adjustments to the team's game plan if the score becomes one-sided or if you're worried about losing a one-goal lead in the waning minutes of the game. Always be prepared to change your lines if your team is having trouble scoring goals. On the other hand, if your team is well in command of the game, you should move your players around to play different positions. Have your less offensively skilled team members play forward, and ask your more offensively skilled players to move back to defense and pass the puck more. Keep in mind that it's considered poor practice to run up the score in youth sports.

You should also make adjustments if your team is leading by a goal late in the game. This is the time to play a simple game, make safe plays, and avoid turnovers in the neutral or defensive zone. Teach your team to play smart at both blue lines. Players should use the boards to chip the puck out near your defensive blue line and get the puck in deep near the offensive blue line. When a team has a lead late in the game, a coach might implement a One-Two-Two Forecheck **D7** to ensure that the team doesn't give up any odd-man rushes, where the other team has a player advantage in moving on your team's goal. Keep the shifts short to help everyone stay involved. When a team is down by a goal late in the game, a coach will sometimes give the defensemen the freedom to become more involved offensively.

What about Statistics?

Individual stats should not be the focus of how a player is performing. It's more important that your team members learn and improve each game, responding to what you're teaching. If you'd like to set team goals, that's OK, but even then the focus shouldn't be on wins and losses. Two goals I like setting for my team are scoring the game's first goal and not allowing the opposition to score more than three goals in any given game.

End the Game Positively

Always respect your opponent. Each game should end with both teams lining up for a handshake followed by your final word of thanks to the other

In youth hockey leagues, the traditional handshake of sportsmanship occurs at the conclusion of each game. It's important to instruct your players to be good sports in victory or defeat.

coach and referees. Good sportsmanship should be a prerequisite for every game.

As soon as the game ends and you're in the locker room, it's important to have a closed-door meeting with your team for a few minutes. Whether you've won or lost the game, your comments should be positive. Have your players quiet down, and then you can acknowledge what they did well during the game. You can point out the positive support they provided for each other and how hard they worked. Don't concentrate on whether you've won or lost because sometimes your team plays well and doesn't win; at other times they win but don't play well. Although this might be a cliché, it's true that "it's not whether you win or lose, but how you play the game," especially in youth sports. Of course, you'll want to point out the areas that need improvement, but remind your players that you'll work on these at practice.

Taking Stock after the Game

After each game, assess where you are and where you want to be. I always look first at how my team played. I don't put a lot of emphasis on winning and losing. I consider a successful game to be one where the kids had fun and played with heart and determination. In fact, I talk to my players between every period and tell them what's going well before I talk about what areas need correction. If we lose a game, I go into the locker room and tell them I understand if they're upset about losing, but I'm not. I remind them that they played great, but the other team played a little bit

Winning and Losing

I learned two important lessons when my team lost a game: first, it's only a game, and second, there's always tomorrow. When I was growing up, I enjoyed winning like everyone else, but I always played hockey to have fun, whether it was a big league championship or a weekend pond hockey game.

better. In my opinion, a good game means my kids played hard, smart, and competitively.

Sometimes kids think that if they beat a certain team the last time, they'll definitely beat them again. But kids come to the rink with different emotional levels and in varying levels of exhaustion. If they've been playing in the snow all day, they might come to the rink already exhausted. Kids are kids. You never know what you're going to get on any given day. In fact, there's a time-honored belief in pro sports that any team can beat any other team on any given day, and that's really the truth.

I believe in being totally honest when assessing how my team plays. There are times that we've played terribly and didn't compete, and I tell my kids just that even if they win. However, I also add that tomorrow is another day. Don't worry about this game; look forward to the next day and the next game. Kids know when they haven't played well. While it's necessary to remind them they need to compete, skate harder, or bear down on the puck when they shoot, it's crazy to get carried away just because they lose. Always leave the kids with something positive, because kids play sports for fun. You certainly don't want them to feel negative or down on themselves.

Questions and Answers

Q. I have a player who is very skilled in practice, but she can't seem to translate her skills into a game situation. What should I do?

A. There are players who are good practice players but who don't perform as well in games. They often feel outside pressure and become nervous when game time arrives. It's important to help your players relax and have fun playing the game. As coach, you want your team to play with intensity, but you want them to understand that they're playing a game. It's all about having fun. Sometimes skilled players who practice well but who can't translate their skills to a game situation need to watch how their favorite professional team plays. This allows them to pick up tips on how to be a better team player.

Q. How do I divide the lines on my team? Do I put all the best players on one line, put players of similar height and weight together, or make the selection randomly?

A. There are two schools of thought on this. Putting your best players together will certainly help your team when that line is on the ice, but if

Troubleshooting Chart

Problem	Analysis	Solution
Your team isn't scoring enough goals.	If your team is having trouble scoring, it's important to get your kids to shoot the puck more often. Your players must learn that when they're on the ice, hockey isn't a spectator sport. Hockey is a team sport, not one where one player skates around the entire opposition and scores by himself. It's equally as important to instruct your players to use the points. Tell your forwards that if the defensemen are open at the blue line, they should pass the puck back to the defensemen and head to the front of the net. No goaltender likes traffic in front, particularly because many goals are scored when the goalie is screened. Often, making passes from behind the offensive zone net creates scoring chances. A goaltender dislikes the opposition setting up behind the net because it's difficult for the goalie to concentrate on the puck while simultaneously reading where the pass from behind might end up.	Shoot, shoot, and shoot some more! Teach your team that on an offensive rush, the player with the puck drives wide to get a shot on goal while a teammate drives to the net for any rebound chance. Never give up a shot to make a low percentage pass. On two-on-one plays, your player's first thought should be to shoot rather than to pass, because shooting can result in a goal scored or a rebound chance. Explain that you want players to pass at the right time without ever giving up a chance to score. Use the Continuous Two-on-One drill GS8 in practice. It's a great drill to teach your players to shoot the puck, drive to the net for rebounds, and fight for position in front, where they can screen the goaltender on the "second chance" puck. Other drills to help build your players' confidence in shooting goals are Two Players, Two Shots, Long Pass F23, Center-Ice Crossover Give-and-Go, Two-on-Zero F25, Timing F30, Umbrella Shooting F42, and Three-Player Cycle 04.
Your team is turning the puck over too frequently.	When a teammate has the puck, the other players need to move to open ice, becoming available for a pass. There are certain areas of the ice where you should *never* turn the puck over to the opponent. Your players should get the puck out of their defensive zone 5 feet inside their own blue line and also get the puck deep into the offensive zone 5 feet outside the opponent's blue line. It's equally important to avoid turning the puck over anywhere in your defensive zone. The ultimate no-no is losing the puck in the scoring area in front of your own net. As coach, you must remind your players to always make the safe, easy pass. It's equally important to recognize and sense danger. Your players will learn they must play the game with a sense of urgency. Use any and all drills that teach quick puck movement.	Teach players to move the puck quickly, making the easiest pass to an open teammate when heading up the ice. They shouldn't try to stickhandle around the opponent. Nor should they get fancy when they reach the red line and aren't facing an outnumbered offensive rush. It's often better to chip the puck softly off the boards behind the opposing defensemen and continue skating to retrieve it or shoot the puck deep into the offensive zone and forecheck to recover it. The name of the game is puck control, but again, one player cannot be expected to do it alone. Use the following drills to encourage your players to move the puck to the open player and avoid turning it over to the opposition: Reverse Four Pass F22, Crossover, Follow Your Pass F21, Center-Ice Crossover Give-and-Go F24, Double Breakout 06, and Three-Player Offensive Drive 07.

(continued next page)

Troubleshooting Chart (continued)

Problem	Analysis	Solution
Your defense is breaking down at key moments.	You need to stress that defense is more than just the defensemen and goaltender working together to prevent goals against. Defense is a total team effort.	Dedicate part of your practice to working on defensive zone coverage. Teach your players to keep the opponent they're covering between themselves and their own net. Players should keep their sticks on the ice in the defensive zone, trying to block any potential passing lane for the opponent. Teach them to feel proud when they win any one-on-one battles in their defensive zone. If you're protecting a lead late in a game, it's even more important to remind your forwards that there must be a player high in the slot area in the offensive zone to prevent any outnumbered rushes against them. All forwards should backcheck as quickly as possible when they lose possession of the puck. Defensemen should never gamble by pinching down the offensive boards in an attempt to keep the puck in unless they are 100 percent certain there won't be a confrontation with an opposing player. Have your players work on recovering the puck in their own end and moving the puck quickly out of the defensive zone while maintaining puck control. Drills to help are Three-on-Three Defensive Zone Coverage D3, One-on-One out of the Corner D1, Two-One-Two Forecheck D6, and Three-Player Offensive Drive O7.
Your team begins to lose momentum during games.	There can be a variety of reasons for losing momentum. First, players may not be in top shape. If this is the case, you need to address the problem in practices by putting the team through conditioning skating drills. Another problem could be their inability to focus.	The best way to deal with loss of momentum is to remind your team of the importance of concentrating for the entire game. Explain to players that they're being asked to focus for an hour to an hour and a half and are expected to do so. Team discipline on and off the ice is equally helpful. You don't need to be a tyrant, but it's OK to ask for respect and full attention when you're speaking. In many ways this disciplined style will help your players focus for the entire game and avoid losing momentum. Lastly, an easy way to keep the momentum up is to keep the shifts short. Make line changes quickly to keep everyone focused and mentally in the game. Short shifts also motivate everyone to go "full out" on every shift. Nothing is more satisfying than watching your players keep the tempo of play high when they go out line after line. You'll find that your players will learn to push each other to greater heights. To help players develop focus, they need to work harder in practice. Use conditioning drills like V-Starts and Control Stops F3 and Two-Skate Power Stops F7. To challenge them to improve and to focus, use intermediate to advanced drills like Reverse Four Pass F22, Blue Line Three Pass F29, or Three-Line Shooting with a Pass F44. If you're coaching a young team, keep in mind that having patience is more important than playing tyrant and confusing them with difficult drills.

you have players with less skill playing together, they may spend much of the next shift in their own zone. I like to mix it up and keep my lines as balanced as possible. I encourage my more-skilled players to help every teammate improve. I find I can accomplish this by splitting up the talent throughout the lineup. You'll discover that your less-skilled players will improve more quickly by skating with teammates of greater skill. At the same time you're also helping mold your skilled players into becoming leaders. The greatest athletes in team sports always make the players around them better athletes.

Q. Should I assign each of my defensemen to cover a specific forward on the other team? We occasionally face a team that has a particularly skilled player.

A. I don't believe it's necessary to have a specific defenseman cover one very skilled player on the opposing team. It's more important to teach your team to play a sound defensive game. Hockey is a team sport, and all players should work together both offensively and defensively. However, depending on the level I'm coaching, I'll try to match certain players or lines against the other team's better players. It's usually enough to tell your team to be aware when the opposition's top players are on the ice. Instruct them to keep a keen eye on where those players are at all times. Remember that if you double-team a skilled player, it always leaves an opposing player wide open for a scoring chance, so you may hurt yourself in the long run. Defending a skilled player takes a team effort, not an individual one.

Q. We lost by a huge margin in our last game. In the practices that followed, my team still seems down about the loss. How do I revive their enthusiasm?

A. It's important to put all losses behind you, no matter what the score may have been. Explain to your team that every dog has his day. Sometimes it just isn't your day. If your team was totally outclassed, it's a good idea to emphasize there's always something to be learned from a loss. Tell your players that they've now seen how good hockey can be played at their level. Remind them that if they're willing to work hard, you'll try your best to get them to the next level, but emphasize that it's up to them to show the dedication and desire needed to achieve this.

Q. Even though I've stressed the importance of respecting the officials, my players were clearly upset at the poor officiating during one of our games. How do I address this?

A. This is one of my rules that I will absolutely not tolerate being broken. Players, parents, or coaches should never be permitted to berate an official. If your players begin to lay the blame on the officials, you must stop them immediately. Tell them that players play, coaches coach, referees officiate. As players, they should focus all their energy on what they need to do to help the team, which includes avoiding negative emotions. Everything a team does should be positive. Remind them the only thing they can control is their own actions, which is exactly where their focus should remain.

Q. I have one player who refuses to pass during games. We've worked on passing repeatedly during practices, but in a game he always chooses to take a shot on goal rather than pass. The other kids on the team are becoming impatient with his selfishness. How should I handle this?

A. This is always a tough situation. I've seen and heard parents and grandparents encourage their kids to score goals for monetary rewards. If this is the case, I would talk with the parents about the importance of team play. If they feel that strongly about rewards, suggest they include assists as well. If the problem lies solely with the player, it's time to sit him down and explain the team concept of the game. Tell him that great players like Wayne Gretzky felt more pleasure setting up his teammates than scoring himself.

Q. I have a player who repeatedly misses practice. Although I've spoken to her and her parents about this, they're upset because she sees very little ice time during the games. I've told both players and parents that those who attend practice consistently will receive more playing time than those who don't. Yet her parents are very angry at my decision. Is my decision reasonable?

A. It's important to have rules and abide by them. If your rule is that missed practices mean less playing time during games, and if you're up front with parents from day one about this, there really isn't any room for disagreement. If you have a problem with a parent or player who's angry about your decision, ask them if they feel it's OK to break team rules. It always helps to have additional support from league officials. Any time you have a problem with a parent or player that cannot be solved reasonably, you need to reach out to your league officials, who will step in to help explain league and team policies.

Q. I coach a young team and can't break them of the habit of following the puck around the ice during games. The players seem to forget their position during the excitement of a game. How do I break them of this habit?

A. Remember that kids play hockey because it's fun. The easiest way to break the habit of "beehive hockey" is to work on positioning during practice. The best way to teach any skill is through repetition. Practice, practice, and more practice. As coach, you need to have patience, though. Your young players may take all year to spread out and play their position, but don't give up or be stressed if they don't catch on. The most important thing is to make sure they're having fun.

Q. In our last game, our team fell behind by three goals early in the first period. I couldn't seem to motivate players to keep trying. How do I keep them playing hard even when we're behind?

A. It's a good idea to instill that "never give up" attitude. Use examples of teams that have come back to win games after falling behind. This is a great opportunity to take a time-out and rally the troops! Explain that a hockey game is three periods long and that the most satisfying victories are the ones in which your team comes from behind to win. Talk about the most admired athletes who keep trying no matter how difficult it is to achieve victory. Tell them you live by the motto "Quitters never win and winners never quit."

CHAPTER 10

Dealing with Parents and Gender Issues

Perspective on Parents

Parents are usually their children's biggest cheerleaders, but in some ways this can pose a number of problems. Because parents want their children to feel good about themselves, they may believe this can happen only if their children excel. However, players don't have to be top performers to have a positive self-image. It's more important for children to set realistic goals for themselves and then try their best to achieve these goals. Part of your job as coach is helping each child to assess realistic goals. If offensive players feel they're a failure unless they score in every game, or if defensemen believe they can never allow a goal to enter their net, they're setting themselves up for failure. It's often said that hockey is a game of mistakes. That mistakes happen is a given, and, of course, it's your job to do your best to correct them. The key is to correct in a positive manner so that you set an example for parents as well as children.

I believe that players are successful if they've improved from the first day of the season until the last. It's your responsibility to teach your players how to improve upon a skill or play-making decision. But coaching is as much about how you say things as it is about what you say. Never hover over players and rant about something they did wrong. Don't be afraid to get down on one knee with younger children and explain the reason you're correcting them. If you pat them on the back and offer an encouraging word, you'll see them break into a big smile. Parents will see their children feeding off your positive energy level, and hopefully they'll take a low-key approach as well.

Help Parents Look at the Big Picture

Parents need to realize that many individuals make up a team and that your concern is for all the players, not just a few. After all, a good team is one where everyone contributes to the betterment of the team, not solely for individual statistics. It's often difficult for parents to be realistic about their child's ability level. They may feel their son or daughter should be used on every power play or should be receiving more ice time. You don't need to justify your decisions, but do be available and willing to answer parents' questions. It's equally important for parents to understand that when they give their child advice that conflicts with your suggestions, it confuses the child and may undermine your role as coach.

Keeping Emotions in Check

Like other team sports, hockey requires strong bonds of trust and encouragement between teammates. If parents are permitted to weaken these bonds by ridiculing their child or someone else's, it can create a great deal of tension and hurt feelings. Unfortunately, "hockey rage" has become a real problem among some parents, so much so that hockey organizations have stepped in to address the problem. USA Hockey has a "zero tolerance" policy that states that any parent or spectator who displays inappropriate behavior will be removed from the game area. This rule also applies to players and coaches. A player can receive an unsportsmanlike conduct penalty and even a misconduct penalty if poor behavior continues. Coaches can be assessed a minor penalty and an additional game misconduct penalty for the same offense. Hockey Canada has instituted a "Relax, it's just a game" ad campaign on television, on the radio, and in newspapers. The ads show what happens when parents put too much pressure on their children and when they lose their temper over simple children's games.

I believe that much of the problem stems from parental dreams of college hockey scholarships and lucrative National Hockey League salaries. Parents fail to realize that the odds that their child will receive huge monetary benefits from playing a sport are incredibly small. It's great for a kid to have dreams of becoming the next Wayne Gretzky or Martin Brodeur, but it's dead wrong for parents to pressure kids or push them in a direction they might not choose for themselves. Any parent who berates an official or a child on either team needs to be reminded that children play hockey to have fun, not to sign an NHL contract.

Addressing Gender Issues

Women's hockey is not a new phenomenon; in fact, it's over a hundred years old. During the past decade, female participation in hockey increased 400 percent! This explosion in enthusiasm certainly helped women's hockey when it became a full-medal Olympic sport at the 2002 Winter Olympics in Salt Lake City.

Girls play hockey for the same reasons as boys: they love its fast pace along with the physical and mental challenges. Girls can play on any team right through the high school level, but many prefer to join a girls' team beginning in the sixth or seventh grade. There are now many female select teams as well as women's varsity high school teams and collegiate divisions. The only differentiation in the rules of girls' ice hockey is that intentional body checking is not permitted. There is still a great deal of body contact, but intentional checking is penalized.

Though girls do tend to be a bit more sensitive to criticism from the coach (on or off the ice), they're quickly closing the gap with boys when it comes to competitiveness and their drive and desire to take their ability to the next level. I firmly believe that this is a great time for girls' sports because there are many more opportunities for girls to play sports they love in college and beyond.

There are some unique challenges for girls who play on mixed-gender teams. Mixed teams allow body checking, so it's up to the individual girl and her parents to determine when, if ever, this becomes a detriment to her play or safety. It's a good idea for coaches to encourage their players to get to the locker room early and be fully dressed at least ten minutes before they go on the ice. Though most kids carry their bag of hockey gear and dress at the rink, this can present a problem on mixed-gender teams. Be assured that every rink is well versed in handling this situation, and most are more than willing to have a girls' changing area. Some girls choose the option of coming to the locker room fully dressed except for their skates. That way they don't miss the pre-practice instruction and bonding that take place between teammates.

If you're a male coaching an all girls' team, you're faced with yet another unique challenge because you'll need help with entry into the locker room. If you're working with a female coach, she can make certain that all the girls are dressed before you walk in. If you don't have a female on staff, ask the mother of one of the players to help out. It's also a good idea never to be the lone adult coach in any locker room.

When coaching a mixed-gender team, I've found that the girls almost always pair up with girls, and boys with boys, when doing partner drills. This is OK initially, since kids almost always want to be paired with someone of the same sex. If someone is left out, have this player join in with a pair of players at an equal ability level. However, if you're working on a skill such as checking, try to take size and ability into account and move kids around accordingly. If you feel it's in the best interest of all the players' development, it's perfectly OK for you to pair up players yourself.

Remember, too, that gender issues aren't the only challenge when it comes to helping every kid on your team feel comfortable. If there's one kid who seems to be without a friend on the team, it's up to you to help make him or her feel accepted.

Questions and Answers

Q. How do I deal with parents who insist on giving their child advice about her performance during a game or practice, especially when I don't agree with the advice?

A. Understand that as a coach, you're not going to change how parents bring up their children, nor should you try. The important issue to address is how this player relates to your coaching style. If the child is learning and responding to what you're teaching within the framework of the team, this is the best you can do. If the parents' advice is negatively affecting their child's play, then you'll have to speak with them. Be sensitive but realistic when sharing your own goals and objectives. Hopefully, they'll understand what you're trying to accomplish and will refrain from filling their child's head with advice that is not productive.

Q. There are some parents who continuously voice their disapproval of the referees' calls or the other team's play during a game. How do I tactfully get them to be supportive of our team without being disrespectful of the other players or officials?

A. Today, many youth sports adhere to a zero tolerance stance regarding parental interference at games and practices. Sportsmanship has become a huge focus point for many youth hockey programs, so much so that the on-ice officials have the authority to stop a game and have disrespectful parents escorted out of the building. The game doesn't resume until the offending parties have left.

   If the actions of a parent go unnoticed by the officials, but not by you or your players, it's critical that you address the offender as soon as possible. Explain that you expect parents to praise and cheer for their son or daughter and the child's teammates, but never at the expense of the feelings of the opponent, the opponent's parents, or the officials. Tell the parents that the players are influenced both by their behavior and yours. A team-wide letter is an effective reminder as well.

Q. How do I address a parent who feels his child isn't getting enough ice time or who complains when she isn't used on a power play or penalty kill?

A. If you're coaching a house-league program, this is rarely a problem because it's your job as coach to give all players equal ice time. It's important to ask your players in advance what they'd like to see happen if they're faced with a situation where winning a game is on the line. Ask them if, in that situation, they'd like to see the best players on the ice or if they'd like you to just "roll the lines." Getting the players involved in the decision making helps when a parent questions you about your decisions. Do understand that no matter what, your coaching decisions will sometimes be questioned. You'll usually hear more from parents about ice time as the level of competition and the team's expectations to win increase. If you tell parents that you've discussed the crucial situations with your players and that you and the team have made the decision, then you've shown that you're stressing team rather than individual play. If the parents report that their child has voiced concern about ice time, it's time to sit down with the parents and child. Formulate a plan to help the player improve her skills, thereby increasing her chance of receiving more ice time. Again, remember that ice time issues should occur only when the level of play is competitive. Sometimes it's difficult for parents to hear, but do explain that at any competitive level, coaches often have to make difficult decisions. You can agree to disagree about whether their child should receive more ice time. Always provide the child with the opportunity to show that she should be the player who receives more ice time.

Q. I feel one parent is being overly critical of her child's performance. If her child doesn't live up to her expectations, the parent demeans him both during and after a game. This is having an adverse effect on this child's attitude and play because he's so fearful of making mistakes. What can I say to this parent?

A. It's very important that you get all parents to respect what you're trying to teach their kids. Explain that all the kids become confused if too many people are giving advice during a game or practice. Remind parents that you're the coach, and that it's your voice alone that players should listen for and respond to. This is a tough situation for a coach to be in, but I've found it best to address it immediately by speaking to the parents. Also, reinforce your message by sending a letter home to each member of the team reminding parents not only of what you're trying to accomplish but what's expected of them and their children as well. Reinforce that positive remarks usually help make for a fun and positive learning environment.

Q. I coach a girls' team and have found that some of the players seem to be taking my corrections as a personal insult. How do I prevent hurt feelings when I am pointing out mistakes or correcting a particular skill problem?

A. When you need to make corrections or point out mistakes, preventing hurt feelings should be foremost in your mind. I don't even like to use the word *criticism*; I prefer to correct in a way that explains what particular part of a skill or play was done incorrectly, sandwiching my remark with a compliment. For example, "Nice effort, Annie. If you bend your knees and straighten your back more, you'll get a stronger, smoother stride. Keep up the good work!"

Q. Some of the boys on my team are unwilling to pass the puck to the girls or rely on their defensive skills. How do I handle this?

A. Boys who are unwilling to pass the puck to the girls on the team need to be reminded of what team play involves. Speak to the boys individually, explaining that the best athletes are the ones who help improve the level of *all* their teammates. The top players in college and in professional sports use team play to make the players around them consistently better.

Q. Are there different teaching strategies that are better received by one gender versus the other?

A. While there are different methods of teaching, none are gender specific. Your teaching strategies should be geared toward the ability level of your team, not gender. A good coach will learn to evaluate the talent level of the team and teach what the team can handle. Be prepared to teach a skill or strategy in a variety of ways. When preparing for your next practice, always have a backup plan in case your team can't handle the drill you'd originally intended to use.

PART TWO

Drills: Foundations for the Growth of Players and Coaches

CHAPTER 11

Fundamental Drills

Fundamental drills should be incorporated in every practice for players of every level. Of course, you should tailor the drills for your players so as they progress you use drills of appropriately increasing difficulty.

When presenting any new drill, a good coach explains and diagrams it using a coach's board in the locker room before practice. While on the ice, sometimes a second explanation and diagram are needed, but physically demonstrating the drill is always a good idea. Always station your assistant coaches around the rink to give direction and encouragement.

Make certain that your players are dressed in full gear for every on-ice practice. Any additional equipment is listed for each drill.

Diagram key.

X	player	\/	V-start
•	puck	M(b)	Mohawk turn to backward
▲	cone	M(f)	Mohawk turn to forward
L	stick	❶ ❷ ❸ ❹	order of skill demonstrated
⬓	net	G	goaltender
( )	C cuts	D	defenseman
ℒ	pivoting	F	forward
--------→	passing	LW	left winger
⊖—→	shooting	RW	right winger
∿∿∿→	stickhandling	C	center
——→	skating	LD	left defenseman
Ⓑ—→	backward skating	RD	right defenseman
⤻	glide turn	C₁ C₂	coaches
=	stopping	⊣	direction player is facing

Skating Drills

Forward Skating C Cuts   F1   ●

Purpose: To help develop the proper skating stride.
Number of Players: All

Additional Equipment: None
Time: 2 to 3 minutes

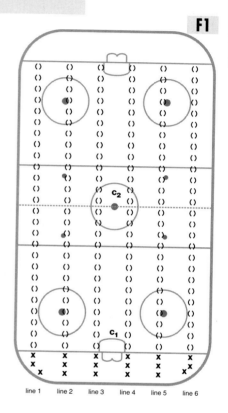

F1

1. Line up players along one goal line in five or six equal lines, with the first player in each line standing on the goal line. Station one coach at the goal line and one at center ice.
2. Blow your whistle to start the first player in each line striding the entire length of the ice using the same leg. Players should extend the stride leg as they're pushing fully through, cutting a C into the ice. Players then recover the stride leg back to the starting position while the opposite glide leg stays in place.
3. When all the players have reached the opposite end, have them stride with the other leg in the opposite direction.
4. When players are striding comfortably, have them skate the length of the ice striding and recovering, changing legs with each stride.

   Remind players to stay low with their knees bent at a 90-degree angle and keeping their head and chest erect. Direct your players to move the arm opposite from their striding leg parallel to the stride, not across the body. Players should keep their stick on the ice in front of their body, as though getting ready to receive a pass from a teammate.

line 1   line 2   line 3   line 4   line 5   line 6

Backward Skating C Cuts   F2   ●

Purpose: To help develop the proper skating stride when skating backward.
Number of Players: All

Additional Equipment: None
Time: 2 to 3 minutes

1. Line up players along one goal line in five or six equal lines, with the first player in each line standing on the goal line. Station one coach at the goal line and one at center ice.
2. The progression is the same as in Forward Skating C Cuts, but this time

F2

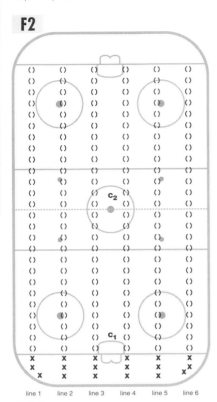

line 1   line 2   line 3   line 4   line 5   line 6

F3

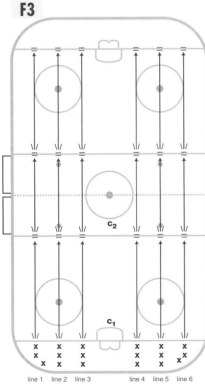

line 1   line 2   line 3   line 4   line 5   line 6

players are striding backward, cutting Cs into the ice one side at a time. The backward C cut is carved starting with the heel of the skate and ending at the toe.

3. Blow your whistle to start the first player in each line striding backward the entire length of the ice. Players should extend the stride leg as they push fully through, cutting a C into the ice. Players then recover the stride leg back to the starting position while the opposite glide leg stays in place.

4. When all the players have reached the opposite end, have them stride with the other leg in the opposite direction.

Remind your players to skate with their stick on the ice in front of their body, not to the side. Generally speaking, defensemen usually skate backward with the top hand on the stick while the opposite hand is held up with the palm facing the opponent. This position aids them in turning the shoulder to pivot when necessary and also puts the player in good position to use the poke check. Once they've mastered this drill, have them skate the length of the ice striding and recovering, changing legs with each stride. Remind players to stay low, with their knees bent at a 90-degree angle and keeping their head and chest erect.

V-Starts and Control Stops F3

Purpose: To develop the ability to start explosively and stop on the ice.	**Number of Players:** All **Additional Equipment:** None **Time:** 2 to 3 minutes

1. Line up players in five or six equal lines. Station one coach at the goal line and one at center ice.
2. Blow your whistle to start the first player in each line skating down the ice.
3. Players stop at each blue line and the opposite goal line. You can ensure they're practicing stopping in both directions by always facing them toward the players' benches.

Glide Turns F4 ●

F4

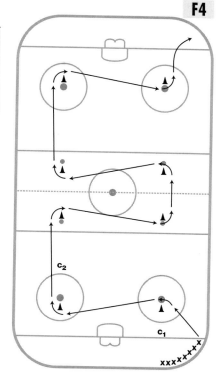

Purpose: To develop the ability to use the inside and outside skate edges when making a glide turn.	**Number of Players:** All **Additional Equipment:** 8 cones **Time:** 2 to 3 minutes

1. Set up a "slalom course" using eight cones placed on all the face-off dots except the one at center ice. Station one coach at the goal line and one near the second face-off circle.
2. All your players line up in one corner of the ice behind the goal line.
3. Have players take off one after the other, spacing them about 10 to 15 feet apart.
4. Players skate the course, making tight turns around each cone.

As players skate the drill, explain the importance of edge control. Demonstrate how to make a perfect turn by being on the outside edge of one skate and the inside edge of the other. You should stress that their stick must lead through the turn first. This enables them to turn with greater ease and still maintain the ability to receive a pass both during and at the conclusion of their turn.

Continuous Glide Turns F5 ●

F5

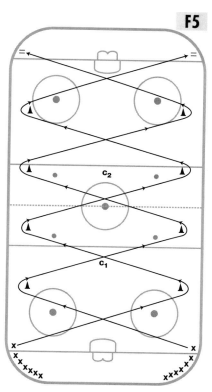

Purpose: To develop the ability to use the inside and outside skate edges when making a glide turn.	**Number of Players:** All **Additional Equipment:** 8 cones **Time:** 2 to 3 minutes

1. Line up four cones on each side of the ice approximately 10 to 12 feet from each side board. Make certain the cones are lined up at the same position across the ice. Station a coach near each blue line.
2. Divide your players into two groups and position a group in each corner at one end of the ice.
3. On the whistle, the first player in each line starts skating, crosses the ice diagonally, does a glide turn around the

F6

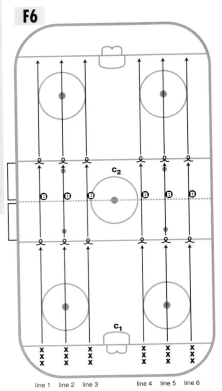

line 1   line 2   line 3   line 4   line 5   line 6

F7

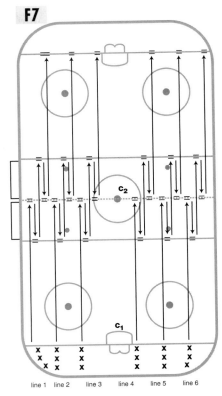

line 1   line 2   line 3   line 4   line 5   line 6

closest cone on the opposite side of the ice, and then skates diagonally back across the ice toward the next cone.

4. Players continue skating in the same pattern and finish by stopping in the corners at the opposite end of the ice. Keep the whistle going and the players moving.

Variation: Have players do a control stop at the cone instead of a glide turn around it. After stopping, they skate diagonally across the ice to the next cone, stop, and skate diagonally across to the next cone until concluding at the other end of the ice.

Pivoting   F6   ●

Purpose: To develop the ability to pivot from forward skating to backward skating and from backward skating to	forward skating. **Number of Players:** All **Additional Equipment:** None **Time:** 2 to 3 minutes

1. Line up players along one goal line in five or six equal lines. Station one coach near the goal net and one near the far blue line.
2. On your whistle, the first player in each line begins skating forward and then pivots from forward to backward at the near blue line. The player then skates backward to the far blue line, pivots from backward to forward, and skates to the far goal line. Make certain everyone pivots in the same direction toward the players' benches.
3. After everyone has skated, players line up and return in the opposite direction. Remind them that they should again pivot toward the players' benches. This ensures that each player practices pivoting in both directions.

Two-Skate Power Stops   F7   ●●

Purpose: To develop the ability to stop quickly and change direction.	**Number of Players:** All **Additional Equipment:** None **Time:** 2 to 3 minutes

1. Line up your players in five or six lines on one goal line. Station one coach near the goal net and one at center ice.

2. The first player in each line skates quickly to center ice and performs a power stop. They change directions, skate forward to the near blue line, and make another power stop.

3. Start the next group when the first group performs their second power stop.

4. The players in the first group must change direction again, skating forward to the far blue line and performing another power stop. Then they change direction again and skate back to center ice.

5. At center ice the players in the first group make a final power stop, change directions, and skate forward to finish by making a control stop on the far goal line.

All these stops are made so your players use momentum to get going quickly in the opposite direction. While players perform the two-skate power stop, make sure every time they stop that they're facing the players' benches. This ensures that players are stopping properly, using both edges of each skate.

Forward Crossovers F8 ●●

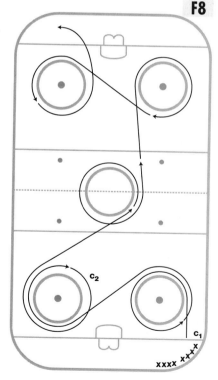

F8

Purpose: To develop the ability to make a turn by crossing the outside skate over the inside skate.	**Number of Players:** All, in groups of 4 **Additional Equipment:** None **Time:** 3 to 4 minutes

1. Line up your players in one corner of the ice behind the goal line. Station a coach near each face-off circle in one end zone.

2. In groups of four, players perform forward crossovers all the way around the closest face-off circle. Space the players 8 to 10 feet apart.

3. After the fourth player skates by the front of the line, start the next four players.

4. When each group finishes one revolution of the first circle, they skate directly across the ice toward the bottom of the other face-off circle in this end zone and perform forward crossovers in the opposite direction.

5. Next players skate to the center-ice face-off circle and perform the crossovers, again in the opposite direction. They finish by skating the crossovers around the last two face-off circles in the opposite end zone, as they did at the near end, in different directions.

F9

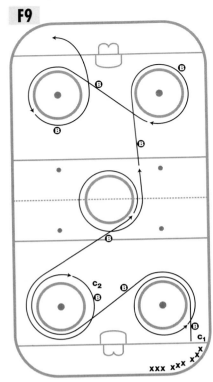

Remember, it's important to have minimal congestion at each circle so you can spot the players who may need extra help with these skills. This is a good warm-up drill.

Variation: Players skate the circles while controlling the puck.

Backward Crossunders F9 ●●

Purpose: To develop the ability to make a turn when skating backward by crossing the inside skate under the outside skate.	**Number of Players:** All, in groups of 3 **Additional Equipment:** None **Time:** 4 to 5 minutes

1. Line up your players in one corner of the ice behind the goal line. Station a coach near each face-off circle in one end zone.
2. In groups of three, players perform backward crossunders all the way around the closest face-off circle. Space the players 10 to 12 feet apart.
3. After the third player skates by the front of the line, start the next three players.
4. When each group finishes one revolution of the first circle, they skate backward directly across the ice toward the bottom of the other face-off circle in this end zone and perform backward crossunders in the opposite direction.
5. Next players skate backward to the center-ice face-off circle and perform the crossunders, again in the opposite direction. They finish by skating the crossunders around the last two face-off circles in the opposite end zone, as they did at the near end zone, in different directions.

Tops and Bottoms F10 ●●

F10

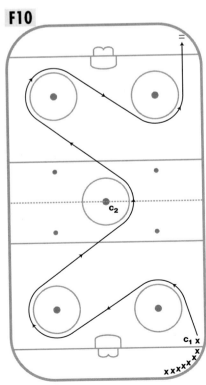

Purpose: To improve the ability to perform forward crossovers and backward crossunders.	**Number of Players:** All **Additional Equipment:** None **Time:** 2 minutes

1. All players line up in one corner of the ice. Station one coach at the goal line and one coach at center ice.

2. One by one, spaced 6 feet apart, players skate a forward crossover around the top of the nearest face-off circle.
3. Players then skate diagonally across the ice to the bottom of the opposite face-off circle in the same end zone and skate forward crossovers in the opposite direction halfway around that circle.
4. Players continue skating diagonally to the center-ice face-off circle, changing the direction of the forward crossovers, and skate halfway around that circle.
5. Players conclude by skating the last two circles in the opposite end zone in the same manner.

Variation: Players skate the same sequence using backward crossunders.

Transition Moves (Mohawk Turns) F11 ●●

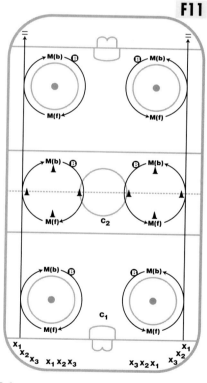

F11

Purpose: To develop the ability to make a transition from forward skating to backward skating and from backward skating to forward skating.

Number of Players: All
Additional Equipment: 8 cones
Time: 3 minutes

1. Set up four cones in a circle on each side of the center-ice face-off circle, lining up the cones with the circles at opposite ends of the ice rink. Station one coach near the goal net and one near center ice.
2. Divide your players into two groups and position one group in each corner at one end of the rink. Instruct the players to face the opposite end of the rink at all times, keeping their eyes on either a flag or scoreboard as a focus point.
3. Three players from each group, spaced about 10 feet apart, skate forward along the boards and perform forward crossovers around the closest face-off circle until they reach the top of the circle. At that point players perform a Mohawk turn from forward to backward, changing to crossunder skating until they reach the bottom of the circle. Remind players to keep their eyes focused on the opposite end of the rink.
4. At the bottom of the circle, players do another Mohawk turn, this time from backward crossunders to forward crossovers, and then skate down the boards to the "cone circle" near center ice, repeating the same skating pattern as the first circle.

F12

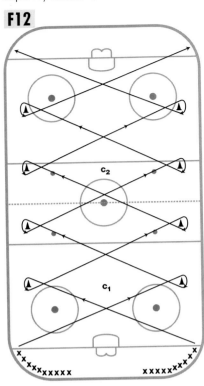

F13

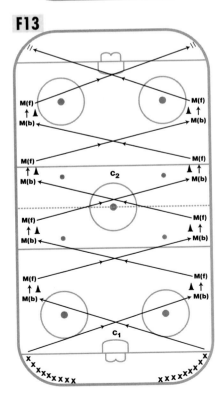

5. Players complete the drill by repeating the same skating pattern at the face-off circle at the farthest end of the ice.
6. When the third player in the first group skates by the front of the line, start the next progression of three players.
7. After players complete the three circles, they line up in opposite corners at the other end of the ice. Now have them perform the drill in the opposite direction to guarantee they have practiced transition moves (Mohawk turns) in both directions.

Continuous Inside-Outs F12

Purpose: To develop the ability to execute a series of tight glide turns while maintaining speed.	**Number of Players:** All **Additional Equipment:** 8 cones **Time:** 3 minutes

1. Line up four cones on each side of the ice approximately 10 to 12 feet from each side board. Make certain the cones are lined up at the same position across the ice.
2. Divide your players into two groups and position one group in each corner at one end of the ice.
3. On the whistle, the first player in each line skates diagonally across the ice, moving toward the inside part of the cone, and turns completely back around the cone. Essentially the player is making a 360-degree turn around the cone in the opposite direction from a glide turn.
4. After circling the cone, the player then skates diagonally across the ice to the next cone and circles it in the same manner.
5. Players continue skating in the same pattern and finish at the opposite end of the ice. Keep your whistle going and the players moving.

Continuous Mohawk Turns F13

Purpose: To develop the ability to execute a series of Mohawk turns.	**Number of Players:** All **Additional Equipment:** 8 cones **Time:** 3 minutes

1. Line up four cones on each side of the ice approximately 10 to 12 feet from each side board. Make certain the cones are lined up at the same position across the ice. Station one coach near the goal net and one at center ice.
2. Divide your players into two groups and position one group in each corner at one end of the ice.
3. On the whistle, the first player in each line skates diagonally across the ice, moving toward the front of the first cone.
4. The player makes a Mohawk turn from forward to backward and immediately makes a second Mohawk turn from backward to forward around the back of the cone. The player then continues skating forward diagonally across the ice to the next cone.
5. Players continue skating in the same pattern and finish at the opposite end of the ice. Keep your whistle going and the players moving.

Passing Drills

Partner Passing and Receiving a Pass F14 ●

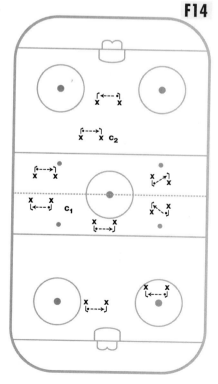

F14

Purpose: To develop accuracy with forehand and backhand passing.
Number of Players: All, in pairs

Additional Equipment: 1 puck per pair
Time: 5 minutes

1. Have your players spread out all over the ice, working in pairs that stand stationary about 10 feet apart. Coaches should move around from pair to pair, observing and teaching proper form.
2. Partners pass one puck back and forth, working on forehand passing and receiving the pass. You and your assistant coaches should move around to each group and aid them in using proper form.
3. Halfway through the allotted time, switch to backhand passing.

F15

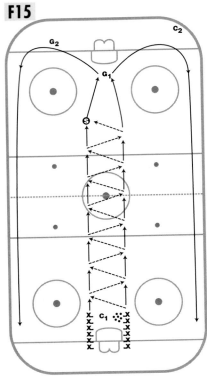

Five-Foot Passing F15 ●

Purpose: To develop the ability to make short, quick, stick-to-stick passes while skating.

Number of Players: All, 1 goalie
Additional Equipment: 20 to 30 pucks
Time: 3 to 5 minutes

1. If you have two goaltenders, position both at the far end of the ice, one in the net and one waiting. Station one coach at the near net and one in the corner at the opposite end of the ice.
2. Line up your players approximately 5 feet apart just in front of the near net.
3. Place the pucks near the front of one line.
4. The first player in each line skates up the middle of the ice. They pass one puck back and forth while attempting to stay no more than 5 feet apart.
5. They continue passing until they reach the far blue line, where they make one last pass.
6. The player that receives the last pass shoots on goal from the top of the circle. The other player drives to the net for a rebound.
7. The players then turn toward the opposite boards and skate back to the end from which they began.
8. The next set of players begins when the first players reach center ice.
9. The coach in the corner should instruct the goaltenders to switch off every ten to fifteen shots.

This is another good warm-up drill that loosens up the players' hands, while allowing them to "feel the puck."

Variations: Add pucks in both corners of the ice near the goalies. After the players have completed the first part of the drill, each player turns toward an opposite corner, retrieves a new puck, and then passes that puck off the boards to himself while skating back to the starting end.

Or, for more-skilled players, add pucks in one corner at the far end of the ice near the goaltenders. When the first part of the drill is complete, each player turns toward an opposite corner. The player on the puck side re-trieves a puck and makes a long pass across the ice to the other player. The players continue these long passes until they reach their initial starting point. Players should exercise caution when skating through "traffic"; they should skate with their heads up, completing their cross-ice passes while not disrupt-ing their teammates who are skating and passing through the middle of the ice.

Cross-Ice Follow Your Pass F16 ●

Purpose: To develop proficiency at making and receiving cross-ice passes.
Number of Players: All, in groups of 3

Additional Equipment: 1 puck per group
Time: 3 minutes

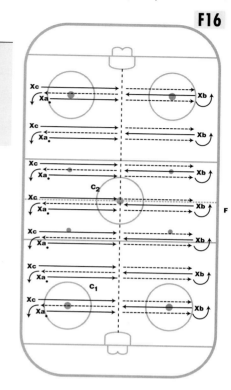

1. Divide your players into groups of three and space the groups evenly along the ice. (If there's a single player left out, you can make one group of four. If there are two players left out, have a coach join them or make two groups of four.) Coaches should move around from group to group, observing and teaching proper form.
2. One player from each group (player Xb) lines up against one side board. The other two players in each group (players Xa and Xc) line up one behind the other directly across the ice from player Xb against the other side board. Each player Xa should have a puck.
3. Player Xa skates with the puck halfway across the ice and then passes it to player Xb. Player Xa follows the pass and takes player Xb's spot across the ice.
4. Player Xb receives the pass and then skates with the puck halfway across the ice in the opposite direction. Player Xb passes to player Xc and takes his spot. Player Xc follows the same pattern as player Xa, continuing the drill.

Two Players, Two Shots, Short Pass F17 ●

Purpose: To develop proficiency at passing, receiving, and shooting while moving.

Number of Players: All, 1 goalie
Additional Equipment: 20 to 30 pucks
Time: 3 to 5 minutes

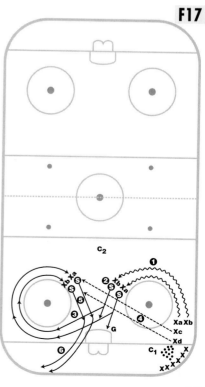

1. Players line up with pucks in one corner behind the goal line. The goalie is in the net. Station one coach near the blue line and one coach near the players.
2. The first two players in line (Players Xa and Xb), spaced 10 feet apart, skate (each stickhandling a puck)

about halfway around the nearest face-off circle (1). Players Xc and Xd wait near the starting point.

3. Player Xa stickhandles the puck while doing forward crossovers around the top of the face-off circle and then takes a shot on goal (2).

4. Player Xb follows the same skating pattern, leaving about 10 feet behind player Xa.

5. After both players have taken a shot, they continue to skate diagonally across the ice toward the bottom of the opposite face-off circle (3).

6. Both players then do forward crossovers in the opposite direction toward the top of that face-off circle. Player Xa receives a pass from player Xc (4) and then takes a second shot on goal (5).

7. Player Xb receives a pass from player Xd and also takes a second shot on goal.

8. After players take their second shots on goal, have them line up in the opposite corner (6); you'll need some pucks here, too. Remember, you or an assistant will need to pass the puck to the last two players in the first line for their second shots on goal because no one will be left in that corner.

9. Players Xc and Xd then follow the same skating pattern as players Xa and Xb.

10. Once all players have taken their second shot, restart the drill from the opposite corner.

This drill is performed using half-ice, so you can run the drill at both ends of the ice simultaneously.

Center-Ice Crossover and Go F18 ●

Purpose: To develop proficiency at performing forward crossovers, passing and receiving, stickhandling, and shooting.	**Number of Players:** All, 2 goalies **Additional Equipment:** 40 pucks, 6 cones (optional) **Time:** 5 minutes

1. Place a goalie in each net. Divide your players into two groups with twenty pucks in each line. Each group lines up behind the centerline facing in opposite directions against the boards. Players will only shoot on the goal that their line is facing. Station a coach near the front of each line against the boards.

2. Player Xa in each line moves diagonally toward the middle of the ice, skating forward crossovers in the same direction fully around the center-ice face-off circle (1).

3. Each player Xa returns to the centerline on the same side of the ice from which he started and receives a pass from player Xb in his group (2).

4. Each player Xa stickhandles the puck across the blue line, shoots on the goal his line is facing (3), and then skates to the end of the opposite line (4).
5. After passing to each player Xa, each player Xb begins to skate in the same pattern, doing forward crossovers around the center-ice face-off circle and then receiving a pass from the next player in line.
6. Change skating directions halfway through the allotted time.

You may want to station a coach in the middle of the ice to direct players, especially younger players, as they skate around the face-off circle, although your players will catch on quickly.

Variation: Add three cones inside each blue line through which players must stickhandle before shooting on goal.

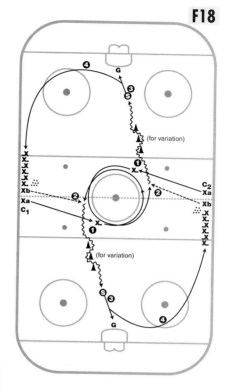

F18

Blue Line Cross Pass F19 ●

Purpose: To develop proficiency at leading the man when passing and receiving.	**Number of Players:** All, in four groups, 2 goalies **Additional Equipment:** 40 pucks **Time:** 3 to 5 minutes

1. Divide players into four equal groups. Place a goalie in each net. Station a coach near each blue line.
2. Each group lines up with ten pucks in one of the four spots where the blue lines touch the boards. Players face the group at the opposite blue line.
3. Players who are diagonally opposite across the ice perform the skating pattern simultaneously. Each player Xa skates diagonally across the ice toward the bottom of the center-ice face-off circle and receives a pass from the player Xb positioned directly across the blue line.
4. Each player Xa skates and stickhandles down the ice toward the opposite end, crosses the blue line, and shoots on the net.
5. Each player Xb then skates diagonally across the ice in the opposite direction to player Xa, receives a pass from the player Xc in the group directly across the ice, stickhandles the puck down the ice, crosses the other blue line, and concludes with a shot on goal.

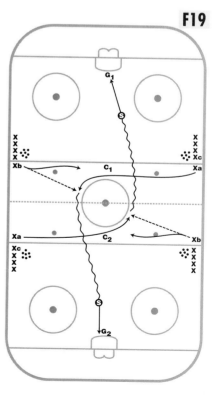

F19

FUNDAMENTAL DRILLS

F20

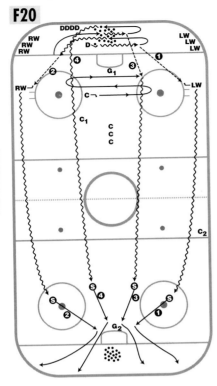

At first it's a good idea to use your coach's whistle to signal when each group of players should start, but with practice, they'll be able to make eye contact with the player diagonally across the ice so they can control the drill.

Four-Player Breakout F20

Purpose: To develop proficiency at making and receiving breakout passes and to learn breakout positioning.

Number of Players: All, in groups of 4, 2 goalies
Additional Equipment: 30 to 40 pucks
Time: 3 to 5 minutes

1. Each group is made up of two wingers, one defenseman, and one center. Place a goalie in each net, and fifteen to twenty pucks behind each net. Station one coach near the high slot area and one coach near the far blue line.
2. Defensemen line up behind the goal line toward one side of the net at one end. Position left and right wingers in the corners of the end zone where the defensemen are. Move one left winger and one right winger to a position against the boards near the hash marks (the breakout position) at that same end of the ice. One center stands in front of the net at the same end, but near the hash marks. The rest of the centers stay in the high slot area waiting for their turn. Even out the lines; if necessary, have some defensemen act as forwards for this drill.
3. One defenseman retrieves a puck behind the net and stickhandles it until he crosses the goal line behind the first left winger (1).
4. At the same time, the center should mirror the movements of the defenseman, staying in front of the net but always facing and watching the defenseman. The center must always be available for a pass from the defenseman, though in this drill the defenseman passes first to the left winger and right winger.
5. The defenseman makes a breakout pass to the left winger, who skates and stickhandles down the length of the ice, takes an angle shot on the goalie (G2), and remains at that end (1).
6. The same defenseman picks up another puck behind the net, crosses the goal line on the other side of the ice, and passes to the right winger (2).
7. The right winger now skates down the length of the ice, takes an angle shot on the goalie from the opposite side of the ice, and remains at that end (2).

8. The same defenseman now skates behind the net again and retrieves another puck.

9. The defenseman passes to the center. The center should be 10 to 15 feet from the defenseman when the pass is made and should be in a position to skate quickly up ice and take a shot on goal (3), remaining at that end.

10. Finally, the same defenseman skates behind the net one last time, retrieves a puck, and skates the length of the ice, finishing with a shot on goal (4), remaining at that end.

11. Each new defenseman begins the sequence until everyone has had a turn to shoot. Then players line up and face the other goalie (G1). You can allow players to switch positions but try to keep the lines equal.

Crossover, Follow Your Pass F21

Purpose: To develop proficiency at stickhandling, performing forward crossovers, passing and receiving, and shooting.	**Number of Players:** All, 2 goalies **Additional Equipment:** 40 pucks, 6 cones **Time:** 5 minutes

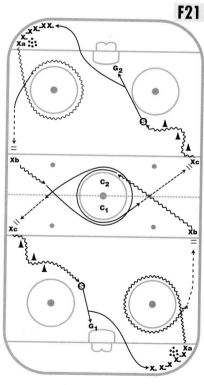

1. Divide players into two groups. Each group lines up at opposite ends of the ice in opposite corners with twenty pucks in each line. Position a goalie in each net and station two coaches at center ice.

2. Station a player (Xb) from each group against the boards outside the near blue line and a player Xc from each group against the boards outside the far blue line. Place three cones just inside each blue line near each player Xc.

3. Player Xa in each group skates directly down the boards, stickhandles the puck, and does forward crossovers around the near face-off circle.

4. Each player Xa completes that circle, makes a pass to his group's player Xb, and continues skating in the direction of the pass, stopping to take the spot of player Xb.

5. Each player Xb stickhandles the puck and, skating in a direction toward the opposite blue line, does forward crossovers around the center-ice face-off circle. The coaches should make sure that the players skate in the same direction around the center-ice circle.

6. Each player Xb then passes to player Xc from his group, and takes player Xc's spot.

7. Each player Xc receives the pass and stickhandles the puck while skating (slaloming) through the three cones.

8. Each player Xc shoots on goal near the top of the face-off circle and then skates to the back of the line at that end of the ice.

9. Halfway through the allotted time, move the pucks and players waiting in the end zones to the opposite corners. Restart the drill so your players skate crossovers in the other direction.

Reverse Four Pass F22 ●●

Purpose: To develop proficiency at passing, moving around the offensive zone, and shooting.	Number of Players: All, 1 goalie Additional Equipment: 20 pucks Time: 5 minutes

1. Place a goalie in the net. Position all your players (Xd players) except three in one corner of the ice with pucks. Station a coach near the blue line.

2. Player Xa is next to the goal but away from the corner where the players are lined up. Player Xb is in the middle of the ice near the blue line. Player Xc is close to the boards near the blue line.

F22

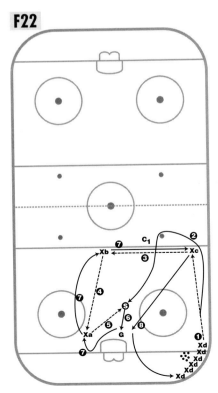

3. The first player in line (Xd) takes a puck, passes it to player Xc (1), and then skates down the boards toward the near blue line, around the face-off dot outside it, and then back in toward the goal (2).

4. Player Xc receives the puck and passes it across the blue line to player Xb (3).

5. Player Xb receives the puck and passes it to player Xa (4).

6. Player Xa receives the puck and passes it back to player Xd near the high slot area (5).

7. Player Xd receives the puck and takes a shot on goal (6).

8. Player Xd now takes player Xa's spot, player Xa takes player Xb's spot, and player Xb takes player Xc's spot (7). Player Xc drives to the net for the rebound of player Xd's shot and then proceeds to the end of the line (8).

9. Drill continues with the next player in line until all players have rotated through each position.

The movement of players here is a key element. All players need to be ready to move after they have made their pass.

Variation: To rotate players through all the positions faster, turn this into a full-ice drill by dividing your players into two groups and running the drill at both ends of the ice.

Two Players, Two Shots, Long Pass F23 ●●

F23

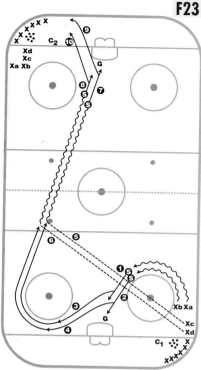

Purpose: To develop proficiency at stickhandling, performing forward cross-overs, making and receiving a long pass, and shooting.

Number of Players: All, 2 goalies
Additional Equipment: 40 pucks
Time: 5 minutes

1. Place a goalie in each net. Divide players into two groups and have them line up in opposite ends of the ice with twenty pucks each in diagonal corners. Station a coach near each goal line.
2. On the whistle, both ends start the drill simultaneously. Each player Xa stickhandles the puck, does forward crossovers around the top of the near face-off circle, and takes a shot on goal (1).
3. Each player Xb starts about half a circle behind player Xa and follows the same skating pattern (2).
4. After the players have taken a shot, they continue to skate diagonally across the ice toward the bottom of the other face-off circle in the same end of the ice (3, 4).
5. Each player Xa receives a diagonal pass near the blue line from each player Xc (5), skates and stickhandles the puck the length of the ice, and then shoots on the opposite goal (7).
6. Each player Xb receives a diagonal pass near the blue line from each player Xd (6), skates and stickhandles the puck the length of the ice, and shoots on the opposite goal (8).
7. As players Xa and Xb are taking their second shots on goal, whistle for the next two players, players Xc and Xd in the above steps, to begin the drill in the same manner as players Xa and Xb. Players Xa and Xb finish by moving to the end of the line at the opposite end of the ice (9, 10).
8. After every player in each line has shot on goal twice, switch sides of the ice so players will skate the forward crossovers in both directions and receive passes on their forehand and backhand. Goalies will also have the opportunity to face shots from different angles.

Center-Ice Crossover Give-and-Go F24 ●●

Purpose: To develop proficiency at stickhandling, performing forward crossovers, passing and receiving, and shooting.

Number of Players: All, 2 goalies
Additional Equipment: 40 pucks
Time: 5 minutes

F24

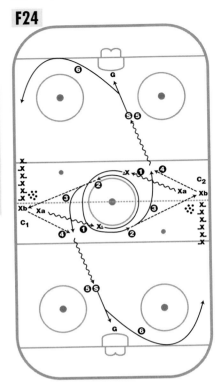

1. Place a goalie in each net. Divide your players into two equal lines and position each line against the boards behind the centerline facing in opposite directions. Have twenty pucks in each line. Players will only shoot on the goal that their line is facing. Station a coach with each group.
2. Each player Xa stickhandles a puck and does forward crossovers around the center-ice face-off circle (1).
3. As each player Xa nears the bottom or three-quarter point of the center-ice face-off circle she passes the puck to player Xb from her group (2). Passing the puck early is the key to completing two passes.
4. Each player Xa continues skating in a direction toward the goal she will be shooting at (3).
5. Each player Xb receives the pass and passes directly back to each player Xa (4). Each player Xa now skates across the blue line, and shoots on goal (5).
6. Each player Xa then skates to the back of the line on the opposite side of the ice (6).
7. Each player Xb now assumes the position of player Xa, and the drill continues with a new group.
8. Halfway through the allotted time, switch directions.

It's a good idea for the coaches to remind younger players to be alert for a pass and to signal when players begin carrying a puck.

Variation: Add some cones just inside the blue line if you want players to stickhandle through them before shooting on goal.

Center-Ice Crossover Give-and-Go, Two-on-Zero F25 ●●

F25

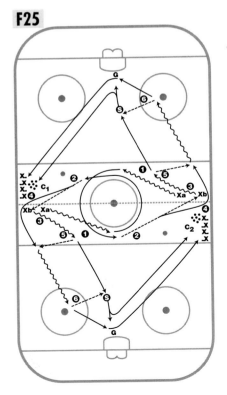

Purpose: To develop proficiency at stickhandling, performing forward crossovers, passing and receiving, and shooting in a two-on-zero.	**Number of Players:** All, 2 goalies **Additional Equipment:** 40 pucks **Time:** 5 minutes

1. Place a goalie in each net. Divide your players into two equal lines and position each line against the boards behind the centerline facing in opposite directions. Have twenty pucks in each line. Players will only shoot on the goal their line is facing. Station a coach with each group.
2. Each player Xa stickhandles a puck toward the center-ice face-off circle and does forward crossovers around the center-ice face-off circle (1).
3. As each player Xa nears the bottom or three-quarter point of the center-ice face-off circle he passes the puck to player Xb from his group (2).
4. Each player Xb immediately breaks toward the middle of the ice (3) while each player Xa skates in a pattern *cutting behind* player Xb (4). Passing the puck early is the key to allowing time for this crisscross movement to work.
5. Players Xa and Xb now pass the puck back and forth in a two-on-zero manner (5), skating in on the goalie. Players should be encouraged to make only one pass after they cross the blue line (6).
6. The player with the puck now shoots on goal, while the other player drives to the net for a rebound.
7. When the shot on goal has been taken, both players skate to the back of the line on the opposite side of the ice.
8. After the first two players have made their crisscross and are approaching the blue line, the next players in line should be ready to start.
9. Halfway through the allotted time, switch directions.

The key to staying onside during this drill lies with each player Xa, who must cut behind player Xb after passing the puck.

Full-Ice Horseshoe Two-on-Zero F26 ●●

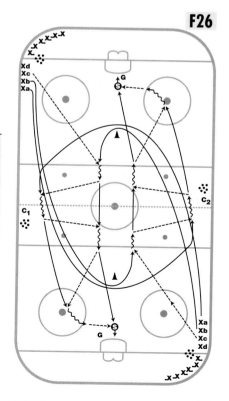

F26

Purpose: To develop proficiency at skating, passing and receiving, and shooting in a two-on-zero.	**Number of Players:** All, 2 goalies **Additional Equipment:** 40 pucks, 2 cones **Time:** 5 minutes

1. Place a cone (or your glove) 20 feet inside each blue line in the middle of the ice.
2. Place a goalie in each net. Split your team into two lines (each with twenty pucks) in diagonally opposite corners of the ice. Station a coach against each side of the boards at center ice with extra pucks.
3. Players Xa and Xb from each end skate simultaneously down the boards without pucks toward the far blue line,

where they skate around the cone at the opposite end of the ice.

4. Each player Xc from the opposite line passes a puck to either player Xa or Xb in the pair that came from the other end of the ice.

5. Each pair of Xa and Xb players then pass the pack back and forth up the ice, two-on-zero, take a shot on the goal at the end they started from, and skate to the end of the line where they began.

6. Once each player Xc makes the pass, players Xc and Xd from both ends proceed toward the far blue line and skate in the same pattern as players Xa and Xb, receiving a pass from new players Xc, and returning to take a shot on the goal at the end they started from.

7. Halfway through the allotted time, move the pucks and players to the other two corners to perform the drill in the opposite direction.

Give-and-Go Mohawks   F27   ●●

Purpose: To develop proficiency at skating, passing and receiving, performing Mohawk turns, pivoting, stickhandling, and shooting.	Number of Players: All, 2 goalies Additional Equipment: 40 pucks Time: 3 to 5 minutes

F27

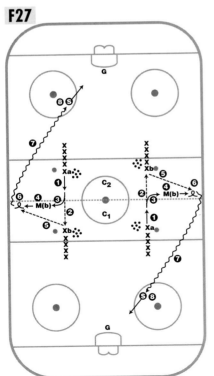

1. Place a goalie in each net. Divide your players into four equal lines near the four neutral zone face-off dots just outside the blue lines. There should be ten pucks in each line. Station two coaches at center ice.

2. On the whistle, each player Xa in the two groups that are diagonally opposite begins to skate (1) and passes a puck to each player Xb in the group directly opposite at the opposing blue line (2).

3. Each player Xa continues to skate toward the centerline (3) and does a Mohawk turn toward the boards (4).

4. Each player Xb receives the pass from player Xa and returns the pass as player Xa approaches the boards (5).

5. Each player Xa does a quick pivot when receiving the pass (6), stickhandles the puck across the blue line (7), and then shoots on the goalie (8).

6. After shooting on goal, each player stays at that end of the ice but switches lines.

7. On the next whistle, each player Xb (the new Xa) then passes directly forward to the next player in line at the opposite blue line (the new Xb), and the drill continues.

Players should proceed only on the whistle until they become so accustomed to executing this drill they're able to look

Flip or Saucer Pass F28 ●●●

Purpose: To develop the ability to make a flip or saucer pass. **Number of Players:** All, in pairs	**Additional Equipment:** 1 puck per pair (plus a few extras), 1 extra cone or stick per pair **Time:** 3 minutes

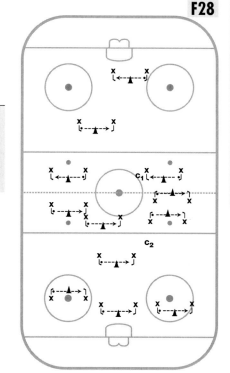

1. Players work in pairs spread out all over the ice. Each pair stands about 10 to 12 feet apart. Place one extra stick or cone between the two players to create an obstacle. Each pair should use one puck but keep an extra one nearby.
2. While staying stationary, players must elevate the puck over the obstacle to complete a pass to their partner. The coaches move around from pair to pair, observing and teaching proper form.

Blue Line Three Pass F29 ●●●

Purpose: To develop proficiency at passing and receiving, skating, and shooting.	**Number of Players:** All, 2 goalies **Additional Equipment:** 40 pucks **Time:** 5 to 7 minutes

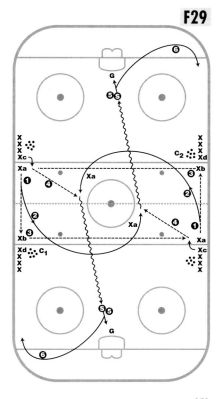

1. Place a goalie in each net. Split your players into four equal groups standing just inside the blue line in each of the four spots where the blue lines touch the boards. Players face the group at the opposite blue line. There should be ten pucks in each group. Station a coach with each group if you can, or with one group at each blue line.
2. Each player Xa, the first player in the two groups that are diagonally opposite, passes a puck to player Xb in the group directly opposite at the other blue line (1).
3. Each player Xa follows the puck, crosses the far blue line, turns to recross the blue line, and skates up toward the middle of the ice (2).

4. Each player Xb now passes directly across the ice to each player Xc (3).

5. Each player Xc receives the pass and then makes a return pass to each player Xa (4).

6. Each player Xa receives the pass while heading up the middle of the ice, skating back toward the end from which he started, and shoots on goal (5).

7. Each player Xb (the new Xa) now passes directly down the boards to each player Xc (the new Xb) and skates down the boards in the same pattern that Xa completed but in the opposite direction.

8. Each player Xc then passes across the ice to each player Xd, who then makes a return pass to each player Xb.

9. Each player Xb receives the pass while heading up the middle of the ice, skating back toward the end from which he started, and shoots on goal.

10. The drill continues with new players starting from the original diagonal positions.

11. After shooting on goal, each player should stay at the same end of the ice but switch lines.

This drill can be confusing, so your players must pay attention and be ready! The coaches can assist by reminding the players to stay alert, instructing them when they'll receive or make a pass, or when they should make a pass and begin skating.

Again, at first it's a good idea to use your coach's whistle to signal when the players should start, but with practice they'll be able to make eye contact with the player diagonally across the ice so they can control the drill. This is a difficult pattern, but as your players catch on, the drill will run smoothly.

F30

Timing F30 ●●●

Purpose: To develop proficiency at precise timing while skating, passing and receiving, and shooting.	**Number of Players:** All, 2 goalies **Additional Equipment:** 40 pucks **Time:** 8 to 10 minutes

1. Place a goalie in each net. Split your players into four equal groups that are numbered line 1 or 2 on each side of the ice. Put twenty pucks at each end. Position one player from each line 1 (Xa) with one of the pucks in the middle of the ice at each blue line. Scatter the remaining pucks toward the board side of the end zone face-off dot closest to line 1 at diagonal ends of the ice. Station a coach near each blue line.

2. On your whistle, each player Xa skates straight in on goal to take a shot (1) and then heads toward the side of the ice where the pucks are located (2).

3. Player Xb in each line 1 skates deep into the face-off circle in that zone and then turns almost directly up the middle of the ice (3).

4. At the same time, the first player in each line 2, player Xc, skates from center ice back toward each blue line and curls toward the boards (4).

5. Each player Xa now makes a diagonal pass to player Xb (5). Each player Xa then goes to the end of his line 1.

6. Each player Xb receives the pass and head-mans the puck to player Xc (6). (If any wayward passes occur, player Xc should continue the drill without the puck and retrieve a new one. Timing is crucial in this drill, so this reinforces the need for players to make good passes.) Each player Xb then goes to the end of his line 2.

7. Each player Xc continues down the ice, takes a shot on goal, retrieves a puck, and continues the drill as the new player Xa.

8. Halfway through the allotted time, move the pucks to the other end zone face-off circle. Tell the players in both lines #1 to to turn around and line up at the opposite blue line. Players in both lines #2 just turn around and start their lines at center ice. Now restart the drill in the opposite direction.

Note that both sides of the ice will be skating at the same time. All players should be aware of each other's destination and function at all times. Stress to your players that this is a difficult drill and that timing is crucial.

Changing sides halfway through the drill ensures that players skate and pass from opposite angles.

Stickhandling Drills

Stationary Stickhandling F31 ●

Purpose: To develop the ability to stickhandle.	**Additional Equipment:** 1 puck per player
Number of Players: All	**Time:** 3 minutes

1. Have players watch from two angles as you demonstrate the skill of stickhandling.

FUNDAMENTAL DRILLS

F31

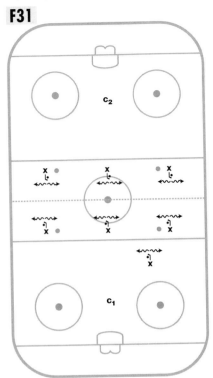

F32

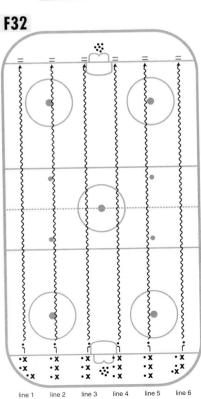

line 1   line 2   line 3   line 4   line 5   line 6

2. Players then spread out all over the ice, stand stationary, and stickhandle a puck in front of their body from side to side.

3. Coaches should move around from player to player, observing and teaching proper form.

Permit young players to look at the puck when they're first learning to stickhandle. However, as they progress, your players should be able to feel the puck on their stick. Only the lower line of their vision should remain on the puck while their head and eyes remain erect. Players may need to move their bottom hand up and down the stick shaft for more control, depending on how far they can reach and how great their control of the puck is.

Stickhandling While Skating F32 ●

Purpose: To develop proficiency at stickhandling while skating.	Additional Equipment: 1 puck per player (plus 20 extras)
Number of Players: All	**Time:** 3 to 5 minutes

1. Divide your players, including the goalies, into six equal lines facing up the ice behind one of the goal lines. Each player has a puck. Place ten extra pucks at each end of the ice behind the goal lines.

2. On your whistle, the first player in each line stickhandles a puck the length of the ice and stops at the far goal line.

3. Start the next six players when the first group reaches the blue line.

4. When all the players have reached the opposite goal line, start them off again the other direction.

Stickhandling While Turning toward the Boards F33 ●

Purpose: To develop proficiency at skating, stickhandling, and turning.	Additional Equipment: 1 puck per player
Number of Players: All	**Time:** 3 minutes

1. Position players around the ice, each with a puck. Station a coach near each blue line.
2. Each player skates in the same direction around the ice while stickhandling a puck.
3. On the whistle, everyone turns toward the boards.
4. While continuing to stickhandle, players take a few quick strides and then slow down.
5. On the next whistle, everyone turns toward the boards again, proceeding in the opposite direction.

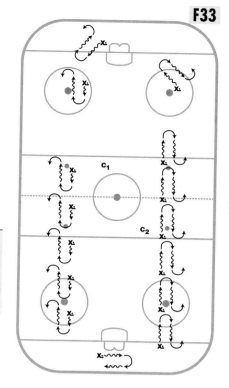

F33

Stickhandling Turnbacks F34 ●

Purpose: To develop proficiency at skating, stickhandling, and turning.
Number of Players: All

Additional Equipment: 1 puck per player (plus 10 to 20 extras)
Time: 3 to 5 minutes

1. Divide your players into five equal lines across one goal line. Each player has a puck. Place 5 to 10 extra pucks behind each goal line. Station one coach near the goal line and one near center ice.
2. On the whistle, the first player in each line stickhandles the puck toward center ice. Then all skating players turn in the *same* direction (they should face the players' benches on every turn to avoid colliding with each other) and skate back toward the near blue line.
3. When the players reach the near blue line, they again turn to face the players' benches, skate to the far blue line, turn to face the players' benches, and then skate back to center ice.
4. To conclude, players turn to face the players' benches and skate down the ice, stopping at the opposite end.
5. Blow your whistle to signal the second wave of players to begin as soon as the first group returns to the closest blue line.

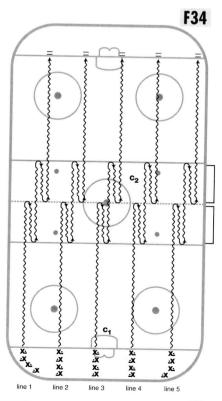

F34

line 1   line 2   line 3   line 4   line 5

F35

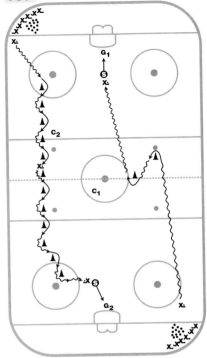

Stickhandling Slalom and Turnbacks F35 ⬤

Purpose: To develop proficiency at skating, stickhandling in a slalom course, turning, and shooting; and to warm up the goalie.

Number of Players: All, 2 goalies
Additional Equipment: 10 to 12 cones for slalom, 2 cones for turnbacks
Time: 3 to 5 minutes

1. Divide your players into two groups and have them line up in each end of the ice diagonally across from each other. Place a goalie in each net. Have pucks at both ends. Station one coach at center ice and one near the far blue line.
2. On one side of the ice, place one cone at the face-off dot just outside the far blue line and a second cone just off the edge of the center-ice face-off circle.
3. Players on that side of the ice skate down the boards until they reach the far cone.
4. Players make a glide turn toward the middle of the ice around that cone, skate to the cone near center ice, make a glide turn in the opposite direction around the cone, stickhandle straight down the ice, and shoot on the goaltender (G1).
5. On the other side of the ice, use ten to twelve cones, placing them 8 to 12 feet apart. Players on this side stickhandle a puck as they slalom through the cones as quickly as possible to the other end of the ice and then shoot on the goaltender (G2).
6. The second player in each line should begin as soon as the first player reaches center ice. All players should finish by moving to the end of the opposite line to perform the drill in the other direction.

This is a good warm-up drill for the goaltenders, so instruct your players to shoot on the goaltenders, not stickhandle around them at close range. This drill enables the goalies to get a feel for the puck while giving the players a good warm-up through shooting and stickhandling.

Skating Figure-Eight Stickhandling

F36 ●●

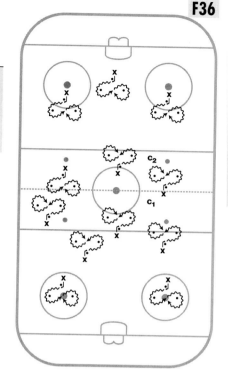

F36

Purpose: To develop the ability to skate and stickhandle in a figure-eight pattern.	**Number of Players:** All **Additional Equipment:** 3 pucks per player **Time:** 3 to 5 minutes

1. Players find their own spot anywhere on the ice and place two pucks about 10 feet apart on the ice in front of them. Coaches move from player to player, observing and teaching proper form.
2. Players skate and stickhandle the third puck in a figure-eight pattern around the other two pucks. Remind your players that the stick blade should be the first thing that leads through each turn.

If you don't have enough pucks to stickhandle around, players can drop their gloves and stickhandle around them. There's a slight safety risk to performing this without gloves on, but remember that this drill (and the next one) are for more-skilled players. Another option is to have players work in groups of three, with one player stickhandling figure eights around the other two players. Players should switch places every thirty seconds to one minute or on your whistle.

Stationary Figure-Eight Stickhandling

F37 ●●●

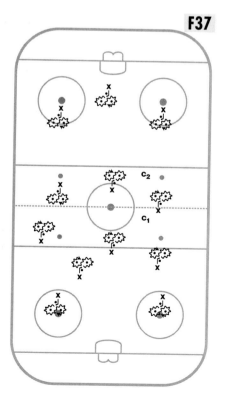

F37

Purpose: To develop the ability to stickhandle in a figure-eight pattern while remaining stationary.	**Number of Players:** All **Additional Equipment:** 3 pucks per player **Time:** 3 minutes

1. Players find their own spot on the ice and place two pucks slightly farther than shoulder width apart on the ice in front of them. Station a coach near each blue line.
2. While standing stationary, each player stickhandles the third puck in a figure-eight pattern around the other two pucks. On the whistle, players change direction to stickhandle figure eights in the opposite direction.

As in the previous drill, if there's a shortage of pucks, players can stick-handle around their gloves.

Shooting Drills

Three-Lane Shooting F38 ●

Purpose: To develop proficiency at stickhandling and shooting.	**Additional Equipment:** 40 pucks
Number of Players: All, 2 goalies	**Time:** 5 minutes

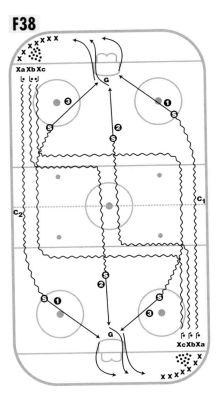

F38

1. Split your players into two lines at opposite ends of the ice diagonally across from one another, with twenty pucks in each line. Place a goalie in each net. Station a coach against each side of the boards at the centerline.
2. On the whistle, the first player in each line (player Xa) skates directly down the boards and takes an angle shot on goal from the top of the face-off circle (1). Each player Xa then skates to the back of the line in that end zone.
3. Each player Xb leaves just behind player Xa but stickhandles the puck to the near blue line and turns toward the middle of the ice, skating directly along the blue line.
4. When each player Xb reaches the middle of the ice, he turns again, skates directly down the middle of the ice to just inside the blue line, and takes a direct shot on goal (2). Each player Xb then skates to the back of the line in that end zone.
5. Each player Xc leaves just behind player Xb, skates while stickhandling to the near blue line, turns, and skates all the way along the blue line toward the other side of the ice. Then player Xc turns to skate down the boards, arrives inside the far blue line, and takes an angle shot on goal from the top of the circle (3). Each player Xc then skates to the back of the line in that end zone.
6. Halfway through the allotted time, move the pucks and players to the opposite corners and restart the drill.

Three-Line Shooting F39

Purpose: To develop proficiency at stickhandling and shooting.

Number of Players: All, 1 goalie
Additional Equipment: 30 to 45 pucks
Time: 3 to 5 minutes

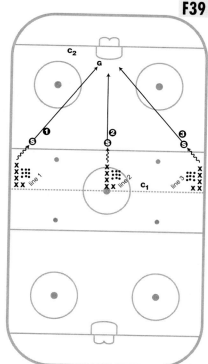

1. Split your team into three equal lines, one against one side board near the centerline, the second at the center-ice face-off circle, and the third against the opposite side boards near the centerline. Each line should have ten to fifteen pucks. Place the goalie in the net. Station one coach near center ice and one coach near the far goal line.

2. The first player in one of the side board lines stick-handles the puck across the blue line and then takes an angle shot on goal from the top of the circle (1).

3. Next the first player from the line in the middle of the ice stickhandles a puck across the blue line and takes a shot on goal from about 10 feet inside the blue line (2).

4. Then the first player in the final line stickhandles a puck inside the blue line and takes an angle shot on goal (3). The drill continues with the second players in each line.

5. Players should move to the end of the next line after each shot (line 1 shooter goes to line 2, line 2 to line 3, line 3 to line 1).

This can be done as a half-ice drill or you can have groups shooting on each goal at once. Note that the goaltender receives a shot from three different angles.

Half-Ice Horseshoe F40 ⬤

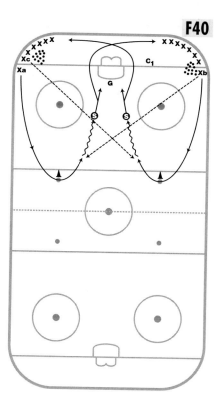

Purpose: To develop proficiency at skating, passing and receiving, and shooting; and to warm up the goalie.

Number of Players: All, 1 goalie
Additional Equipment: 40 pucks, 2 cones
Time: 3 minutes

1. Place a cone on each neutral zone face-off dot.

2. Divide the players in half and line them up in each corner at one end of the ice. Have twenty pucks in each corner. Place the goalie in the net. Station a coach at the goal line.

3. Player Xa (the first player in one of the lines) skates down the boards toward the near blue line without a puck, glides around the nearest cone, and skates toward the middle of the ice.
4. Player Xa then receives a pass from player Xb, the first player in the opposite line, shoots on goal from the high slot area, and finishes by going to the end of the other line.
5. Immediately after the pass, player Xb skates down the boards, performs a glide turn around the opposite cone, and skates back toward the goalie.
6. Player Xb receives a pass from player Xc, the first player in the opposite line, shoots on goal, and finishes by going to the end of the other line, and the drill continues.

This is a great pregame goalie warm-up that can be done using half-ice or both ends. If you're using it as a pregame warm-up, remember that cones cannot be used during game warm-ups. Instead, rely on the neutral zone face-off circles just outside the blue line.

Full-Ice Horseshoe F41

F41

Purpose: To develop proficiency at skating, passing and receiving, stickhandling, and shooting.	Number of Players: All, 2 goalies
	Additional Equipment: 40 pucks, 2 cones
	Time: 5 minutes

1. Place a cone (or your glove) 20 feet inside each blue line in the middle of the ice.
2. Split your players into two lines in diagonally opposite corners of the ice. Have twenty pucks in each line. Place a goalie in each net. Position a coach against the boards on each side of the centerline with extra pucks in case of errant passes.
3. Each player Xa from each line skates down the boards toward the far blue line, skates around the cone, and receives a pass from the player Xb at that end of the ice.
4. Each player Xa then stickhandles the puck back to the starting end of the ice and takes a shot from inside the blue line. Player Xa then goes to the end of the line in that end zone.
5. After passing to player Xa, each player Xb (the new Xa) skates toward the far blue line, turns around the cone at the opposite end of the ice, and receives a pass from the

new player Xb, and so on. After her shot, player Xb goes to the end of the line in that end zone.

6. Halfway through the allotted time, move pucks and players to opposite corners and restart the drill in the opposite direction.

It's important to stress to your players that in order for their teammate to maintain speed, they should pass the puck to the oncoming player as he begins heading back up ice. Turning on a slightly flat angle and accurate passing are both crucial. This drill is excellent for concentration because it requires skating, passing, stickhandling, and shooting. It requires your players to work in harmony, which emphasizes the importance of teamwork.

Variations: To increase the difficulty level of the drill, have two players from each line skate at the same time, receive one puck, and pass it between them as they approach the goalie. This is called a two-on-zero because both players are acting as forwards without any defensemen opposing them.

Or add a defenseman to make it a two-on-one in the returning direction. Place an additional cone at each blue line for the defensemen to pivot around.

Umbrella Shooting F42 ●

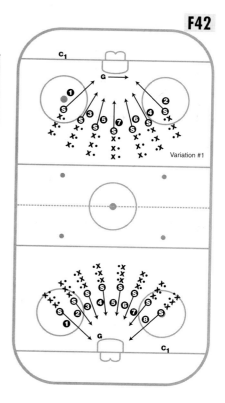

F42

Purpose: To develop proficiency at shooting, and to warm up the goalie.	**Number of Players:** All, 1 goalie **Additional Equipment:** 40 pucks **Time:** 3 to 5 minutes

1. Line up your players in eight lines forming an "umbrella" shape, starting from the top of the end zone face-off circle on one side across the ice to the top of the other face-off circle. Make sure each player has a puck. Place the goalie in the net. Station a coach near the goal line.
2. Beginning on one side of the ice, the first player in each line shoots a puck on goal. Each player should make sure the goalie is set before she takes her shot.
3. After shooting, each player rotates to the end of the line to the right (the player in the last line moves to the end of the first line).
4. The drill continues with the next player in each line.

This can be used as a game warm-up drill or for a warm-up shooting drill during practice. Use as a half-ice drill or at both ends of the ice.

Variations: Have the player on one end of the umbrella shoot first. The player on the opposite end of the umbrella shoots next; then players alternate sides, concluding with the middle shooter. This makes the goaltender work on lateral movement and angles.

Or, station a coach in the corner with the pucks. The coach randomly passes a puck to any player, who then shoots on goal. All players should be ready to receive a pass and then shoot the puck. This also helps the goaltender's lateral movements and angles. The goalie must be positioned on the puck side post, react to a pass from the corner, and move to play the angle of the shooter who receives the puck.

Wrist Shots, Backhand Shots, Snap Shots, and Slap Shots F43 ● ➤ ●●●

Purpose: To develop the ability to make wrist shots, backhand shots, snap shots, and slap shots.	**Number of Players:** All **Additional Equipment:** 1 puck per player **Time:** 4 to 8 minutes

F43

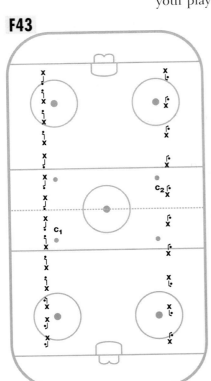

1. Start by demonstrating and explaining the mechanics of each shot. Have your players watch from different angles.
2. Players then find a spot on the ice about 10 feet from the side boards for wrist shots and backhand shots and 15 to 20 feet from the boards for snap shots and slap shots. They should spread out and allow plenty of room between them.
3. Players pick a spot on the boards to aim for. Explain to them that the goal of the drill is to work on proper form (not to see who can make the loudest noise by shooting the puck off the glass).
4. Coaches move from player to player to give individual instruction. Blow your whistle every few minutes to signal players to work on a different shot.

The time for this drill will vary according to the skill level of your players. Remember that snap shots and slap shots are for the more-skilled players.

Variations: After players have mastered all these shots, they can take a few strides, slowly skating toward the puck, and attempt a slap shot.

Or, they can work in pairs facing each other about 15 feet apart. One player passes to the other, who attempts to shoot the pass or one-time the puck toward the boards using either the snap shot or slap shot. Players should understand that they must first pass the puck softly and progress to stronger passing as they master the shot.

Three-Line Shooting with a Pass F44 ●●

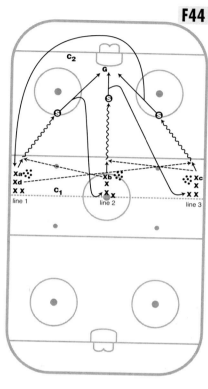

F44

Purpose: To develop proficiency at skating, passing and receiving, and shooting.
Number of Players: All, 1 goalie

Additional Equipment: 30 to 45 pucks
Time: 3 to 5 minutes

1. Divide your players into three lines, one against one side of the boards near the centerline, the second near the center-ice face-off dot, and the third on the opposite side of the boards near the centerline. Have ten to fifteen pucks in each line. Place the goalie in the net. Station one coach near center ice and one coach near the goal line.

2. The first player in one of the side lines, player Xa, skates without a puck, receives a pass from player Xb (the first player in the center-ice group), stickhandles across the blue line, and takes an angle shot on goal from the top of the circle.

3. Player Xb then skates without a puck and receives a pass from player Xc, the first player in the other group against the boards.

4. Player Xb skates across the blue line and takes a shot from 10 feet inside the offensive zone.

5. Player Xc skates without a puck, receives a pass from player Xd (the next player in player Xa's group), stickhandles across the blue line, and takes an angle shot on goal, and so on.

6. Players should move to the end of the next line after each shot (line 1 shooter goes to line 2, line 2 to line 3, line 3 to line 1).

This can be used as a half-ice drill or a drill at both ends of the ice. Goaltenders receive shots from three angles, and skating players have the additional challenge of making a stick-to-stick pass.

F45

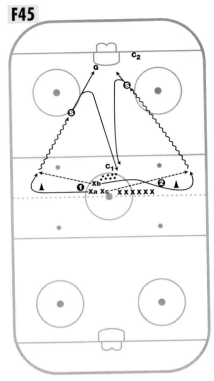

Curl-Out Shooting F45 ●●

Purpose: To develop proficiency at skating, making glide turns, passing and receiving, and shooting.

Number of Players: All, 1 goalie
Additional Equipment: 40 pucks, 2 cones
Time: 3 to 5 minutes

1. Have all players (and pucks) in the center-ice face-off circle. Place the goalie in the net. Position the cones approximately 6 feet toward the blue line from the centerline and approximately 10 feet from the boards on either side. Station one coach near center ice and one near the goal line.
2. The first player in line, player Xa, starts skating along the centerline, does a glide turn around the cone near the boards, and receives a pass from player Xb (the next player in line) (1).
3. Player Xa stickhandles the puck across the blue line and takes a shot on goal from the top of the circle and goes to the back of the line.
4. Player Xb then skates in the opposite direction along the centerline, makes a glide turn around the cone on the opposite side of the ice, receives a pass from player Xc (the next player in line) (2), stickhandles across the blue line, and takes a shot from the opposite angle. Player Xb then goes to the back of the line.
5. Continue with the rest of the players skating the pattern. Players should skate the drill in the other direction when they get back to the head of the line.

This can be used as a half-ice drill or a drill at both ends of the ice.

F46

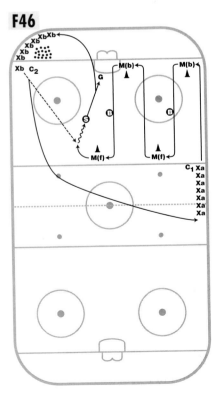

Mohawk Shooting F46 ●●

Purpose: To develop proficiency at forward and backward skating, making Mohawk turns, passing and receiving, and shooting.

Number of Players: All, 1 goalie
Additional Equipment: 20 pucks, 4 cones
Time: 5 minutes

1. Place the first cone about 3 feet from the side boards and 6 feet from the goal line. Place the second cone about 18

feet from the same side boards and 10 feet above the top of the end zone circle. Place the third cone about 30 feet from the same side boards and 6 feet from the goal line. Place the fourth cone about 45 feet from the same side boards and 10 feet above the high slot near the middle of the ice.

2. Divide your players into two lines, one line outside the blue line against the boards facing the cones, and the other line in the opposite corner behind the goal line with the twenty pucks. Place the goalie in the net. Station a coach near the front of each line of players.

3. The first player in the line outside the blue line, player Xa, skates forward down the boards toward the first cone, makes a Mohawk turn to face backward, and then skates backward toward the blue line.

4. At the second cone, player Xa does a Mohawk turn to face forward, skates forward down toward the goal, and does a Mohawk turn to backward around the third cone.

5. Player Xa now skates backward toward the blue line, executes another Mohawk turn to forward around the fourth cone, skates in on the goalie, and receives a pass from player Xb, the first player in line in the corner.

6. Player Xa shoots and then skates to the end of the line in the corner.

7. Player Xb now skates out to the end of the line outside the blue line.

8. To keep your players in motion, when player Xa reaches the second cone, the second player in the line near the blue line (a new player Xa) begins skating the same drill pattern.

9. Halfway through the allotted time, move pucks, players, and cones to the opposite side of the ice and restart the drill in the opposite direction.

This can be used as a half-ice drill or a drill at both ends of the ice.

Checking Drills

One-on-One Battle (Stick Lift and Stick Press) F47 ●

Purpose: To develop proficiency at competing for the puck and performing the stick lift or stick press.	**Number of Players:** All, 1 goalie **Additional Equipment:** 30 to 40 pucks, 2 cones **Time:** 8 to 10 minutes

1. Place a cone on each of the face-off dots just outside the blue lines.
2. Have players form two equal lines about 20 feet on either side of the net,

F47

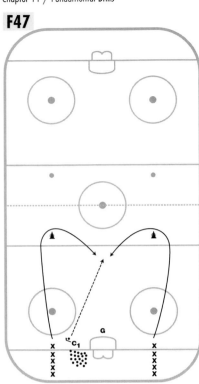

with the skates of the first player in each line touching the goal line. Place the goalie in the net. Station a coach with the pucks between one line of players and the net.

3. On the whistle, the first player in each line races to the nearest cone.
4. Players do a tight glide turn around that cone and then skate back toward the net.
5. As players approach, the coach passes a puck toward the slot area. The players compete for the puck and attempt to score a goal. Encourage them to perform either a stick lift or stick press to stop the other player from controlling the puck.
6. If the puck slides by the players, they continue to battle for the offensive scoring chance.
7. Blow the whistle for the next two players to begin as soon as the first two players are approaching the puck.
8. After each scoring attempt, the players should go to the end of the opposite line.

This can be used as a half-ice drill or a drill at both ends of the ice. I like to use this drill near the end of practices to provide competition and conditioning.

F48

Angle Checking F48

Purpose: To develop the ability to execute angle checks.	**Additional Equipment:** 30 pucks, 4 cones
Number of Players: All, 1 goalie	**Time:** 5 minutes

1. Place two cones about 3 feet apart near each neutral zone face-off dot the players are facing.
2. Position four equal lines of players about 5 feet apart on each side of the center-ice face-off circle and facing the opposite net. Place a goalie in each net. Station a coach with the pucks just inside each blue line the players are facing.
3. On the whistle, the first player in each line skates quickly toward the cones.
4. The player in the line closest to the boards, player Xa, skates around the far cone and receives a pass from the coach, becoming the offensive player.
5. The first player in the other line, player Xb, skates around the near cone, becoming the defensive player.

6. Player Xb attempts to angle-check player Xa toward the boards, lifting his stick and trying to separate player Xa from the puck and gain possession.

7. Both players skate down the boards, continuing to battle for the puck and attempting to score on the goalie. They finish by going to the end of the opposite line.

8. Halfway through the allotted time, move players, pucks, and cones to the other side of the ice to perform angle checks in the opposite direction.

This can be done going in both directions at the same time (as shown). To make it a half-ice drill, line up the players at the blue line and position the coach at center ice.

Variation: Have players perform body checks or shoulders checks instead of angle checks.

Poke Check F49   F49

Purpose: To develop the ability to execute poke checks.	**Additional Equipment:** 40 pucks, 6 cones (optional)
Number of Players: All, 2 goalies	**Time:** 5 minutes

1. Divide your players into equal groups of forwards and defensemen. Have the forwards line up in two diagonally opposite groups in each end of the ice along the boards near the hash marks. Each forward has a puck. Station a coach near each group of forwards.

2. Position the defensemen in two groups, one at each blue line against the boards, and facing the forwards.

3. On your whistle, the first forward in each line attempts to skate with a puck the length of the ice while the first defenseman in each line skates backward defending one-on-one in an attempt to perform a poke check and get the puck away from the forward. (You can use the six cones to separate the ice diagonally and prevent players starting at opposite ends from crashing into each other in the neutral ice area.)

4. The forward attempts to beat the defenseman and score on the opposite goal. If the defenseman breaks up the one-on-one, their turn ends then.

5. To finish, the forward goes to the end of the opposite line of forwards and the defenseman goes to the end of his original line.

6. Halfway through the allotted time, move pucks, players, and cones to the opposite end of the ice and restart the drill in the opposite direction.

F50

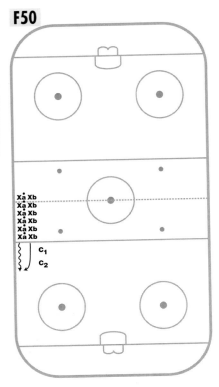

Giving and Receiving Shoulder Checks, Body Checks, and Hip Checks F50

Purpose: To develop the ability to give and receive body checks, shoulder checks, and hip checks.	**Number of Players:** All **Additional Equipment:** 1 puck per pair **Time:** 5 minutes

1. Have players form two lines, 3 feet apart, near one side of the boards at each blue line. Station a coach with each group, demonstrating proper technique and body position for both giving and receiving a check.
2. The player in line closest to the boards, player Xa, carries the puck down the boards while the forward-skating defensive player (player Xb) in the other line shoulder-checks player Xa into the boards. Player Xa should skate at medium speed and directly down the boards to allow both players to feel the contact. Don't allow player Xa to cut back in front of or behind player Xb.
3. After players have crossed the goal line, they go to the end of the opposite line.
4. Halfway through the allotted time, move pucks and players to the other side of the ice and restart the drill in the opposite direction.

For half-ice practices, teach this drill on both sides of the ice simultaneously. For full-ice practices, utilize your entire coaching staff to work on this drill in different areas around the rink.

Variation: Once players become comfortable with shoulder checks, move on to body checks and then hip checks. Note that for hip checks, the defensive players (players Xb) will skate backward.

Successive One-on-Ones F51

Purpose: To promote quickness and develop proficiency at executing poke checks.	**Number of Players:** Defensemen, 1 goalie **Additional Equipment:** 20 pucks **Time:** Each defenseman defends once

F51

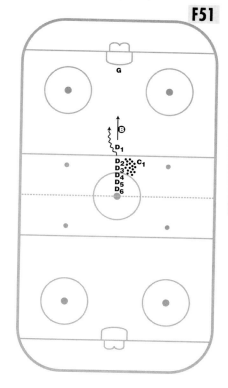

1. Line up all the defensemen outside the blue line at one end of the ice with a coach and pucks. Place the goalie in the net. (Forwards can work on any different half-ice drill at the other end of the ice; try **F17**, **F22**, **F28**, **F36**, **F39**, **F40**, **F42**, **F44**, **F45**, **F48**, or **F50**.)

2. Have one defenseman (D1) just inside the blue line ready to face a one-on-one situation against each of the other defensemen.

3. The first defenseman in line (D2) drives to the net with a puck, attempting to get around player D1.

4. Player D1 begins to retreat while trying to poke the puck off player D2's stick or, at the very least, keeping player D2 to the outside.

5. If player D2 does beat player D1, player D2 attempts to score on the goalie. Regardless of whether player D1 stops player D2, player D1 quickly moves toward the blue line, closing the gap on the next player in line (D3), who attempts the next one-on-one on your signal. You may have to tell player D1 when to abandon a one-on-one and move back toward the blue line to start again.

6. Player D1 continues the drill until he's faced all of the other defensemen, at which point a new defenseman becomes the defender.

7. Drill continues until each defensemen has had to defend the goal.

This is a half-ice drill. Although it's very demanding, it's a great way to improve foot quickness and poke-checking skills. Vary when you signal each attacking defensemen to start to challenge the foot quickness of the defending defenseman.

Hook Check and Sweep Check **F52** ●●●

F52

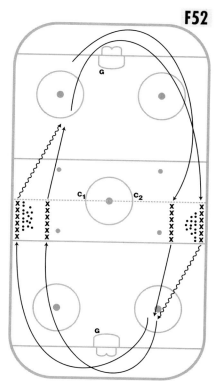

Purpose: To develop the ability to execute hook checks and sweep checks.	**Number of Players:** All, 2 goalies
	Additional Equipment: 40 pucks
	Time: 5 minutes

1. Start with two lines of players 6 to 8 feet apart facing one net near the boards on the centerline and another two lines near the other side of the boards on the centerline facing the opposite net. Have twenty pucks in each line

closest to the boards. Station a coach on either side of the center-ice face-off circle.

2. On the whistle, the first player in each line closest to the boards skates forward toward the net they are facing. When they reach the top of the end zone face-off circle, they drive to the net and attempt to score.

3. The first player in each inside line leaves a split second later, chases the offensive player, and attempts to either hook-check or sweep-check the puck from the offensive skater to stop the scoring chance.

4. After the scoring attempt or successful check, the offensive player goes to the end of the opposite inside line, and the defensive player goes to the end of the opposite outside line.

5. Start the next player in each line as the hook check, sweep check, or shot on goal occurs.

6. Halfway through the allotted time, turn the lines around and restart the drill in the opposite direction.

CHAPTER 12

Offensive Drills

Offensive drills use one or more of the fundamental skills of skating, shooting, passing, and stickhandling. They will also help teach your players how to work together as an offensive team. For example, each player should utilize his teammates when attempting to create outnumbered situations. Offensive players without the puck will learn to support the puck carrier or move to open ice to receive a pass. Players with puck possession will discover creative ways to generate scoring opportunities. Remember that a puck moves faster than a player can skate, so passing and receiving a pass become the keys to puck possession and creating scoring chances.

Half-Ice Two-on-Zero Drive 01 ⬤

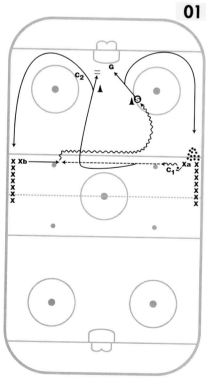

01

Purpose: To develop proficiency at driving wide with the puck, shooting while driving to the net, and driving to the front of the net for rebounds.

Number of Players: All, 1 goalie
Additional Equipment: 30 pucks, 2 cones
Time: 5 minutes

1. Divide your players in half and line them up against the boards between the centerline and the blue line. One line has the pucks. Place the goalie in the net. Position two cones in the offensive zone as shown on the diagram. Station one coach near the line with the pucks and one coach near the net.
2. The first player in the line with the pucks, player Xa, begins skating with a puck along the blue line toward the opposite line.

3. The first player in the line on the opposite side of the ice, player Xb, begins skating toward player Xa.
4. Within a stride or two, player Xa should quickly and accurately pass the puck to player Xb. Timing is very important here.
5. Player Xb, now with the puck, and player Xa cross, switching sides at the blue line while staying onside. Player Xb should skate closer to the blue line to avoid a collision.
6. Player Xb then carries the puck around the cone placed slightly inside the face-off circle, while player Xa drives around the cone positioned in front of the net and stops.
7. Player Xb then takes an angle shot on goal, with player Xa looking for a rebound. The coach at the net should encourage player Xa to go for the rebound.
8. Players then go to the end of the opposite line.
9. Start the next two players when the first pair have crossed and are attacking near the top of the end zone face-off circles.
10. Halfway through the allotted time, move the cones and pucks to the other end of the ice and restart the drill in the opposite direction.

This drill can be done using half-ice or both ends of the ice.

Variation: Have the puck carrier pass the puck to the driving teammate instead of shooting. Remember to switch sides so the goalie is facing shots from different angles.

02

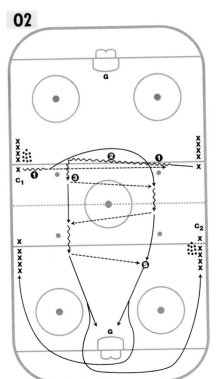

Blue Line Two-on-Zero 02

Purpose: To develop proficiency at passing, receiving, shooting, and driving to the net in a two-on-zero.

Number of Players: All, 2 goalies
Additional Equipment: 40 pucks
Time: 6 to 8 minutes

1. Split your players into four equal lines against the boards near the blue line. Players should face each other. Two lines that are diagonally opposite one another each have twenty pucks. Station a coach with each of those lines. Place a goalie in each net.
2. Start at one end of the ice. The player in the line with the pucks retrieves a puck and begins skating along the blue line, passing to the first player in the opposite line, who receives the pass and then also skates along the blue line (1). Remind players to pass the puck early and accurately when they begin the drill.

3. Those two players cross, switching sides of the ice (2). The player with the puck should skate closer to the blue line to avoid a collision.

4. They continue passing back and forth down the ice (3) in a two-on-zero rush, then take a shot on goal, and go to the end of the other line in the end zone where they finished. In other words, the player with the puck goes to the end of the line of players without pucks in the end zone opposite to where he started.

5. As those players cross their offensive blue line, the two players at the opposite end begin the drill. The player on the puck side starts with the puck, skates directly along the blue line, and passes to the first player in line across the ice.

6. The two players cross, switching sides of the ice, passing back and forth down the ice in a two-on-zero rush, taking a shot on goal, and so on.

Encourage your players to stop in front of the net on any shot that's taken because you're working on shooting on goal and driving to the net for rebounds.

Full-Ice Two-on-Zero 03

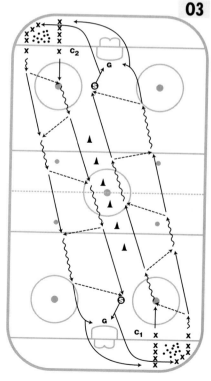

03

Purpose: To develop proficiency at forehand and backhand passing and receiving, shooting, and driving to the net in a two-on-zero.	**Number of Players:** All, 2 goalies **Additional Equipment:** 40 pucks, 6 to 8 cones **Time:** 5 minutes

1. Place six to eight cones diagonally through the middle of the ice, dividing the ice in half in the neutral zone. Station a coach near each goal line.

2. Split players into two lines at each end of the rink in two diagonally opposite corners. The lines closest to the boards each have twenty pucks. Place a goalie in each net.

3. The first four players (one from each line) begin by skating down the ice, passing and receiving the puck in a two-on-zero rush.

4. Once each pair crosses the opposite blue line, they should make one final pass, with the receiver taking an immediate shot on goal and the passer driving to the net for the rebound. Encourage your players to make as many accurate passes as possible as they move down the ice.

5. After the rush, players go to the end of the other line in the end zone

where they finished. This ensures they will work on both their forehand and backhand passing and receiving.

6. The next four players should start the drill as soon as the ones in front of them reach center ice.

7. Halfway through the allotted time, move pucks and players to the other side of the ice and restart the drill in the opposite direction.

Make sure players shoot from different angles.

Three-Player Cycle 04 ⬤

Purpose: To develop proficiency at offensive zone puck control.
Number of Players: All, in groups of 3, 1 goalie

Additional Equipment: 20 pucks
Time: 5 minutes

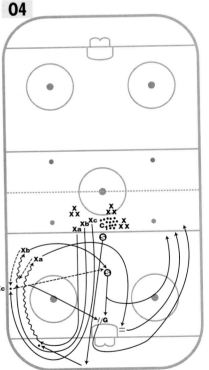

04

1. Line up all players outside the blue line with pucks. Station a coach with the pucks there too. Place the goalie in the net. Players work in groups of three.

2. The coach shoots a puck into one corner of the ice.

3. Player Xa skates from the middle of the ice toward the puck. As player Xa reaches the top of the face-off circle, player Xb begins to follow her.

4. When player Xb reaches the top of the circle, player Xc follows him.

5. Player Xa retrieves the puck, turns toward the side boards, and skates directly back toward the blue line. Player Xa approaches the top of the circle and passes the puck softly off the boards back toward the goal line.

6. At this point, player Xb retrieves the puck, skates to the top of the circle, and passes the puck back softly off the boards.

7. Player Xc now retrieves the puck. Player Xa continues skating through the high slot, stopping in front of the net. Player Xb continues in a pattern across the top of the circle toward the high slot.

8. Player Xc looks to make a cross-ice pass to player Xb, who is positioned in the high slot for a shot on goal. Player Xc continues to drive to the net for a rebound.

9. After one scoring attempt, all three players sprint out of the end zone. The coach shoots another puck into the opposite corner, and the next three players start the drill.

10. Halfway through the allotted time, switch sides of the ice so your players work out of both corners. This ensures everyone is working on passing the puck with both the backhand and forehand. It also allows goaltenders to face passes and shots coming at them from varying angles.

This drill can be done using half-ice or both ends of the ice.
Variation: Allow the last player who retrieves the puck to skate away from the side boards and shoot directly on goal or to pass to the player who is driving to the net.

Timed Three-on-Zero 05

Purpose: To develop proficiency at passing, receiving, and working as a team to score as quickly as possible. **Number of Players:** All, in groups of 3, 1 goalie	**Additional Equipment:** 3 pucks per group **Time:** 10 minutes

1. Split your players into groups of three. Place the goalie in the net.
2. The first group lines up on the blue line with one puck. Station a coach nearby with a stopwatch and the extra pucks.
3. On the whistle, all three players advance toward the goal, passing the puck between them.
4. Each player must touch the puck before anyone can shoot on goal. It's your decision whether you require each group to score one, two, or three goals before the group's time is up.
5. After the three players score with the first puck, they must all skate back toward the same blue line, where one player retrieves a second puck. Once more, the three players pass the puck to each other.
6. The preset number of goals must be scored before all three players skate hard out of the zone and over the blue line, stopping the clock.
7. Then the next team of players starts the drill.
8. Depending on how many groups you have and how much time you want to spend on this drill, you can have each group go one, two, or three times.

This is a great competitive drill that can be used at the end of practice and that can be run as a half-ice drill or as a

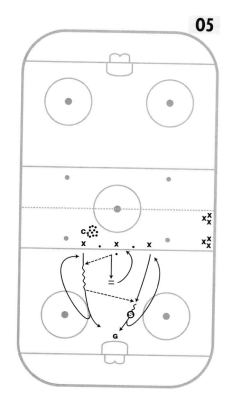

05

drill at both ends of the ice. Based on the time you've set aside for this drill and the ability level of your players and goalies, you'll need to decide on how many goals each group needs to score to complete the drill. You should keep a record of each team's time; obviously the winner is the team that performs the drill fastest. Kids are guaranteed to have fun with this one!

Double Breakout 06 ⬤

Purpose: To teach player positions during breakouts and offensive zone plays.

Number of Players: All, in groups of 5, 2 goalies
Additional Equipment: 20 pucks
Time: 10 minutes

1. Each group is made up of two wingers, two defensemen, and one center. Have one group on the ice, with the remaining players on the bench. Place a goalie in each net.
2. Have the pucks situated either on the boards or near the boards at center ice. Station one coach at center ice (C1) and one with the players on the bench (C2).
3. The center (C), right and left wingers (RW, LW), and two defensemen (RD, LD) are positioned as shown in the diagram. Players should take their positions as if readying for a center-ice face-off (diagram 1 shows steps 3 through 9).
4. The coach at center ice begins by shooting a puck into one corner of the ice.
5. The defenseman closest to the puck skates backward, pivoting toward the puck to retrieve it.
6. The left and right wingers skate toward their breakout position, stopping against the boards near the hash marks of each face-off circle in the defensive zone and facing slightly up-ice.
7. The remaining defenseman skates backward and then pivots to protect the area in the front of the net in case of a turnover. The center skates into a supporting position for the puck-retrieving defenseman. The center should always mirror the puck-retrieving defenseman but stay in front of the goal line about 10 to 15 feet away, always available for a pass.
8. The defenseman who retrieved the puck has a few options: immediately pass up the boards to the winger or the center, or retrieve the puck, skate behind the net, and pass the puck to the winger on the opposite side of the ice or the center.

06

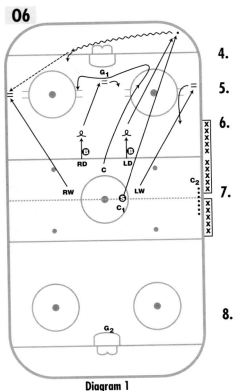

Diagram 1

9. The front-of-the-net defenseman can either stay in that position or move to the opposite side of the net to receive a pass from the other defenseman. As coach, decide if your players have the ability to make consecutive passes before offering this option.

10. The actual breakout occurs when one of the defensemen passes to a winger or center, and all five players move offensively up the ice with the forwards passing the puck back and forth and taking a shot on the goalie (G2) at the opposite end of the ice (diagram 2, 1).

11. On the coach's whistle, or if a goal is scored, the five players immediately skate out into the neutral zone, returning to a similar starting position at center ice but lined up in the opposite face-off position to begin a new breakout from the other end (diagram 2, 2).

12. At this point, the coach shoots a new puck into the end opposite where the drill began, signaling the players to move to make another breakout and passing the puck back and forth as they skate up ice in an attempt to score on that goaltender (not shown).

13. For the last part of the drill, the coach pushes a puck into the corner or uses a whistle to signal a forward to retrieve the puck and pass it back to a defenseman, who is standing at the offensive blue line, ready to take a shot on the goalie (G1) (diagram 3, 1).

14. The forwards now converge on the net, one screening the goalie, one trying to move in for a rebound, and one in the high slot area, trying to score from a rebound of the defenseman's shot on goal (diagram 3, 2).

15. On your final whistle, the five players sprint to the players' bench, and the next group of players comes off the bench to begin the drill, starting from the opposite end of the ice (diagram 3, 3).

Variation: Dump the puck around the boards, forcing the goaltender to go behind the net to stop the puck so his defensemen can retrieve it to start the breakout.

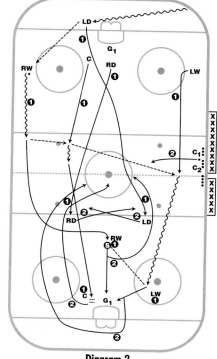

Diagram 2

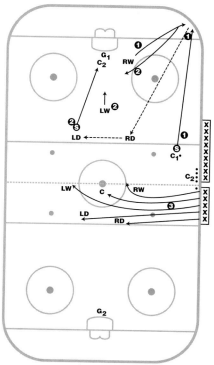

Diagram 3

OFFENSIVE DRILLS

Three-Player Offensive Drive 07

Purpose: To develop proficiency at offensive zone play and determining when to pass, when to shoot.

Number of Players: All, 1 goalie
Additional Equipment: 20 pucks
Time: 5 to 10 minutes

1. Players line up on the centerline in three groups: one line of players against each side of the boards and one line in the center-ice face-off circle with the pucks. Place the goalie in the net. Station a coach near the centerline.
2. The player in the center of the ice starts with a puck and, on the coach's voice command, passes to either winger.
3. The winger who receives the pass begins driving wide, but on an angle toward the net.
4. After passing the puck, the center immediately breaks to the front of the net, making certain to stay onside.
5. The winger who is away from the puck initially skates wide as well and then cuts laterally toward the middle of the ice, in the high slot area. The winger with the puck now has three options: shoot, pass the puck to the winger in the high slot, or pass to the center driving to the front of the net for a tip-in.
6. The group of forwards should attempt to score a goal. Blow your whistle to signal the end of this group's turn, perhaps after one scoring attempt and one rebound scoring attempt.
7. On your whistle, this group hustles out of the end zone and goes to the end of the line to their right; that is, the left winger goes to the center's line, the center goes to the right winger's line, and the right winger goes to end of the left winger's line. Simultaneously, the next group of three begins the drill.

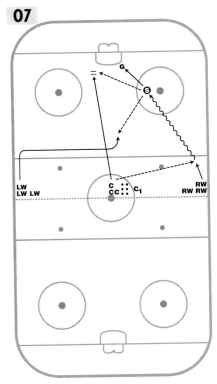

Although this drill can be run using the full-ice, I prefer half-ice because you can have groups of three performing the drill simultaneously in both directions from center ice.

The object here is to stress the offensive posture of a player driving wide with the puck toward the goal, a second player driving and stopping in front, and a third player skating in a pattern toward the high slot area. This is a great drill for teaching the importance of having the third player high in the slot. Your players will learn offensive zone play as well as transitioning to defense because a player in the high slot area is in a good position to help the defenseman in a backchecking situation.

Variation: Do the drill as a three-on-one or a three-on-two by position-ing defensemen at the blue line. You'll find that when doing a three-on-two, the player driving wide with the puck backs up one defenseman. The player driving to the net backs up the other defenseman, with the high slot area re-maining open for the third player.

Basic Offensive Zone Face-Off 08 ⬤

Purpose: To practice face-offs in the offensive zone.
Number of Players: All, in groups of 5, 1 goalie

Additional Equipment: 1 puck
Time: 8 to 10 minutes

1. The first group of five has two wingers, two defensemen, and one center. The left winger lines up on the hash marks, the center lines up to take the face-off, and the right winger lines up on the other hash marks. The defensemen line up just inside the blue line. The second group of five (the X players) lines up in a defensive posture as shown on the diagram. Place the goalie in the net.

2. The aim of any offensive zone face-off is to generate a scoring chance, so the center's responsibility is to attempt to win the face-off and send the puck back to a defenseman stationed at the blue line.

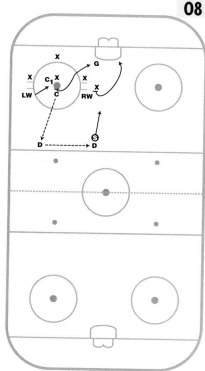

08

3. That defenseman then has the option of shooting the puck directly on goal, passing to the other defenseman to shoot, or finding an open teammate to pass to.

4. The responsibility of the forwards doesn't end if the face-off is won. The center should momentarily block out the other center from pursuing the puck and then imme-diately head to the net to act as a screen or recover a rebound shot from a defenseman.

5. As shown in the diagram, the left winger also tries to fight toward the front of the net or head to the high slot area. The right winger should also momentarily block out the player beside her and then either head to the net or move to get open for a pass. It's vital that all three forwards move their feet to help out. The bottom line is that when your team wins the draw, players block the opposing forwards from putting pressure on your defensemen, release, and either break to the front of the net or move to get open for a pass.

6. If your players lose the face-off, it's time to pressure and recover the puck. In the example shown in the diagram,

either the center or left winger would try to pressure the puck carrier (the other team's defenseman). The right winger would now be the high player in the slot.

7. If the other team's defenseman is able to skate behind his own net with puck control, then your right winger should move to pressure him. In this situation, it's a good idea for both your center and left winger to avoid chasing the defenseman behind the net; instead, they should begin skating to backcheck by cutting short of the net. One player should move immediately to the high slot area, and the other should move to cover any open, weak-side (away from the puck) opposing forward. Allow your players to be creative in offensive zone face-offs because there are a variety of alignments that can be used.

This drill is an opportunity for some situation teaching. If a player is not moving to the area indicated in the steps above, blow your whistle to stop play. Keep in mind, however, that hockey is a read-and-react sport, so players—especially on offense—need to use some creativity.

Instead of dropping the puck between the centers, try dropping it in a different area to see how your players react. Remember to switch and start from the opposite face-off circle to work on positioning on the other side of the ice. Have the groups of five switch from offensive to defensive face-off positions and vice versa. Rotate groups of players in from defensive position to offensive position to resting. When they're "resting," have your other coaches work with them on skating, passing, or stickhandling drills in the neutral zone. Use your imagination!

09

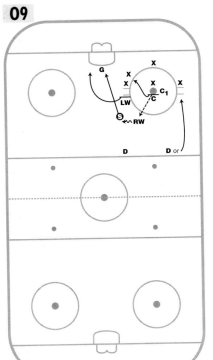

Offensive Zone Face-Off, Winger behind Center 09 ●

Purpose: To practice face-offs in the offensive zone. **Number of Players:** All, in groups of 5, 1 goalie	**Additional Equipment:** 1 puck **Time:** 8 to 10 minutes

1. The first group of five has two wingers, two defensemen, and one center. They line up for an end zone face-off in the right face-off circle. The second group of five (the X players) lines up in a defensive posture. Place the goalie in the net.

2. The center lines up across from the opposing center, and the right winger is directly behind the center or on an angle where the center can direct the puck back to that winger.

3. This allows the right winger the option of taking an immediate shot on goal or tipping the puck back to his defenseman and then moving to an open area of the ice to be in a scoring position. The defensemen can be lined up at the blue line, or one defenseman can be on the hash marks that the right winger has vacated and the other defenseman can remain back for the offensive zone draw.

4. The inside winger (here, the left winger) is key in blocking out any player who's trying to pressure the shooter (here, the right winger).

5. Again, if they lose the face-off, your players must move quickly to pressure and recover the puck (see **08**, steps 6 and 7).

This drill also is an opportunity for some situation teaching. If a player is not moving to the area indicated in the steps above, blow your whistle to stop play. Keep in mind, however, that hockey is a read-and-react sport, so players—especially on offense—need to use some creativity.

Instead of dropping the puck between the centers, try dropping it in a different area to see how your players react. Remember to switch and start from the opposite face-off circle to work on positioning on the other side of the ice. Have the groups of five switch from offensive to defensive face-off positions and vice versa. Rotate groups of players in from defensive position to offensive position to resting. When they're "resting," have your other coaches work with them on skating, passing, or stickhandling drills in the neutral zone. Use your imagination!

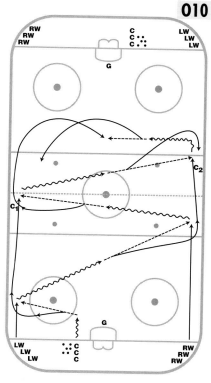

010

Three-on-Zero Rush, Return 010 ●→●●

Purpose: To develop proficiency at skating, passing and receiving, and filling the lanes in a three-player rush and return.

Number of Players: All, in groups of 3, 2 goalies
Additional Equipment: 40 pucks
Time: 8 to 10 minutes

1. Position half the players at each end of the ice behind the goal line in three equal lines. Players will be acting as a left winger, a right winger, and a center. Each line of centers has twenty pucks. The centers should position themselves a few feet from the goaltender and net so they aren't in danger of being hit by stray shots that come toward the goal. Place a goalie in each goal. Initially, the coaches should be stationed at each end to instruct players when to begin the drill.

2. Start at one end of the ice with the first player in each line skating up the ice. The center immediately passes the puck to one of the wingers, who then cuts toward the middle of the ice.
3. The center now cuts behind that winger toward the boards.
4. The three players pass the puck back and forth as they skate up the length of the ice, following their passes, and filling each lane until they reach the far blue line.
5. Then all three players turn around and skate back to where they started, maintaining their speed, following their passes, and filling each lane. They finish by taking a shot on goal. Remind your players that when attacking the net, the objective is to attack as though they were doing the Three-Player Offensive Drive **07** . That is, at the near blue line, the puck carrier drives wide toward the net, the player in the middle drives to the front of the net, and the third player moves into the high slot.
6. As the first group begins their return, the first players from each line at the opposite end of the ice begin the drill.

If you're coaching younger or inexperienced players, you'll probably want your players to stay in their lanes, pass the puck up ice in a three-on-zero rush, turn inside the far blue line, and then return. With older, more skilled players, have them follow their pass, head-manning the puck to a teammate while moving up the ice in a three-on-zero rush.

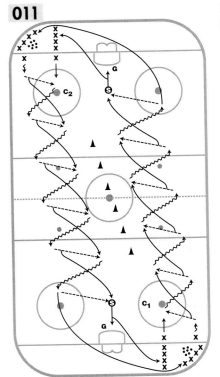

011

Full-Ice Two-on-Zero Follow Your Pass

011

Purpose: To develop proficiency at skating in a diagonal pattern and passing and receiving in a two-on-zero.	**Number of Players:** All, 2 goalies **Additional Equipment:** 40 pucks, 6 to 8 cones **Time:** 5 to 8 minutes

1. This is a variation of Full-Ice Two-on-Zero **03** that should be used when your players are skilled enough to complete passes with speed and agility. Place six to eight cones diagonally through the neutral zone to divide the ice in half. Split players into two lines at each end of the rink in two diagonally opposite corners. The lines closest to the boards each have twenty pucks. Place a goalie in each net. Position a coach near each goal line.

2. At each end of the ice, the first player in the line with the pucks begins skating and then passes a puck to the first player in the other line.

3. The passer cuts behind the receiver, who must immediately cross in front of the player who passed the puck, switching sides of the ice.

4. The receiver skates, stickhandles the puck, and returns a pass to the passer.

5. The receiver skates in front of the passer, switching sides of the ice again, and continues to follow or pass down the ice until both players reach the far blue line.

6. The players make one pass inside the blue line, take a shot on goal, drive to the net for a rebound, and then go to the end of the other line in the end zone where they finished.

7. As soon as the first groups of two players reach center ice, the next players should begin.

8. Halfway through the allotted time, switch ends of the ice.

The most difficult part of this drill involves the crossing movement. The player receiving the puck must immediately skate diagonally across the ice, and the passer must also remember to cut behind the player receiving the pass, which maintains the flow of the drill.

Blue Line Three-Pass Two-on-Zero

012 ●●→●●●

Purpose: To develop proficiency at skating, passing and receiving, and shooting in a two-player rush.

Number of Players: All, 2 goalies
Additional Equipment: 40 pucks
Time: 5 to 7 minutes

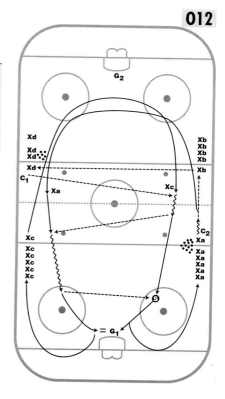

1. Split your players into four equal lines against the boards near each end of the blue lines. Players should face each other. Twenty pucks are positioned with two lines of players who are diagonally opposite. Station a coach with each of those lines.

2. Starting at one end, the first player in the line with the pucks, player Xa, passes a puck straight down the boards to a player at the opposite blue line, player Xb.

3. Player Xa follows his pass. At the same time, the first player in the line directly across the blue line from player Xa's line, player Xc, starts skating down the boards toward the opposite blue line.

4. Players Xa and Xc swing inside the far blue line, cross

paths with one another, and then turn back in the opposite direction, filling the wide lanes of the ice.

5. Player Xb immediately passes the puck directly across the blue line to player Xd.

6. Player Xd receives the pass and makes a return pass to either player Xa or Xc, who are heading back up ice.

7. Players Xa and Xc make a two-on-zero rush against the goaltender (G1) and then go to the end of the other line in the end zone where they finished.

8. Player Xd gets a new puck and begins the drill in the opposite direction by passing the puck down the boards to the new player Xc at the far blue line.

9. The new player Xc receives the pass and then passes the puck directly across the blue line to the new player Xa.

10. Players Xb and Xd at the opposite end skate toward the near blue line, turn inside it, switch lanes, and skate back in the opposite direction. They receive a pass from the new player Xa, go two-on-zero against the other goaltender (G2), and then go to the end of the other line in the end zone where they finished. The drill continues with a new player Xa.

CHAPTER 13

Defensive Drills

Regardless of their position, all players on your team must learn to play effective defense. These drills will help your players learn to transition quickly from offense to defense and backcheck either the puck carrier or an opponent. Some of the drills will also help your players to better understand their positioning whether for face-off alignment or playing in the defensive zone. They will learn their coverage area and which player they are responsible for covering. As I've often said, offense begins with good defense, and defense requires patience, timing, and hard work.

One-on-One out of the Corner D1

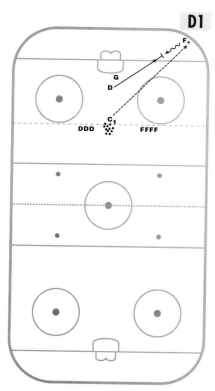

Purpose: To develop proficiency at defending against a forward who is attacking the goal.	**Number of Players:** All, 1 goalie **Additional Equipment:** 20 pucks **Time:** 8 to 10 minutes

1. Have all players, pucks, and a coach in the high slot area. Divide players into defensemen and forwards. Place the goalie in the net.

2. Position one defenseman in front of the net and one forward in a corner.

3. The coach passes the puck to the corner forward, who then attacks the net in an attempt to beat the defenseman and score.

4. The defenseman leaves the front of the net and skates to close the gap between herself and the forward. The defenseman attempts to stop the forward from scoring by gaining possession of the puck.

5. When either the forward scores, the defenseman gains

possession, or the coach stops the action with a whistle (after thirty seconds), each player goes to the end of their original line.

6. The next forward and defenseman move to their starting positions in the opposite corner, and the drill continues, with players switching corners each time.

It's important to teach your defensemen not to skate forward in a direct line to body-check or separate the forward from the puck. Quite often defensemen will get beat trying to check while skating forward at their opponent. The stick of the defensemen should always be on the ice while they try to anticipate and take away the most dangerous passing lane their opponent might have. They must always keep that forward between themselves and the goal, even if it means stopping in front of the opponent, retreating in a backward position, and playing the forward one-on-one back toward the front of the net. Through repetition, your defensemen will develop a good sense of the amount of time and space they're giving up. They'll also learn how to use their stick to block passes and attempted shots on goal.

This drill is performed using half-ice, so you can run the drill at both ends of the ice simultaneously.

D2

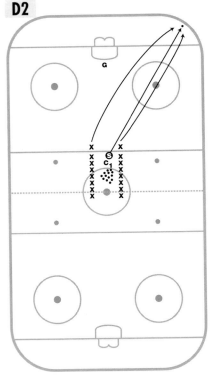

Combat One-on-One D2 ⬮

Purpose: To develop proficiency at battling for a loose puck and shifting between offense and defense.	**Number of Players:** All, 1 goalie **Additional Equipment:** 20 pucks **Time:** 8 to 10 minutes

1. Divide players into two equal lines and position them outside the blue line. Station a coach with the pucks between the two lines.

2. The coach dumps a puck into the corner. The first player in each line skates toward the puck, competing one-on-one to get possession of the puck and score a goal. Both players are considered offensive and defensive players. This gets players to recognize they must move quickly from an offensive to defensive posture to prevent a goal from being scored.

3. After twenty seconds, the coach blows his whistle and the two players sprint out of the end zone.

4. The coach then dumps another puck into the opposite corner and the next two players in line begin.

It's important to teach your players not to check in a straight line. During this drill, the best teaching technique is angle checking.

Variation: Turn this drill into a two-on-two by adding two more lines.

Three-on-Three Defensive Zone Coverage **D3** ●

Purpose: To develop proficiency at defending the goal by staying between the opponent and the goal in a three-on-three situation.	**Number of Players:** All, in groups of 6, 1 goalie **Additional Equipment:** 20 pucks **Time:** 10 minutes

1. Line up players and coaches at the top of the face-off circle. Place the goalie in the net.
2. Position three defensive players (two defensemen and a center) on their knees in front of the net (1). The three offensive players (the three forwards) can be anywhere on the ice inside the top of the end zone face-off circles.
3. When the coach passes a puck to one of the offensive forwards, the three defensive players move quickly to their feet toward the player they're about to cover. Remind your players that one defenseman should always be protecting the front of the net. The other defenseman should move to attack the puck carrier while the defensive center plays a supporting role by looking to move toward an open offensive forward (2).
4. As the offensive forwards move or pass the puck in an attempt to score, the three defensive players should play man on man and try to gain possession of the puck.
5. Continue for twenty to thirty seconds, then have the defensive players pass you the puck to end their turn, and put in a new group.

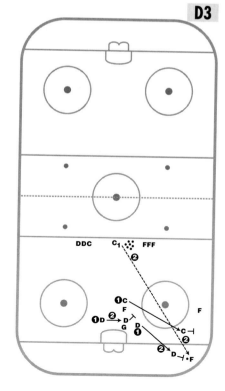

This drill is performed using half-ice, so you can run the drill at both ends of the ice simultaneously.

Instruct all players in a defensive posture to keep the player they're covering between themselves and the goal they're defending and never to move to the offensive side of the puck. It's a good idea to keep play below the top of the circles when playing a three-on-three because this is the area most frequently used by offensive forwards during a game. It's important to teach your players to keep their sticks on the ice when defending to cut down the passing lanes and block attempted shots.

One-Four Neutral Zone Face-Off D4 ●

Purpose: To practice a passive formation in a neutral zone face-off.
Number of Players: All, in groups of 5, 2 goalies

Additional Equipment: 20 pucks
Time: 8 to 10 minutes

D4

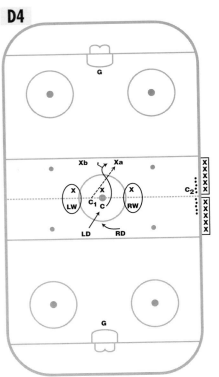

1. The first group of five has two wingers, two defensemen, and one center. They line up for a neutral zone face-off at center ice. The second group of five (the X players) lines up opposite them for a center-ice face-off. The rest of the players are on the bench. Place a goalie in each net. Station one coach with a puck at the center-ice face-off dot and one coach against the boards near the players' benches with the rest of the pucks.

2. The players receive a live puck from a controlled face-off drop. In the example shown in the diagram, the coach tosses the puck to player Xa.

3. The opposing players (the Xs) try to offensively move the puck up the ice while the defensive players move to their positions and try to recover the puck. The center tries to force a turnover by attacking player Xa from the middle of the ice, angling player Xa toward the boards. The center's stick should be in the passing lane to block any attempt by player Xa to pass to his defensive partner, player Xb.

4. At the same time, the wingers (LW, RW) each stay with and cover their opposing winger. The left defenseman (LD) moves forward to cover the opposing center and the right defenseman (RD) moves forward toward the middle of the ice to read and react to any opposing rush or missed assignment. (If the puck goes to player Xb at the face-off, the roles of LD and RD are reversed and the center angles toward player Xb.)

5. After one minute, the coach blows the whistle and the defensive players go to the benches. The X players become the new defensive players, and the new X players come off the bench and start with another neutral zone face-off.

6. Continue to rotate the players every minute.

Left-Wing Lock, Neutral Zone Face-Off D5 ●

Purpose: To practice assignments for a neutral zone face-off.
Number of Players: All, in groups of 5, 2 goalies

Additional Equipment: 20 pucks
Time: 8 to 10 minutes

1. The first group of five has two wingers, two defensemen, and one center. They line up for a neutral zone face-off at center ice. The second group of five (Xa, Xb, Xc, Xd, Xe) lines up opposite them for a center-ice face-off. The rest of the players are on the bench. Place a goalie in each net. Station one coach with a puck at the center-ice face-off dot and one coach against the boards near the players' benches with the rest of the pucks.

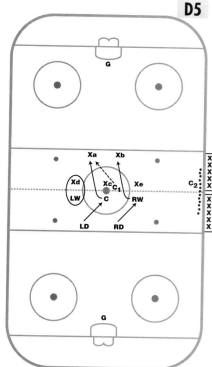

D5

2. The players receive a live puck from a controlled face-off drop. In the example shown in the diagram, the coach tosses the puck to player Xa.

3. The opposing players (the Xs) try to offensively move the puck up the ice while the defensive players move to their positions and try to recover the puck. The center immediately breaks through to try and recover the puck or force player Xa into a turnover.

4. At the same time, the right winger (RW) skates to cover player Xb to prevent him from receiving a pass from his defensive partner, player Xa. The left winger (LW) stays with and covers the opposing winger (player Xd) that he is lined up beside. The left defenseman (LD) moves forward to cover the opposing center (Xc) and the right defenseman (RD) moves forward to cover the other opposing winger (Xe). (If the puck goes to player Xb at the face-off, all players cover the same opponent, but RW will try to create the turnover instead of C because RW is covering Xb.)

5. After one minute, the coach blows the whistle and the defensive players go to the benches. The X players become the new defensive players, and the new X players come off the bench and start with another neutral zone face-off.

6. Continue to rotate the players every minute.

   This is a more aggressive formation than the previous drill, but it is still a sound defensive posture.

D6

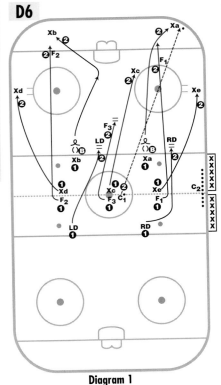

Diagram 1

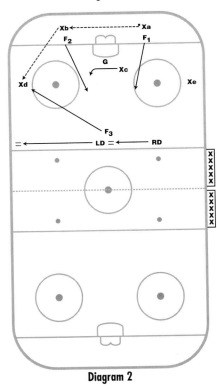

Diagram 2

Two-One-Two Forecheck D6

Purpose: To develop the ability to agressively forecheck an opponent.

Number of Players: All, in groups of 5, 1 goalie
Additional Equipment: 20 pucks
Time: 8 to 10 minutes

1. The first group of five has three forwards (F1, F2, F3) and two defensemen (LD, RD). They line up for a neutral zone face-off at center ice. The second group of five (Xa, Xb, Xc, Xd, Xe) lines up opposite them for a center-ice face-off (diagram 1, 1). The rest of the players are on the bench. Place the goalie in the net. Station one coach with a puck at the center-ice face-off dot and one coach against the boards near the players' benches with the rest of the pucks.

2. The players receive a live puck from a controlled face-off drop. In the example shown in the diagram, the coach dumps the puck into the opponent's corner and player Xa retrieves it (diagram 1, 2).

3. The opposing players (the Xs) move to their breakout positions and try to move the puck out of their zone. The defensive players begin forechecking to try and recover the puck. When player Xa retrieves the puck, player F1 immediately forechecks to try to recover the puck or force player Xa into a turnover (diagram 1, 2).

4. At the same time, the player F2 skates to cover player Xb to prevent him from receiving a pass from his defensive partner, player Xa. Player F3 skates to a position in the high slot, reading and reacting to any pass made by either defenseman (Xa or Xb) to breakout forwards Xc, Xd, or Xe. The forechecking group's defensemen (LD, RD) move up to the blue line to keep any errant pass in the zone (diagram 1, 2).

5. If Xa or Xb are able to complete a breakout pass to one of their forwards (Xc, Xd, or Xe), player F3 should pressure the puck carrier immediately, and F1 and F2 should skate back through the middle of the ice to begin backchecking (diagram 2).

6. After one minute or if the X players break the puck out of their zone, the coach blows the whistle and the forechecking players go to the benches. The X players become the new forecheckers, and the new X players come off the bench.

7. Continue to rotate the players every minute.

This is a more aggressive formation than the next drill. You can use this drill in a full-ice situation where you change ends every time the coach dumps the puck in, or you can use half-ice.

Variation: Use this as a controlled scrimmage where, if the forecheck is improperly executed, you blow your whistle to instruct proper angles and positioning.

One-Two-Two Forecheck D7 ● → ●●

Purpose: To develop the ability to forecheck an opponent to force a turnover.	**Number of Players:** All, in groups of 5, 1 goalie **Additional Equipment:** 20 pucks **Time:** 8 to 10 minutes

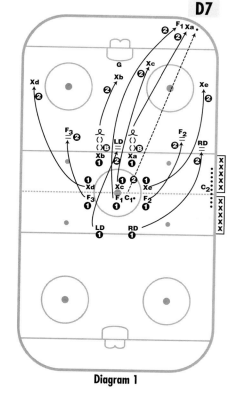

D7

Diagram 1

1. The first group of five has three forwards (F1, F2, F3) and two defensemen (LD, RD). They line up for a neutral zone face-off at center ice. The second group of five (Xa, Xb, Xc, Xd, Xe) lines up opposite them for a center-ice face-off (diagram 1, 1). The rest of the players are on the bench. Place the goalie in the net. Station one coach with a puck at the center-ice face-off dot and one coach against the boards near the players' benches with the rest of the pucks.

2. The players receive a live puck from a controlled face-off drop. In the example shown in the diagram, the coach dumps the puck into the opponent's corner and player Xa retrieves it (diagram 1, 2).

3. The opposing players (the Xs) move to their breakout positions and try to move the puck out of their zone. The defensive players begin forechecking to try and recover the puck. When player Xa retrieves the puck, player F1 immediately forechecks by skating on an angle from the middle of the ice toward player Xa to force player Xa to make a pass around the boards (diagram 1, 2). *Note:* If F1 can't pressure quickly enough, he should remain in the slot area and attack player Xa as Xa attempts to skate out from behind the net with the puck (diagram 3).

4. At the same time, player F2 skates to the puck side near the top of the circle and waits to react to any pass by player Xa to player Xd or Xc. Player F3 skates to a position at the top of the circle away from the puck

D7

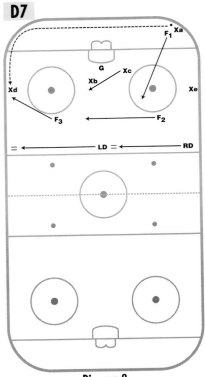

Diagram 2

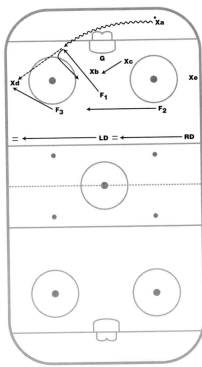

Diagram 3

and waits to react to any pass by player Xa to player Xd or Xc only if Xc has moved to player F3's side of the ice. The forechecking group's defensemen (LD, RD) move up to the blue line to keep any errant pass in the zone (diagram 1, 2).

5. If Xa or Xb are able to complete a breakout pass to one of their forwards (Xc, Xd, or Xe), player F2 or F3 (depending on which side of the ice the puck is passed to) should pressure the puck carrier immediately, and F1 should skate toward the blue line to begin backchecking. The nonpressuring forward (F2 or F3) should also begin backchecking toward the middle of the ice (diagram 2).

6. After one minute or if the X players break the puck out of their zone, the coach blows the whistle and the forechecking players go to the benches. The X players become the new forecheckers, and the new X players come off the bench.

7. Continue to rotate the players every minute.

You can use this drill in a full-ice situation where you change ends every time the coach dumps the puck in, or use half-ice.

Variation: Use this as a controlled scrimmage where, if the forecheck is improperly executed, you blow your whistle to instruct proper angles and positioning.

Defensive Zone Face-Off D8 ●●

Purpose: To practice face-offs in the defensive zone.	**Additional Equipment:** 12 pucks
Number of Players: 2 groups of 5, 1 goalie	**Time:** 8 to 10 minutes

1. The first group of five has two wingers, two defensemen, and one center. They line up for a defensive zone face-off in one of the end zone circles. The second group of five (Xa, Xb, Xc, Xd, Xe) lines up opposite them in an offensive formation. Place the goalie in the net. Station one coach with a puck at the defensive zone face-off dot with an extra puck in his pocket. The rest of the pucks are in the net. The rest of the players should be in the neutral zone with a coach and about

ten pucks working on a skating, passing, or stickhandling drill.

2. The players receive a live puck from a controlled face-off drop. In the left-hand example shown in the diagram, the coach starts the drill from the left-side face-off dot by tossing the puck to player Xa. This means the defensive team loses the face-off.

3. The opposing players (the Xs) try to offensively move the puck to score a goal while the defensive players move to their positions to cover their opponents and try to recover the puck. The center immediately stays with and covers the opponent's center, player Xc. The board-side defenseman (LD) lines up on the board-side hash marks and covers the opponent's right wing, player Xe, and the net-side defenseman (RD) lines up on the net-side hash marks and covers the opponent's left wing, player Xd. The left winger (LW) lines up on the edge of the face-off circle just off the right defenseman's (RD) shoulder. His assignment is to skate diagonally through the face-off circle and cover the opponent's right defenseman, player Xa. The right winger (RW) lines up in between the hash marks in front of the net to skate straight out to and cover the opponent's left defenseman, player Xb.

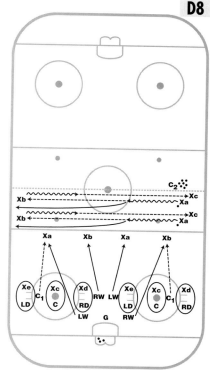

D8

4. In the right-hand example shown in the diagram, the coach starts the drill from the right-side face-off dot by tossing the puck to player Xb. The center immediately stays with and covers the opponent's center, player Xc. The board-side defenseman (RD) lines up on the board-side hash marks and covers the opponent's left wing, player Xd, and the net-side defenseman (LD) lines up on the net-side hash marks and covers the opponent's right wing, player Xe. The right winger (RW) lines up on the edge of the face-off circle just off the left defenseman's (LD) shoulder. His assignment is to skate diagonally through the face-off circle and cover the opponent's left defenseman, player Xb. The left winger (LW) lines up in between the hash marks in front of the net to skate straight out to and cover the opponent's right defenseman, player Xa.

5. After thirty seconds, or if the X players clear the puck out of their zone, the coach blows the whistle and the defensive players go to the neutral zone. The X players become the new defensive players, and the new X players come from the neutral zone group.

6. Continue to rotate the players every thirty seconds.

The diagram shows left- and right-side face-offs, but in a real practice you should only have one face-off at a time. This teaching drill will find kids standing around a bit, so it's important to utilize other areas of the ice with idle players. Players not involved in this drill should be working on skating, passing, or shooting drills with a coach in the neutral zone.

Before every defensive zone face-off the defensive team should assume they are going to lose the draw. During a practice or game when the defensive team wins a defensive zone face-off, all defensive players should move to their breakout positions.

I teach the above defensive zone face-off alignment because in the defensive zone coverage system I use, the defensive defensemen are responsible for covering two of the opposing forwards, and the defensive center always helps out in front of the net, in the corners as support, or covering the third opposing forward. The defensive left and right wingers are responsible for covering the opposing team's defensemen.

I don't suggest teaching this defensive zone face-off alignment to very young players because they'll have a difficult time remembering where they're supposed to line up.

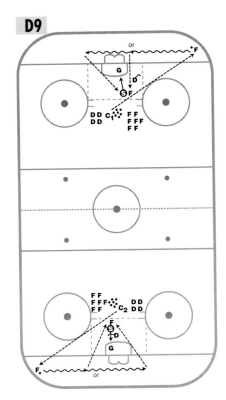

Two-on-One in Tight D9 ●●

Purpose: To develop proficiency at defending against a two-on-one close into the net.

Number of Players: All, in groups of 3, 1 goalie
Additional Equipment: 20 pucks
Time: 10 minutes

1. Divide players into forwards and defenders in the high slot area. Station a coach there too, with the pucks. Place the goalie in the net.
2. One forward begins in one corner; a second forward starts in front of the net, remaining between the hash marks of the face-off circle and the goal line. Also, position one defenseman in front of the net.
3. The coach passes a puck to the forward in the corner. On the whistle, that forward attacks along the goal line toward the net and then has the option of passing the puck to a teammate in front of the net or skating behind the net and attempting to pass to the same forward from there.
4. The two-on-one continues until either a goal is scored, the goalie recovers the puck, or the defenseman breaks up the

play by clearing the puck away from the front of the net. The players then return to the high slot area and the next group begins.

The responsibility of the defenseman in front of the net is to play in between both forwards, keeping his stick in the passing lane to prevent the front-of-the-net forward from taking a shot on goal. The defenseman must also react to the most dangerous player if the puck-carrying forward instead decides to skate to the front of the net to shoot on goal.

This drill is performed using half-ice, so you can run the drill at both ends of the ice simultaneously. It's a difficult drill, but it's excellent for teaching defensemen to recognize the most dangerous player. Defensemen should work with the goaltender to, at worst, give up the least dangerous scoring chance.

CHAPTER 14

Game Situation Drills

These drills are used to re-create actual situations that occur during a game. Some are used with smaller groups of players to zero in on a specific game situation. You will also find that some of the drills teach players what to do when they find themselves in outnumbered situations while others combine offensive and defensive skills. All of them help kids learn to read and react to the ever-changing circumstances of a game.

Full-Ice Two-on-One GS1

GS1

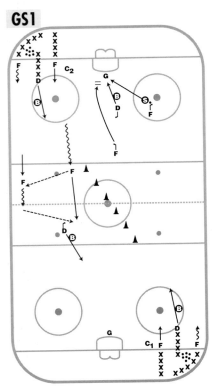

Purpose: To simulate a game setting involving a two-on-one rush.	**Additional Equipment:** 40 pucks, 6 to 8 cones
	Time: 8 to 10 minutes
Number of Players: All, in groups of 3, 2 goalies	

1. Place six to eight cones so they divide the ice diagonally in half through the neutral zone. Split players into three lines (two lines of forwards, one line of defensemen) at each end of the rink in two diagonally opposite corners. The lines closest to the boards each have twenty pucks. Place a goalie in each net. Station a coach in each end zone.

2. On the whistle, the first defenseman in each line skates backward toward the opposite end of the ice. As each reaches the top of the near end zone circle, the first forwards in each line begin skating to create a two-on-one rush. (The forward from the line closest to the boards has a puck.)

3. The forwards attempt to pass a puck back and forth while skating the length of the ice. The defenseman stays in

between them with his stick on the ice in front of him trying to intercept the pass and stop the rush.

4. As the forwards cross the far blue lines, they should make one attempt to score a goal. One forward shoots on goal, and the other forward drives to the net for a rebound. After their shot, or when the defenseman stops the rush, the three players in each group skate to the back of any line in the end where they finished.

5. As each group crosses the centerline, the next two groups begin the drill.

6. Halfway through the allotted time, move the pucks and players to the opposite end zone corners, and move the cones to the opposite diagonal.

This is a progression from the offensive drill Full-Ice Two-on-Zero **03** .

Variation: If your players are becoming accomplished passers, the beginning forwards can have the option to pass the puck to the backward-skating defenseman, who then returns the pass to begin the two-on-one drill up the ice.

Full Circle One-on-One GS2 ●

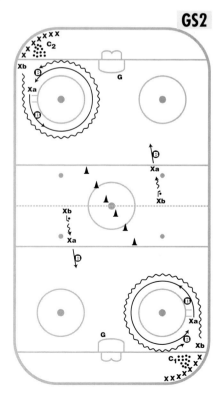

GS2

Purpose: To simulate a game setting involving a one-on-one rush.	**Additional Equipment:** 40 pucks, 6 to 8 cones
Number of Players: All, in pairs, 2 goalies	**Time:** 8 to 10 minutes

1. Place six to eight cones so they divide the ice diagonally in half through the neutral zone. Split your players into two equal lines at each end of the rink in two diagonally opposite corners. Each line has twenty pucks. Place a goalie in each net. Station two coaches at center ice. Station a coach with each line.

2. The first player in each line, player Xa, starts on the hash mark and acts as the defenseman. The second player in each line, player Xb, begins on the goal line with a puck and acts as the forward.

3. On your whistle, each player Xa skates backward crossunders completely around the end zone circle and then retreats backward straight down the boards toward center ice. At the same time, each player Xb stickhandles a puck and skates forward crossovers completely around the same circle while attacking the defenseman (player Xa) one-on-one up the ice.

4. The one-on-one continues until each player Xb takes a

GAME SITUATION DRILLS

shot on goal or each player Xa recovers the puck. Then each pair goes to the back of the line in the end zone where they finished. Players should alternate positions.

5. When the pairs reach center ice, or on the coach's whistle, the next pairs of skaters begin.

6. Halfway through the allotted time, move the pucks and players to the opposite corners, and move the cones to the opposite diagonal.

One-on-One Battle GS3 ●

Purpose: To improve conditioning and one-on-one play through skating and controlling the puck.
Number of Players: All, in pairs, 1 goalie

Additional Equipment: 30 to 40 pucks, 2 cones
Time: 8 to 10 minutes

GS3

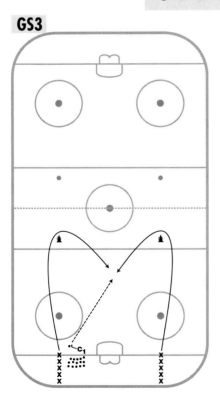

1. Place a cone on each of the face-off dots just outside the blue line. Split your players into two equal lines about 20 feet on either side of the net. The skates of the first player in each line should be touching the goal line. Place the goalie in the net. Station a coach with the pucks about 10 feet to one side of the net.

2. On the whistle, the first player in each line races to the nearest cone, does a tight glide turn around the cone, and then skates back toward the net.

3. As the players approach the net, the coach passes a puck toward the slot area. Both players compete for the puck and attempt to score. If the puck slides by the players, they should recover it and then continue to battle for the offensive scoring chance.

4. As soon as the first two players approach the puck, the coach should blow his whistle to start the next pair.

5. After one scoring attempt, the players in the first pair should go the end of the opposite line so they will perform turns around the cones in both directions.

This drill is performed using half-ice, so you can run the drill at both ends of the ice simultaneously. This is a good conditioning drill that can also be used as a competition drill at the end of practice. In some instances, it helps to match players of equal ability levels so players competing for the puck don't become discouraged.

Cross-Ice Three-on-Three GS4 ●

Purpose: To simulate a game setting playing three-on-three across the ice in the end zone.
Number of Players: All, in groups of 3, 2 to 4 goalies

Additional Equipment: 10 pucks, 2 nets at each end (optional)
Time: 10 minutes

1. Place two nets across the ice from each other in the end zone, 6 to 8 feet from the boards as shown. Divide players into groups of three (two forwards and one defenseman) outside the blue line. All three players work together offensively to score and defensively to stop their opponents. Place a goalie in each net. Station a coach outside the blue line with the pucks. On the diagram, one group is shown as Xs and the other as Os. The coach chooses which net each group attacks.
2. The coach shoots a puck into the end zone, and the first X and O groups race after the puck to try and gain possession.
3. They contine to play three-on-three for thirty to forty-five seconds. If one group scores before time is up, the goalie puts the puck back in play. When time is up, the coach blows his whistle, and the player with the puck passes it to the coach. The players in the end zone sprint out to the blue line, the coach passes a puck into the end zone, and the next two groups race after the puck.

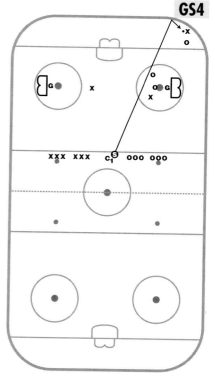

If you have use of the whole rink and enough nets (four) and goalies (four), you can run this drill in both end zones. Most arenas have extra nets, so ask rink personnel beforehand if some are available.

If only one goalie is available, try one of the following options. Some rinks also have a device that covers the goal net but has five cutouts for targets, which could be used in place of a missing goaltender. Or, place cones in the corners of one net and instruct players to shoot for the cones, or count hitting the post as a goal. You can also place the net on its side, with the crossbar touching the ice; here, players score only if their shots hit the lower part of the exposed netting, not the piping.

Although this drill is great for all ages, it is particularly useful for players ten and under who are playing under USA Hockey's Cross-Ice Program. In this program, the ice is cut into three sections using 2-foot-high foam dividers on the blue lines. Sixty to ninety children can be on one rink at one time playing ninety-second shifts. The emphasis with young hockey players

GAME SITUATION DRILLS

should be on skill development; thus, with a smaller ice surface, kids actually get more playing time. There's no scoring record kept, and it's recommended that each child play every position.

Mad Dog One-on-One GS5 ●

Purpose: To simulate a game setting involving a defenseman making a breakout pass to a forward, then involving them in a one-on-one situation.

Number of Players: All, 1 goalie
Additional Equipment: 20 pucks, 2 cones
Time: 8 to 10 minutes

GS5

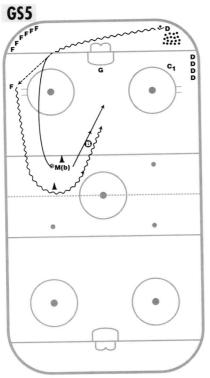

1. Split the players into two lines (one of forwards and one of defensemen) in opposite corners of one end zone. The forwards face up the ice and the defensemen face the net. The line of defensemen has the pucks. Position two cones outside the blue line as shown. Place the goalie in the net. Station a coach near the line of defensemen.

2. On the whistle, the first defenseman skates with a puck behind the goal and then passes to the first forward, who is standing at the breakout position against the boards.

3. After passing the puck, the defenseman skates forward to the near cone (just outside the blue line), executes a Mohawk turn to backward, and prepares to defend a one-on-one rush by the forward against the goalie.

4. The forward receives the pass from the defenseman, skates down the boards directly outside the blue line, goes around the far cone, and then skates back toward the goal in a one-on-one rush against the defenseman to try and score.

5. After one scoring attempt or when the defenseman stops the forward, both players go to the end of the opposite line.

6. Signal the next two players to begin as soon as the first two players approach the cones near the blue line.

7. Halfway through the allotted time, move the pucks to the opposite corner, switch the lines of players, and move the cones to the other side of the ice.

This drill can be done on half-ice or at both ends of the rink simultaneously.

Mad Dog Two-on-One GS6 ●●

Purpose: To simulate a game setting involving a breakout pass and a two-on-one.

Number of Players: All, 1 goalie
Additional Equipment: 20 pucks
Time: 8 to 10 minutes

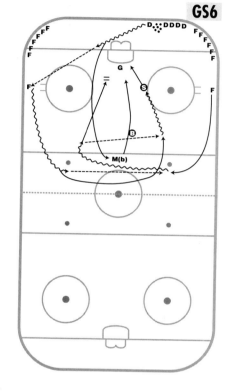

GS6

1. Split players into two equal lines of forwards and one line of defensemen. Line up the forwards in opposite corners of one end zone facing up the ice. One forward is stationed near each side board at the hash marks. Defensemen are situated against the boards about 20 feet from the net with the pucks. Place the goalie in the net.
2. The first defenseman skates out from behind the net with a puck and passes it to one of the first two forwards.
3. After passing to the forward, the defenseman keeps the gap close by skating forward to the near blue line and then executing a backward Mohawk turn to face the two-on-one rush back toward the goal.
4. Both forwards skate toward the outside of the blue line, at which point the forward with the puck passes it directly across ice to the other forward. The forwards then switch sides of the ice and attack two-on-one against the defenseman to try and score. The defenseman stays between the forwards with his stick on the ice in front of him to try and intercept the pass and stop the rush.
5. As the players approach the net, the coach blows his whistle to signal the next three players to begin.
6. After one scoring attempt, or when the defensman stops the forwards, the three players skate to the back of any line.

  This drill can be done on half-ice or at both ends of the rink simultaneously.

Blue Line Two-on-One GS7 ●●

Purpose: To simulate a game setting involving a two-on-one.
Number of Players: All, 2 goalies

Additional Equipment: 40 pucks
Time: 8 to 10 minutes

1. Split your forwards into four equal lines and have them stand against the boards at each blue line. The pucks are positioned with two lines that are diagonally opposite. Defensemen are at center ice against the boards on one side. Place a goalie in each net. Station one coach with the

GS7

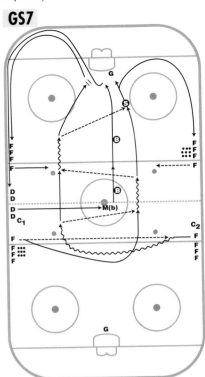

defensmen and one coach on the opposite side of the ice in the neutral zone.

2. The drill starts at one end of the ice with the forward on the puck side quickly passing a puck directly along the blue line to the first forward in the other line.

3. These two players skate toward each other, then cross and switch sides as they head toward the opposite goal and try to score.

4. As these players begin skating and passing down the ice, one defenseman skates into the center-ice face-off circle and does a backward Mohawk turn to defend against the two-on-one rush down the ice. He should stay in between the two forwards with his stick on the ice in front of him to try and intercept the pass and stop the rush.

5. When these three players move across the far blue line near the goal, the next two forwards start out from the opposite end, skating the same pattern in the opposite direction against a new defenseman.

6. After one scoring chance or when the defenseman stops the rush, the two forwards go to the end of the opposite line of forwards in the end zone where they finished. The defenseman skates to the end of the defenseman's line.

GS8

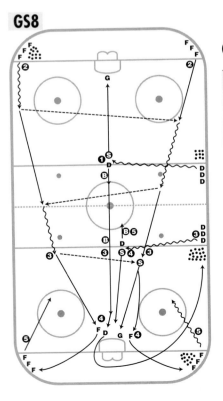

Continuous Two-on-One GS8

Purpose: To simulate a game setting involving a continuous two-on-one rush with a second scoring chance added from a point shot.

Number of Players: All, 2 goalies
Additional Equipment: 50 pucks
Time: 10 minutes

1. Divide the forwards into four equal lines in the four corners of the ice facing up the ice. Two lines that are diagonally opposite have about ten pucks each. All the defenseman are on the same side of the ice, divided so that half of them line up outside each blue line facing the near end zone. Each line has about fifteen pucks. Place a goalie in each net.

2. Begin the drill at one end of the ice with the first defenseman in line skating with a puck along the blue line, taking a shot on goal from the middle of the ice, and then retreating while skating backward toward the opposite end (1).

3. Just after the defenseman takes his shot, the first forward in the line with the pucks from the same end of the ice starts stickhandling with a puck while skating toward the opposite end. At the same time, the forward from the line without pucks starts skating. The two forwards pass the puck back and forth forming a two-on-one rush against the defenseman up the full length of the ice (2). The defenseman should stay in between the two forwards with his stick on the ice in front of him to try and intercept the pass and stop the rush. As the forwards enter the defensive zone, they should take a shot on goal.

4. As the three players cross the offensive blue line, the first defenseman from that end of the ice skates with a puck to the middle of the ice and waits (3).

5. As the players on the rush complete their first scoring chance, or if the original defenseman stops the rush, the coach's whistle signals a second chance on goal. With all three players in front of the net, the new defenseman takes a low point shot with the new puck while the original defenseman plays the second two-on-one in front. The original defenseman should use a stick lift to try and eliminate one of the forwards in his group (4).

6. The original forwards try to score on the rebound of the new defenseman's shot or tip the puck into the net. After this scoring chance the forwards skate to the end of the opposite line in the end where they finished. The original defenseman skates to the end of the defenseman's line at the closest blue line.

7. Meanwhile, after the new defenseman's point shot, he begins to retreat, skating backward. Immediately, the first forward in each line where the rush finished now begin skating and passing the puck back and forth, forming a two-on-one rush in the opposite direction (5), and the drill continues.

Instruct your players to move continuously back and forth up the ice, with the forwards working on passing, shooting, driving to the net, and stopping in front for rebounds. Remind all players that they should remain in front of the net after the initial rush to compete for the second scoring chance.

Keep in mind that this drill is not recommended for younger players who have not yet mastered a hard shot from the blue line.

GAME SITUATION DRILLS

Two-on-Two Continuous GS9 ●●

Purpose: To simulate a game setting involving a continuous two-on-two.
Number of Players: All, 2 goalies

Additional Equipment: 20 pucks
Time: 10 minutes

GS9

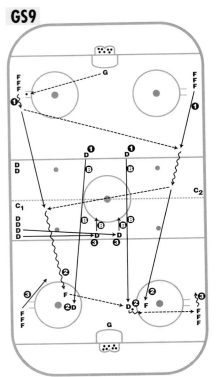

1. Divide the forwards into four equal lines near the side board hash marks at both ends of the ice. The defensemen are split into two lines at each blue line in the neutral zone. Place a goalie and half the pucks in each net. Station a coach on each end of the centerline.

2. Two defensemen take an offensive stance on one blue line. The first forward in each line at that end begins the drill (1). Using one puck (received from the goalie), the two forwards start skating in a two-on-two rush up the ice, trying to score on the goalie at the far end of the rink.

3. As the rush develops, the two defensemen attempt to break up the two-on-two. If they gain possession of the puck, they immediately pass to one of the new forwards in their defensive end (2). If a goal is scored, one of the defensemen or the goalie digs a puck out of the net and passes it to one of the new forwards.

4. The two new forwards then quickly rush up ice two-on-two in the opposite direction against two new defensemen, who—as the original rush passed by them—moved to their positions on the near blue line (3). These new defensemen retreat skating backward, defending the two-on-two rush and attempting to stop the new forwards by gaining possession of the puck.

5. Whether or not a goal is scored, a defenseman or goalie can make the breakout pass to the next forwards to continue the two-on-two drill moving in the opposite direction. Each time this occurs, the forwards who have just completed the rush go to the end of the opposite line in the end where they finished. The two defensemen go to the end of the opposite line of defensemen.

Canadian Olympic One-on-One GS10 ●●

Purpose: To simulate a game setting in which players improve their skating speed and their reaction time.

Number of Players: All, 2 goalies
Additional Equipment: 40 pucks
Time: 5 to 10 minutes

1. Begin with an equal number of forwards in each corner at one end of the ice. Each group has twenty pucks. One defenseman is positioned on one of the end zone hash marks toward the middle of the ice; all other defensemen are lined up in front of the goal. Place a goalie in each net. Station a coach near the goal line where the drill begins.
2. The forwards must start with their skates behind the goal line. The defenseman must start with at least one skate touching the hash marks. On the whistle, the first forward on the side of the ice where the defenseman is lined up skates with the puck from the goal line directly up the ice, remaining close to the boards. At the same time, the defenseman retreats, skating backward as quickly as possible.
3. The forward and defenseman skate one-on-one the full length of the ice with the forward attempting a shot on goal and the defenseman trying to stop him.
4. When the first group crosses the centerline, the coach whistles to start the forward in the opposite corner and a new defenseman, who has lined up on the opposite side hash marks.
5. The forwards should stay at the far end of the ice as they complete the drill, but the defensemen should return to the starting end until all the forwards have completed the drill.
6. Repeat the drill in the opposite direction to face the other goalie.

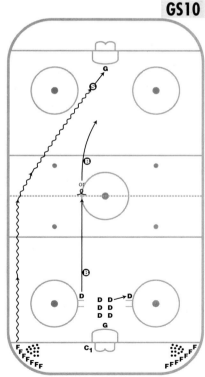

GS10

Encourage all players to skate at full speed. This drill will improve the quickness of forwards and defensemen. Instruct the defensemen that even if the forward skates past them along the boards and is moving on a breakaway, they shouldn't turn to skate forward and chase the forward until they reach center ice.

Variation: If you have a large number of players on the ice or two teams practicing simultaneously, push both nets to the opposite end of the ice so two groups can execute the drill at the same time. Locate the nets on the goal line, in line with the face-off dots at the opposite end of the ice. Also, place six to eight cones along the midline of the ice between the two blue lines, essentially splitting the ice in half. Both sides of the ice now work the drill at the same time. It's important to instruct all players to return to the starting point by skating directly up the middle of the ice, remaining close to the cones, to avoid any unexpected collisions.

GS11

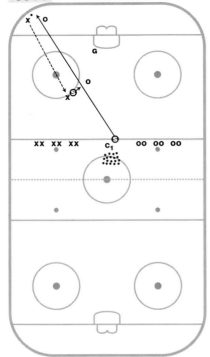

One-Pass Two-on-Two GS11 ●●

Purpose: To simulate a game setting involving transitions between offense and defense in a two-on-two.

Number of Players: All, in pairs, 1 goalie
Additional Equipment: 15 pucks
Time: 10 minutes

1. Divide players into pairs and position them outside the blue line. The players will work together offensively to score and defensively to stop the opponent regardless of their position on the team. On the diagram, the pairs are shown as Xs and Os. Place a goalie in the net. Station a coach outside the blue line with about fifteen pucks and the noninvolved players, who will work to keep the puck in play inside the end zone.

2. When the coach shoots a puck into the zone, one pair of Xs and Os races into the end zone to try and gain possession of the puck. One player from each pair should attempt to retrieve the loose puck while the other player tries to get open for a pass from his teammate.

3. The player who gains possession of the puck becomes an offensive player and must now make at least one pass to his teammate before they can attempt to score. The other pair is now the defensive team, and should try to stop them.

4. If a player on the defensive team steals the puck, that team becomes the offensive team, and the offensive team becomes the defensive team. The same passing rules in step 3 apply to the new offensive team.

5. The drill ends for these pairs when a goal is scored or, in the face of strong defensive play, after a certain period of time. A good rule of thumb is to keep the two-on-two play to approximately twenty seconds to minimize the time your players are uninvolved.

Variation: Have a coach stand stationary inside the blue line, acting as the third player on each team. If a turnover occurs, the player may pass the puck to the coach, who makes a return pass to the same player or his teammate to attempt a shot on goal.

Four-Player Breakout One-on-Zero, Two-on-One **GS12** ●●

Purpose: To simulate a game setting involving passing and receiving, stickhandling, and shooting in a one-on-zero and a two-on-one.

Number of Players: All, in groups of 4, 1 goalie
Additional Equipment: 20 pucks
Time: 10 minutes

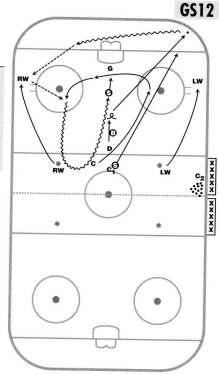

Diagram 1

1. Divide players into groups of four: two wingers, one defenseman, and one center. Only one group is on the ice at a time. The rest of the players are on the benches. Place the pucks near the boards close to the players' benches. Place the goalie in the net. Station one coach at center ice and one at the benches.

2. The defenseman in the first group should take a waiting position in the middle of the ice at the defensive zone blue line. The three forwards (RW, LW, C) should be ready and waiting, filling the three lanes just outside the blue line (diagram 1 shows steps 2 through 7).

3. The drill begins when the coach at center ice shoots a puck into the corner. The defenseman (D) skates backward, pivoting toward the puck.

4. The left and right wingers (LW, RW) skate to their breakout positions in the end zone against the boards, near the hash marks.

5. The center (C) skates as support for the defenseman, always in position to receive a pass.

6. The defenseman retrieves the puck, skates behind the net, and passes to the winger (LW or RW) in breakout position on the boards. As the defenseman goes behind the net, the center mirrors the defenseman, staying within 15 to 20 feet of the defenseman but skating in front of the net.

7. The winger who received the puck passes it to the center and then remains on the hash marks. The center skates over the blue line with the puck and then turns back toward the goal, skating one-on-zero on the goalie, and tries to score a goal. The center's part in the drill has now finished and he skates out of the end zone to the players' benches.

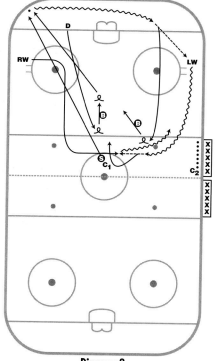

Diagram 2

8. The defenseman now moves back up to the blue line while the coach at center ice dumps a second puck into the opposite corner (diagram 2 shows steps 8 through 10).

9. Again, the defenseman skates backward, pivots toward that corner, retrieves the puck, and skates toward the back of the net, passing to the winger who is at the hash marks on the opposite side of the ice.

10. The defenseman then begins to move up toward the blue line. At the same time, both the left and right wingers skate over the blue line, crossing and passing the puck in the neutral zone before returning in a two-on-one rush against the same defenseman in an attempt to score. After the scoring attempt, or when the defenseman stops the rush, all three players sprint out of the end zone to the players' benches.

11. When this action is complete, the coach at the players' benches whistles for the next group to hustle onto the ice. Each group should perform the drill three times. The coach at the benches should make sure that a different forward takes the center's position on their second and third turns.

Two-Pass Three-on-Three GS13

GS13

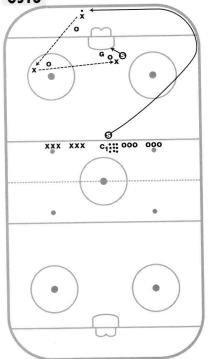

Purpose: To simulate a game setting involving passing and receiving in a three-on-three.

Number of Players: All, in groups of 3, 1 goalie
Additional Equipment: 15 pucks
Time: 10 minutes

1. Divide players into groups of three and position them outside the blue line. The groups will work together offensively to score and defensively to stop the opponent regardless of their position on the team. On the diagram, the groups are shown as Xs and Os. Place a goalie in the net. Station a coach outside the blue line with about fifteen pucks and the noninvolved players, who will work to keep the puck in play inside the end zone.

2. When the coach shoots a puck into the zone, one group of Xs and one group of Os race into the end zone to try and gain possession of the puck. One player from each group attempts to retrieve the loose puck. The other players from each group attempt to get open for a pass from their teammate.

3. The player who gains possession of the puck becomes an offensive player and his team must now make at least two passes among teammates before they can attempt to score.

The other group is now the defensive team, and should try to stop them.

4. If a player on the defensive team steals the puck, that team becomes the offensive team, and the offensive team becomes the defensive team. The same passing rules in step 3 apply to the new offensive team.

5. The drill ends for these groups when a goal is scored or, in the face of strong defensive play, after a certain period of time. A good rule of thumb is to keep the three-on-three play to approximately thirty seconds to minimize the time your players are uninvolved.

Variation: Sometimes groups of younger or less-skilled players will find it hard to complete two passes without losing possession of the puck. If this is the case, then allow the groups to try to score after completing only one pass. I only use this option if the goalie is not receiving any action or the players are becoming discouraged because they can't complete two passes. Often, though, encouraging them to complete two passes will force your players to move toward open ice, getting ready for a pass from a teammate instead of just watching the puck.

All in One GS14

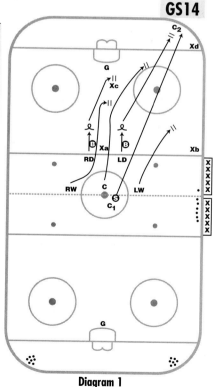

GS14

Diagram 1

Purpose: To simulate a game setting involving defensive zone coverage, breakouts, forechecking, offensive zone plays, and a three-on-two return.

Number of Players: All, in groups of 5, 2 goalies
Additional Equipment: 25 to 30 pucks
Time: 10 minutes

1. Each group is made up of two wingers (RW, LW), two defensemen (RD, LD), and one center (C). Only one group is on the ice at a time. The players start in their center-ice face-off positions. The remaining players are on the bench. Place a goalie in each net. Station one coach (C1) at the center-ice face-off dot with one puck and one (C2) in one corner. Place about fifteen pucks against the boards at center ice and five to ten pucks in each corner at the opposite end of the ice.

2. The coach at center ice (C1) starts the drill by passing a puck to the coach in the corner (C2), who is acting as an opposing forward (the other opposing players are imaginary; on the diagram, they are represented by Xs). The players at center ice move to their defensive coverage positions and stop. The nearest defenseman (LD) stops in front of the coach/forward (diagram 1 shows steps 2 through 6.)

GS14

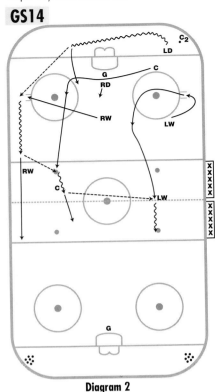

Diagram 2

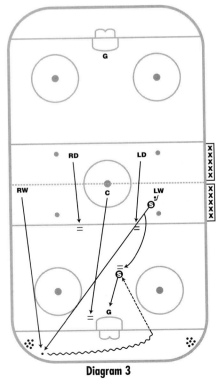

Diagram 3

3. The other defenseman (RD) skates to protect the front of the net and covers one of the imaginary opposing forwards (Xc).

4. The winger farthest from the puck (weak-side winger, RW) skates into the high slot and must face in a direction that allows her to see the imaginary opposing defenseman (Xa) at the blue line and to keep an eye on the puck. Her job is to cover this imaginary defenseman in the middle of the ice near the blue line and to help prevent a goal being scored if there is a breakdown in coverage in front of the net.

5. The winger on the near side of the puck (strong-side winger, LW) covers the other imaginary opposing defenseman (Xb) stationed at the blue line. Her job is to watch both the puck in the corner and the imaginary defenseman. The winger can do this by facing the boards and keeping the imaginary defenseman toward those boards.

6. The center (C) moves to a position to support the defenseman (LD) who is pressuring the puck carrier in the corner and must also keep the last imaginary opposing forward (Xd) between herself and the net. Both coaches should make sure that all players stop in their coverage positions, and should show any players who are out of position where they should stand.

7. On the whistle, players then move to their breakout position, with wingers moving to the boards on either side of the ice to the hash marks (diagram 2 shows steps 7 through 11).

8. One defenseman (LD) retrieves the puck from the coach/forward (C2), skates behind the net, and makes the breakout pass to the winger (RW).

9. The center (C) supports and mirrors the defenseman (LD) by staying within 15 or 20 feet of him but skating in front of the net; the center always remains in position to receive a pass.

10. The weak-side winger (LW) should come across the middle to support the center (C) and the winger receiving the puck (RW). She also protects the front of the net in case of a turnover.

11. At this time, the three forwards (LW, C, RW) skate the length of the ice, with the defensemen (LD, RD) supporting the attack.

12. As the forwards cross center ice, the forward with the puck (LW) dumps it across the ice into the opposite corner.

This signals to the winger on that side (RW) to retrieve the puck (diagram 3 shows steps 12 through 15).

13. Both defensemen (LD, RD) stop at the offensive blue line.

14. The center (C) drives to the net, stopping on the puck side while the winger who dumped in the puck (LW) stops in the high slot area.

15. The puck-retrieving winger (RW) skates with the puck behind the net and passes to either the winger in the slot (LW) or the center (C), who has driven to the net on the opposite side of the ice to set up a scoring chance.

16. For the next part of the drill, one of the forwards (C) retrieves a new puck from the corner and passes it back to the two defensemen (LD, RD), who supported the attack and stopped at the offensive blue line. The defenseman who receives the puck (RD) passes it to the other defenseman (LD), who takes a shot on goal. The forwards (LW, C, RW) are alert to tipping in the point shot or attacking the goal for a quick rebound shot. One forward (RW) tries to screen the goalie's view of the puck when a shot is taken from the point, while the other forward (LW) remains in the slot area (diagram 4).

17. On the coach's signal, one of the three forwards (RW) retrieves another new puck, and all three forwards (LW, C, RW) begin a three-on-two attack in the opposite direction against the same two defensemen (LD, RD). The forwards attempt to score on the three-on-two rush, creating an offensive zone play and driving to the net (diagram 5).

18. After this scoring attempt, or when the defensemen stop the rush, the coach blows his whistle. These five players sprint to the players' benches and the next five players skate onto the ice.

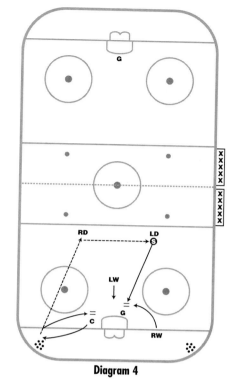

Diagram 4

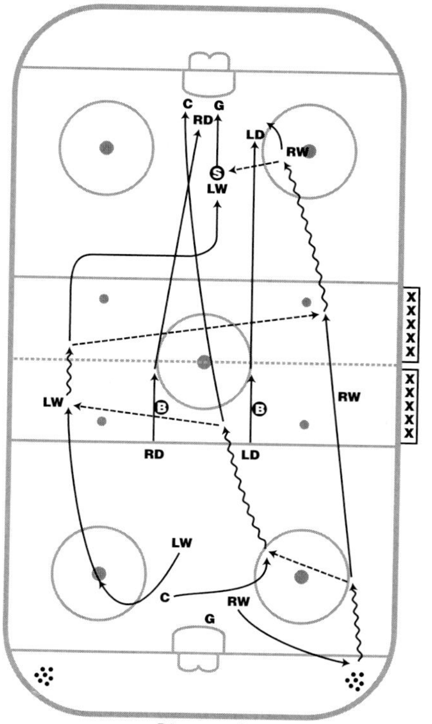

Although there is a bit of downtime for players on the benches, it's important for them to pay attention. They can learn a great deal about defensive positioning and making offensive zone plays.

The coach in the corner should vary the defensive corner so all players understand their positioning in their defensive end on both sides of the ice.

It's also a good idea to have your goalies switch ends of the ice halfway through the time allotment for this drill. Remind your players that during all drills, they should give 100

Diagram 5

percent while on the ice because they have adequate rest time while waiting for their turn.

Pivoting One-on-One GS15 ●●●

Purpose: To simulate a game setting involving pivoting, forward and backward skating, and passing and receiving in a one-on-one.

Number of Players: All, 2 goalies
Additional Equipment: 40 pucks, 2 cones
Time: 10 minutes

GS15

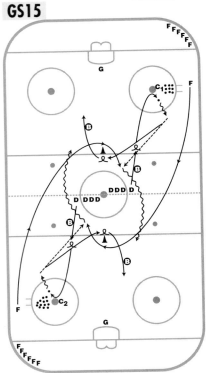

1. Divide your forwards into two lines in two diagonally opposite corners of the ice. All the defensemen are lined up at center ice, half on each side of the face-off circle. Place a cone in the middle of each blue line. Place about twenty pucks in each end zone face-off circle nearest the forwards. Station a coach in each circle to manage the pucks.

2. The first forward in each line is positioned against the boards just behind the end zone face-off circle hash marks. The first defenseman in line on each side of the center-ice face-off circle stands on the red line, prepared to retreat straight back toward the puck.

3. On the whistle, the first defenseman on each side of the center-ice face-off circle skates backward to the blue line, pivots forward, and skates toward the pucks.

4. The coach in each end zone face-off circle pushes a puck toward the boards, where each defenseman, who's also turning toward the boards, must receive it.

5. At the same time, the first forward in each line skates hard toward the far blue line, makes a turn around the cone on the blue line, and returns in the opposite direction.

6. Each defenseman passes to the forward who has made the turn around the cone nearest them.

7. Each forward receives the pass from the defenseman and drives back down the opposite side of the ice to try and score.

8. After making the pass, each defenseman skates forward quickly to get around the cone on the blue line, pivots to backward, and plays the oncoming forward in an attempt to stop him from scoring.

9. After the defensemen pivot around the cone to face the one-on-one, the coach blows his whistle to start the next four players.

10. After the scoring attempt, or when the defenseman stop the rush, each forward goes to the end of the line they started from. The defensemen go to the end of the other line of defensemen.

11. Halfway through the allotted time, move the pucks and players to opposite corners and begin the drill in the opposite direction.

Use this drill only with players who are able to skate extremely well and can pass accurately to players moving with great speed.

Breakout, Regroup Three-on-Two GS16 ●●●

Purpose: To simulate a game setting involving a breakout, a regroup, and a three-on-two.	**Number of Players:** All, in groups of 7, 2 goalies **Additional Equipment:** 15 pucks **Time:** 10 minutes

1. Each group is made up of three forwards (RW, C, LW) and four defense-men (RD1, LD1, RD2, LD2). Only one group is on the ice at a time. The remaining forwards and defensemen are on separate benches. Place a goalie in each net. Station one coach (C2) near one of the players' benches with the pucks. This coach is responsible for pairing up defensemen and giving each group of forwards their positions. Station another coach (C1) in the neutral zone.

2. The players in the first group should line up in one half of the neutral zone as shown. Two of the defense-men (RD1, LD1) are on the defensive blue line. The other two defensemen (RD2, LD2) are lined up opposite them on the centerline. The three forwards should be in between the four defensemen (diagram 1 shows steps 2 through 9).

3. The coach in the neutral zone (C1) starts the drill by shooting a puck around the boards so the goalie can stop the puck behind his own net.

4. The defenseman near the blue line (LD1) retreats, skating backward, then pivots to forward to retrieve the puck from behind the net. At the same time, his defensive partner (RD1) retreats, skating backward, then pivots to forward and skates toward the front of the net. When RD1 sees his partner, LD1, getting close to the puck, he can either stay in front of the net or move to a position on the opposite side of the net, about 10 feet from the net and below the goal line, to get in position to receive a pass.

5. Meanwhile, the three forwards (RW, C, LW) move to their breakout positions in the zone. The wingers (RW, LW) skate to the hash marks on their side of the ice and the center (C)

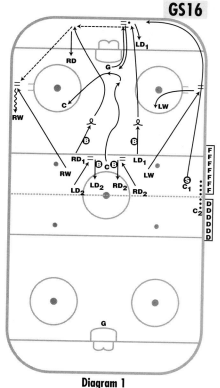

GS16

Diagram 1

GS16

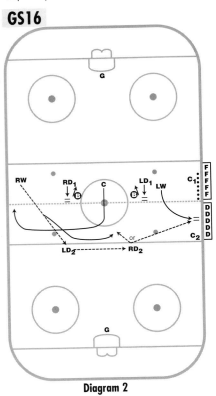

Diagram 2

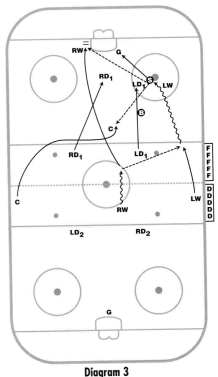

Diagram 3

supports the puck-retrieving defenseman (LD1) by mirroring him but staying in front of the net.

6. The remaining two defensemen (RD2, LD2) move to take a position at their offensive zone blue line.

7. Now the breakout begins. The puck-retrieving defenseman (LD1) either makes a pass to his partner (RD1) or (as shown) skates with the puck behind the net and passes to the winger on the boards (RW).

8. The three forwards (LW, C, RW) now move with the puck out of their zone, passing it back and forth while the defensemen who started the breakout (LD1, RD1) support them from behind (not shown).

9. Meanwhile, the two defensemen not involved in the breakout (LD2, RD2) retreat from the blue line, skating backward toward their own defensive blue line.

10. As soon as one of the forwards cross the forwards' defensive blue line, the retreating defensemen (LD2, RD2) should be at their defensive blue line (diagram 2 shows steps 10 through 12).

11. The drill now changes. The forward with the puck passes it directly to one of defensemen at the far blue line (LD2, RD2). The three forwards now work with this pair of defensemen, following after the puck, and beginning to turn to fill all three lanes. (It's important for the forwards to skate quickly to create speed when they attack in the opposite direction.)

12. The defenseman with the puck (LD2 or RD2) now quickly passes across the blue line to his partner, who returns the puck to one of the forwards. At the same time, the defensemen who started the breakout (LD1, RD1) skate to center ice and begin retreating back toward their defensive end.

13. The forwards fill all three lanes and return, attacking in a three-on-two rush (on LD1 and RD1) in the opposite direction (diagram 3 shows steps 13 and 14).

14. As the forwards cross the offensive blue line, the forward with the puck (LW) drives wide while another forward (RW) drives to the net. The last forward (C) fills the open space in the high slot area. They try to score while RD1 and LD1 attempt to stop them.

15. After one scoring attempt, or when the defensemen stop the rush, the coach in the neutral zone blows his whistle. The forwards sprint to the forwards' bench. The breakout defensemen (RD1, LD1) sprint to the defensemen's bench. The coach near the players' benches sends out three new forwards and two defensemen. The defensemen held over are the new breakout defensemen.

16. The drill begins again from the opposite end.

APPENDIX: Referee Signals

1. Boarding.

2. Body checking.

3. Butt ending.

4. Charging.

5. Checking from behind.

6. Cross-checking.

7. Delayed calling of penalty.

8. Delay of game.

9. Delayed offside.

10. Elbowing.

11. Goal scored.

12. Grasping the face mask.

13. High-sticking.

14. Holding.

15. Hooking.

16. Icing.

Courtesy National Federation of State High School Associations

17. Interference.

18. Kneeing.

19. Misconduct.

20. Penalty shot.

21. Roughing and Fighting.

22. Slashing.

23. Spearing.

24. Time-out and unsportsmanlike conduct.

25. Tripping.

26. Washout.

Glossary

Angle checking: Skating toward an opponent with the puck on an angle rather than head-on to steer him in the desired direction. Stick- or body-checking skills are then used to gain possession of the puck.

Assist: Awarded when a player shoots or passes to the player ultimately responsible for a goal. A maximum of two players may be awarded assists on the same goal.

Backchecking: An act of transitioning from offense to defense in which a player in the *offensive* or *neutral zone* attempts to regain possession of the puck by skating back to check the opponent in the direction of the *defensive zone*.

Backhand shot: A shot that's taken with the puck on the same side of the stick blade as the back of the bottom hand is positioned.

Blue lines: Two parallel lines on either side of the *centerline* approximately 27 feet from it and 57 feet from the nearest goal. They divide the rink into the *offensive*, *defensive*, and *neutral* (center) *zones*.

Boarding: A minor or major penalty that's called when a player checks an opponent into the boards in a dangerous manner.

Boards or **side boards:** A wooden or fiberglass wall 3.5 to 4 feet high that surrounds the rink.

Body checking: When a player uses her hip or shoulder to knock an opponent away from the puck.

Breakaway: When a player with possession of the puck skates in alone on the opposing goaltender.

Breakout: During a breakout, players are positioned in a defensive zone setup. In order to keep puck possession, the players pass the puck to each other while skating out of their end.

Butt ending: A major penalty that's called when a player uses the top end of the stick to jab an opponent.

Center: An offensive player who takes most of the *face-offs*. As one of three forwards, this position is mainly responsible for making offensive plays to help score goals and working defensively with his *defensemen* to stop the opponent.

Center ice: The area between the two *blue lines*. Also called the *neutral zone*.

Centerline: The red line in the middle of the ice that divides the rink in half.

Centering the puck: A pass from an attacking player toward the middle of the ice to a teammate in the offensive zone.

Changing on the fly: When a player or entire line that's been sitting on the players' bench takes to the ice, exchanging positions with a player or players as play continues without a stoppage.

Charging: A minor or major penalty that's called when a player takes more than two strides or steps before checking an opponent.

Checking: Guarding an opponent or attempting to strip him of puck control by using the body or stick.

Checking from behind: A minor or major penalty that's called when a player pushes, checks, or *cross-checks* an opponent from behind in a violent manner that has the potential for injury.

Control stop: A full, sideways stop using the inside and outside edges of both skates.

Crossbar: The tubular steel bar that frames the top of the *goal net*.

Cross-checking: A minor or major penalty that's called when a player holds the shaft of the stick between her hands and uses it to check an opponent. The major penalty is called on a *head check* or violent act performed with the intent to injure.

Crossover skating: A skating move that enables the skater to move sideways by crossing one skate over the other.

Crossunder skating: A skating move that enables the skater to move sideways by crossing one skate under the other while skating backward.

Defenseman: One of the two defensive players whose main job is to prevent goals from being scored against their team.

Defensive zone: The end of the ice where a team's goaltender defends the net, from the end boards to the nearest *blue line*.

Delayed penalty: When an official raises his arm but does not blow his whistle, waiting to see the outcome of a play before calling a penalty. This is done to avoid penalizing the nonoffending team by stopping its momentum while it is in possession of the puck. The official will blow his whistle to call the penalty when a player on the offending team has touched the puck.

Double-teaming: When two players guard one specific offensive player on the opposing team.

Draw: A *face-off*.

Elbowing: A minor or major penalty that's called when a player checks an opponent with his elbow. The major penalty is called when there's a *head check* or intent to injure.

Face-off: A method of starting play in which the referee standing between the two team's centers drops the puck at the beginning of the game or after any other stoppage of play.

Fighting: A major penalty that's called when two players engage in a physical altercation. This is *never* permitted in youth hockey.

Five hole: The area between the goalkeeper's legs. It is the most vulnerable spot for a goaltender.

Forechecking: An attempt to pressure the other team, primarily by a player in the *offensive zone* especially after the puck is dumped into the zone, and to keep the team from gaining control of the puck and clearing the puck out of its zone.

Forward: An offensive player (a left or right *winger* or a *center*), whose main task is goal scoring.

Four hole: The area located high to the goaltender's blocker (stick) side.

Game misconduct: A *penalty* that results in a player or team official being suspended for the duration of the game and that usually carries a suspension for the next game as well.

Glide turn: Used to change direction while maintaining speed using the inside and outside edges of both skates.

Goal: A goal is awarded when the puck completely crosses the goal line between the three pipes of the *goal net*.

Goal crease: The area in front of the *goal net* bordered in red that denotes the playing area of the goaltender. Attacking players may not enter the goal crease unless the puck lies there.

Goal line: A 2-inch-wide red line that extends from one side board to the other, including between the *goal posts*.

Goal net: Mesh netting that is 6 feet wide and 4 feet tall and that's attached to posts of tubular steel resting on the center of the *goal line*.

Goal posts: The tubular steel bar that frames the sides of the *goal net*.

Goaltender or goalie: The player responsible for preventing goals from entering the net. He's also known as the last line of defense and is the only player permitted to cover the puck within the *goal crease*.

Hat trick: When one player scores three goals in the same game.

Head checking: A major penalty that's called when a player checks an opponent in the head.

Head-man the puck: Passing the puck to an open teammate who's farther up the ice.

High slot: The area in the middle of the ice at the top of the offensive zone face-off circles.

High-sticking: A minor, double minor, or major penalty that's called when a player checks an opponent with her stick held above the normal height of the shoulders. The major penalty is called if blood is drawn.

Holding: A minor penalty that's called when a player grabs the stick, jersey, or any part of an opponent's body.

Hook check: A stick-checking maneuver made by a player with one hand on the stick and one knee so low it is practically on the ice. His stick's shaft and blade remain flat on the ice to pull the puck away from an opponent.

Hooking: A minor penalty that's called when a player uses her stick to tug on an opponent's stick or body to stop or slow her progress.

House league: Generally admits all children who desire to play.

Icing: A violation that occurs when a player shoots a puck that travels untouched from his team's side of the centerline past the opposing goal line. Icing is not called if a goal is scored or if the team is playing shorthanded.

Interference: A minor penalty that's called when a player obstructs the motion of an opponent who doesn't have the puck.

Lateral T-glide: A goaltender's sideways skating movement in which he turns the toe of the lead foot forming a T with the back foot, pushing off to glide across to the intended position.

Line change: An entire forward line and/or defensive pair replaced at the same time.

Linesmen: The two officials who drop the puck for face-offs and determine icing and offside infractions.

Major penalty: A five-minute penalty.

Match penalty: A penalty that's called on a player or team official, resulting in her immediate removal from the game and often an additional suspension. Match penalties are usually called when a player deliberately attempts to injure an opponent.

Minor penalty: A two-minute penalty.

Misconduct: A penalty that removes a player from the game for ten minutes; however, another player immediately replaces him, so the team doesn't play shorthanded.

Mohawk turn: A turn performed while transitioning from forward to backward skating or backward to forward skating.

Natural hat trick: When one player scores three consecutive goals in the same game.

Neutral zone: The center ice section between the two *blue lines*.

Offensive zone: The area inside the *blue line* farthest away from your team's *goal net*; also called the attacking zone.

Offside: A violation that's called when an offensive player precedes the puck over his team's offensive blue line into the attacking zone and he or a teammate then touches the puck.

One hole: The area located low to the goaltender's stick side. In competitive play, most goals are scored here.

Open ice: The area of the ice surface that's free of any opponents.

Overtime: One or more additional periods of playing time that are added when the score is tied at the end of three periods. The first goal scored during overtime is the winning goal.

Parallel shuffle: A goaltender's sideways skating movement, pushing off and sliding with opposite skates to arrive at the intended position.

Passing lane: An unobstructed pathway that allows for a pass between players.

Penalty: An infraction of a hockey rule that usually results in the player serving time in the *penalty box*.

Penalty box: An area off the ice where players serve their penalty time.

Penalty kill: The defensive situation when one or more of your players is serving a *penalty* and your team must play shorthanded. Your team will have to play with one or two fewer players on the ice for a given period of time.

Penalty shot: A shot awarded to a player who's been fouled from behind while on a *breakaway* and thereby prevented from getting a clear scoring chance. The player and defending goalkeeper are the only two permitted on the ice during this play.

Pinching: A defenseman's forward skating move at the offensive blue line used with the intention of keeping the puck deep in the *offensive zone*.

Poke check: A technique used by a defensive player when an opponent is carrying the puck. The defenseman uses her stick to jab or thrust toward the puck in an attempt to separate the puck from the opponent.

Power play: An advantage that occurs when one team takes a minor or major penalty that isn't offset by one taken by the other team. The offending player must serve the *penalty* in the *penalty box*, so the nonoffending team has a one-player advantage for the length of the penalty or until a goal is scored.

Power stop: A two-foot, momentary sideways stop that enables the player to transition quickly to change direction.

Pulling the goalie: When the goaltender is taken out of the game and replaced by a skating teammate to improve a team's chances of scoring.

Ready position: The basic stance in hockey. The player's knees and waist are bent, and the stick is centered and flat on the ice.

Rebound: A puck that has popped free after an initial save by the goalkeeper.

Referee: An official who calls penalties and signals when a goal is scored.

Retaliation penalty: A penalty called on a player for retaliating against a player who has fouled him.

Roughing: A minor penalty that occurs when an altercation between players is more of a pushing and shoving match. The penalty is less severe than *fighting*.

Rush: An individual or combined offensive attack by a team in possession of the puck.

Screened shot: A shot taken on goal when a goalkeeper's view is partially obstructed by one or more players.

Shift: The duration of time a player or line spends on the ice at one given time.

Shoulder checking: When a player uses his shoulder to knock an opponent away from the puck.

Slap shot: A shot in which a player raises her stick in a backswing to shoulder height, with her bottom hand held slightly lower on the shaft and her top hand at the end of the stick. As the stick blade moves in a downward motion, it makes contact with the ice about 1 to 2 inches behind the puck, and the player leans onto the stick to put power behind the shot and add velocity to the puck.

Slashing: A minor or major penalty that's called when a player hits an opponent with his stick. The major penalty will be called if the slash was done in a violent manner with the intent to injure.

Slot: The area in the middle of the ice between the face-off hash marks and the top of the offensive zone circle.

Snap shot: A quick shot taken in the same manner as the slap shot, but without the big backswing. The shot begins with the blade slightly off the ice and behind the puck, and as the stick blade moves forward, the player places downward pressure on the ice slightly behind the puck, with wrists and forearms helping the blade snap through the puck to complete the shot.

Spearing: A major penalty that's called when a player uses his stick or part of his body to trip an opponent.

Stick checking: Any legal use of the stick to knock the puck away from an opponent so he loses possession (poke, sweep, hook check, stick lift, or stick press).

Stickhandling: Continuously moving the puck back and forth along the ice from the forehand to the backhand side of the stick blade

Stick lift: A stick-checking maneuver made by a player who lifts the opponent's stick, thereby preventing him from receiving a pass or gaining a scoring chance.

Stick press: A stick-checking maneuver made by a player who presses on top of the opponent's stick, thereby preventing him from receiving a pass or gaining a scoring chance.

Strong side: The side of the ice that the puck is on.

Sudden death: When regulation time runs out and the score is tied. The game goes into overtime and the team who scores the first goal is the winner.

Sweep checking: A stick-checking maneuver made by a player with one hand on the stick and one knee so low it is practically on the ice. His stick's shaft and blade remain flat on the ice to push the puck away from an opponent.

Three hole: The area located high to the goaltender's catching glove side.

T-glide: See *lateral T-glide*.

Travel team: A team that has a more extensive game schedule and range of travel. Players are required to try out for travel teams.

Tripping: A minor penalty that's called when a player uses her stick or part of her body to trip an opponent.

Turnover: Losing possession of the puck.

Two hole: The area located low to the goaltender's catching glove side.

Two-line pass: A type of *offside* violation that occurs when an offensive player passes the puck from his defensive zone to an awaiting teammate who's already across the centerline.

V-start: A skating move in which the skates are pointed out in a V, and the skater can push out off the inside edge of either foot.

Weak side: The side of the ice farther away from the puck.

Winger: One of the two players who flank the *center* on his right or left side and, with him, make up the forward line.

Wrist shot: A shot made using a strong flick of the wrist and forearm muscles while the stick blade remains on the ice. It is slower than a slap shot but more accurate.

Resources

Associations and Organizations

American Sports Education Program
P.O. Box 5076
Champaign IL 61825-5076
800-747-5698; 217-351-5076
E-mail: asep@hkusa.com
www.asep.com
The American Sports Education Program offers both online and instructional education courses and resources for coaches, officials, sports administrators, athletes, and parents of athletes. The ASEP also offers a course on sports first aid.

Hockey Canada
Ottawa office: 801 King Edward Ave., Suite N204
Ottawa ON Kln 6N5
CANADA
613-562-5677; Fax: 613-562-5676
www.hockeycanada.ca
The sole governing body for amateur hockey in Canada. It provides programs in initiation, coaching, officiating, safety, and female hockey. Its five Centres of Excellence house the world's largest collection of instructional videos for all levels of hockey.

International Ice Hockey Federation
Brandschenkestrasse 50
Postfach
8039 Zürich
SWITZERLAND
41-1-562-22-00
E-mail: office@iihf.com; www.iihf.com
Founded in 1908, the IIHF governs the sports of ice hockey and in-line hockey for both men and women. Its objectives are to govern, develop, and promote ice and in-line hockey throughout the world.

National Alliance for Youth Sports
2050 Vista Pkwy.
West Palm Beach FL 33411
800-688-KIDS (800-688-5437); 561-684-1141
E-mail: nays@nays.org
www.nays.org
NAYS offers programs and services for everyone involved in youth sports experiences including volunteers, coaches, officials, parents, and young athletes. Its goal is to make sports and activities safe and fun.

National Youth Sports Safety Foundation
One Beacon St., Suite 3333
Boston MA 02108
617-277-1171
E-mail: NYSSF@aol.com
www.nyssf.org
This national, nonprofit education organization is dedicated to reducing the number and severity of injuries that young players sustain in sports and fitness activities.

North American Youth Sports Institute
4985 Oak Garden Dr.
Kernersville NC 27284-9520
800-767-4916; 336-784-4926
E-mail: Jack@NAYSI.com
www.naysi.com
This website provides assistance and resources in fitness, recreation, and education for teachers, coaches, parents, and youth-work professionals.

Ontario Minor Hockey Association
25 Brodie Dr., Unit 2
Richmond Hill ON L4B 3K7
CANADA

905-780-OMHA (905-780-6642)
E-mail: rropchan@omha.net
www.omha.net
Ontario Minor Hockey Association publishes *Rinkside* newspaper and *Hometown Hockey* magazine. Both contain excellent information and insights for coaches, players, and hockey fans.

Ontario Women's Hockey Association
5155 Spectrum Way, Unit 3
Mississauga ON L4W 5A1
CANADA
905-282-9980
E-mail: info@owha.on.ca
www.owha.on.ca
The OWHA is one of the oldest organizations for women's hockey. It provides a wealth of information on women's and girls' hockey in North America.

USA Hockey, Inc.
1775 Bob Johnson Dr.
Colorado Springs CO 80906
719-576-USAH (719-576-8724)
E-mail: comments@usahockey.org
www.usahockey.com
USA Hockey is the national governing body for youth hockey. The USA Hockey Initiation Program provides a systematic, level-by-level guideline of skill analysis, leadership techniques, and age-appropriate drills for each level of hockey. It also has an in-depth Hockey Coaching Education Program.

Websites and Electronic Newsletters

CANCoach
www.cancoach.com
Offers a large selection of coaching software and online applications for the advancement of sport skills and education including hockey planners and online instruction.

Foundation for Hockey Development
www.fhd.net
The FHD's goal is to develop hockey players, create a positive experience, and keep young men and women participating in the game.

HockeyCoach.com
www.hockeycoach.com
This site provides drills, game strategies, bulletin boards for coaches, and a coaching and player development section. It has one of the largest grassroots hockey coaching followings on the Internet.

I Teach Positive Attitudes in Youth Sports
www.danbylsma.com/IPInit.htm
IT PAYS, started by Dan Bylsma, assistant captain of the Mighty Ducks of Anaheim, promotes playing ice hockey for each player's enjoyment, athletic development, and understanding of the game. It also uses the game of hockey to teach life lessons.

LeagueAthletics.com
www.leagueathletics.com
This is a "put your team online" newsletter.

PlayBetterHockey.com
www.playbetterhockey.com
Coaches can look to this site for drills, strategies, tips, and general knowledge for use with their hockey teams.

Sports Coach
www.brianmac.demon.co.uk/stretch.htm
This site contains detailed stretching exercises as well as links to book and journal pages for additional information.

Index